12/24/15

Freedom of Expression

Dear Mama Julie,

Merry Christmas.
I wrote a book!
Thank you for
everything you do.
Love,
Chris

Freedom of Expression

Interviews with Women in Jazz

Chris Becker

Copyedited by Peter Feder
Proofreading and additional
copyediting by Julie Lytz

Frontpiece: Carmen Lundy.
Photo by Victor Dlamini.

ISBN-13: 978-0692543603
ISBN-10: 0692543600

Library of Congress Control
Number: 2015916416

Beckeresque Press,
Houston, Texas

Contents

Acknowledgments

First and foremost, I want to thank my wife and soul mate Lainie Diamond. Lainie is the one who initially pushed me to pursue a career as a professional writer, and her support and creative input throughout this project has been invaluable. I love you, Lainie!

Very special thanks to my mother, Doris Murdock. This book's subject resonated with her from the very beginning, and her encouragement has helped bring it to fruition. I also want to thank my stepfather, James Murdock, who shares my enthusiasm for both great music and great writing.

My father, Richard Becker, introduced me to jazz when I was a teenager. He took me to my first jazz concerts, including what was, for me, a life-changing performance by the Pat Metheny Group at a club called the Agora in Columbus, Ohio. Back then, he often made it a point to tell adults that his son "has very sophisticated tastes in music." It still makes me smile when I remember that! I am quite sure if he were alive, he would enjoy reading this book. Thanks, Dad.

I thank Kelly Johanns-DiCillo, former tour publicist at Concord Music Group, who secured the first round of interviews for this book. Her enthusiasm for my work and the time she took to secure those interviews helped get this project off the ground.

Attorney Kelly Kocinski has helped many artists and performers with their legal questions and needs, and I am grateful for the advice and services she provided throughout this project.

Thank you to authors Michael Veal, Ned Sublette, and Mark Segal Kemp, who each encouraged me to complete this project and have greatly inspired me with their writing. I also want to thank professor Guthrie Ramsey who, in the early stages of this project, challenged me to compose what became its introduction. At the time, it was a push I needed to begin coalescing the larger themes that were emerging from these interviews.

A big hug and thank you to my friend and fellow writer Meredith Nudo, who has encouraged my writing endeavors from the very first day we met.

Meredith is one of the most talented and funniest people I've ever met, and her enthusiasm for the creative aspirations of her friends is truly something special.

Thank you to my friend trumpeter Lewis "Flip" Barnes for suggesting I interview Connie Crothers, Mazz Swift, Samantha Boshnack, Jean Cook, and Nicole Rampersaud. Flip is a strong advocate for musicians who push the envelope and challenge listeners, and each of these women do just that in their own unique way.

I thank my good friend Robert Landry who was the first to suggest I self-publish this book. At the time, that sounded crazy to me. Now, it seems prophetic. Thanks to author and musician Kevin Moore and pianist, composer, and author Adam Tendler, who each took time to give me advice about self-publishing.

Special thanks to Bonnie and Bruce Diamond, Nita Fowler Chapman, and Harry Connick, Sr. for being so supportive of this project.

I want to express my gratitude and respect to the musicians interviewed in this book. They were all incredibly gracious with their time, and many supported the project on social media and other promotional platforms. Each musician expressed great enthusiasm for the book and its subject, and I am grateful for their patience as I took time to make sure the final product wasn't anything less than spectacular.

Speaking of patience, thank you to my Indiegogo campaign donors (see below). It takes a special person to make a contribution to an independent project like this, and I don't take your support for granted:

Alexandra Adshead, Joseph Benzola, Jacqueline Bishop, Jennifer Collins, Rachel Cohen, Rachel Dvoretzky, Jennifer Hancock, Douglas Henderson, Donnie and Mimi Hughes, Uchenna Ikonne, Eva Kapanadze, Fumiyo Krall, Kristin Lanphier, Steve Layton, Joe LoCascio, Lisa Maxwell, Michael McDonald, Adán Medrano, Doris Murdock, Alisha Pattillo, Joseph Phillips, Jr., Julie Lytz, Louis Romanos, Natalie D. Sacha, Ellen Seeling, Alex Shapiro, SPIKE the Percussionist, Debbie Thompson, Hsin-Jung Tsai, John Walthour, Melody Warren, and Rachel Winer.

Finally, thank you for opening up this book and reading it. I truly hope it is both informative and inspiring.

Introduction

....

We're moving! Jazz is not dead! In fact, we're heading
into something incredible.
—*Connie Crothers to the author, 2013*

In the years since the arrival of the 21st century, jazz has evolved into a truly cross-generational, multicultural musical art form that is assimilating an unprecedented array of musical styles and techniques. At the same time, the male-dominated paradigm that for decades has defined the historical narrative of jazz and shaped the business that promotes and distributes the music is no more. Women are shaking up the music industry while the general public is becoming much more aware of the contributions female musicians have made to the art of jazz since its inception at the turn of the 20th century.

This collection of interviews with 37 female musicians, musicians of all ages, nationalities, and races and representing nearly every style of jazz one can imagine, provides evidence of this profound evolution. The evolution includes the emergence of new musical hybrids born out of musical traditions from around the planet, new approaches to free improvisation that bridge the divide between playing standards and spontaneous improvisation, and new business models designed by and for the benefit of creative musicians who wish to control the financing, marketing, and quality of their music.

We indeed are "heading into something incredible," and women are leading the way.

1. A (Very) Brief History of Women in Jazz

Director Judy Chaikin's 2011 film, *The Girls in the Band*, effectively and entertainingly corrects the widespread misconception that the contributions of women musicians to the development of jazz are so minor as to be inconsequential. Beginning with Art Kane's well-known 1958 group photograph "A Great Day in Harlem"—which includes just three women (singer Maxine Sullivan, pianist Marian McPartland, and pianist Mary Lou Williams) among a total of 57 jazz musicians—the film features interviews with several female jazz musicians, including many who played in big bands during World War II. Their recollections do not negate the contributions of men to the music, and musicians such as Woody Herman, Stanley Kay, and Dr. Billy Taylor are given due credit for employing and advocating for female musicians. Instead, the film offers a refreshing and very entertaining alternate history of the music and its development.

At one point in the film, McPartland says she doesn't know why there weren't more women included in the "A Great Day in Harlem" group photo, as there were plenty of women around at that time playing jazz. To bring things full circle, the film concludes poignantly with a restaging of the classic photo, this time featuring 68 female musicians, including McPartland, as well as Jan Leder, Roberta Piket, Sherrie Maricle, Anat Cohen, Jennifer Leitham, Helen Sung, and Sharel Cassity, who are each interviewed in this book.

These interviews, like those conducted in Chaikin's film, are transcriptions presented in question and answer format that, when presented together as a whole, provide a unique and under-reported perspective on the history and current state of jazz. Although my goal is not to provide a comprehensive history of jazz, I offer some guideposts in this introduction that will help the reader navigate what amounts to several decades of contributions by women to the development of this music and provide some additional context for the 37 interviews herein.

A Definition of Jazz

I don't doubt my connection with [jazz], because I don't look at it as a certain thing. It's creative music. Duke Ellington said, "Jazz means freedom of expression." And I think that everything that I do, for the most part, feels like jazz.
—*Terri Lyne Carrington to the author, 2012*

Jazz emerged in New Orleans at the beginning of the 20th century as an amalgam of blues, ragtime, gospel, military brass marching music, and key elements of European classical music. From its earliest beginnings, a heavily syncopated, almost visceral rhythmic feel that emphasized the second and fourth beat in 4/4 time helped to define this sometimes slow, sometimes fast, yet always danceable new music. It was played by both ensembles and soloists, in bars, brothels, dance halls, and on the street, perhaps most famously as accompaniment to New Orleans' "jazz funeral" processions. Though it was originated by and for African Americans, almost immediately, musicians of European descent began playing the music as well.

The word "jazz" was not used in New Orleans to describe this music. The word—a slang term that originally meant "energy and liveliness"—first appeared in writing about baseball. Dr. Lewis Porter, pianist and professor of music at Rutgers University in Newark, writes: "Whites started to call the new music 'jazz' in Chicago and possibly California in 1915. Because it was a new word, and because it was slang, spellings varied at first (jazz, jas, jaz, jass, jasz), but since 1918 it has been 'jazz.'"[1] Despite its use in cringe-inducing racist lyrics of minstrel songs (e.g., Gus Kahn and Henry Marshall's 1917 recording "That Funny Jas Band from Dixieland"), the word began to be used, by people of all colors, to refer to what was then a new and exciting musical form.

Musical improvisation, including collective improvisation, solo improvisation with the melodies of popular songs (also known as "standards"), and improvised accompaniment (or "comping") is an essential component of this music, although the same can be said for several other musical genres, including European classical music before 1900.

Though labeled by some as "America's classical music," jazz has never stopped developing, and from the beginning embraced and incorporated new technologies and concepts. For example, its earliest practitioners saw the potential for a range of sophisticated musical expression on instruments that at the time were relatively utilitarian in their use, such as the drum kit and the saxophone. This spirit of exploration in jazz continues to this day. As guitarist and composer Pat Metheny writes in the liner notes to his 2010 album, *Orchestrion*: "One of the inspiring hallmarks of the jazz tradition through the decades has been the way that the form has willfully ushered in fresh musical contexts. . . . This pursuit of change, and the way that various restless souls along the way have bridged the roots of the form with the new possibilities of their own time, has been a major defining element . . . in the music's evolution."[2]

The Birth of Jazz

Women did contribute to New Orleans jazz, in many and significant ways. They played bawdy piano in the famous red-light district of Storyville. They were instrumentalists, vocalists, dancers, and bandleaders. —Sherrie Tucker, "Rocking the Cradle of Jazz."[3]

The history in the film *The Girls in the Band* goes back to the 1920s to include the great pianist, composer, and promoter Lillian (or "Lil") Hardin, later known as Lil Hardin Armstrong after her marriage to the now-famous Louis Armstrong, whom she decided to mentor upon his arrival in Chicago from New Orleans in 1922.

"Louis Armstrong's Hot Five was originally Lil Hardin's band," Connie Crothers explains in her interview for this book. "She was a bandleader. Not only was she a bandleader, she was a promoter. Bear in mind that when she was in the Hot Five she was still in her 20s. She was an extremely accomplished musician and jumped over hurdles to accomplish what she did."

Going even further back, we find that women instrumentalists were an active part of New Orleans' pre-1920s jazz community, which emerged in the parlors of the city's notorious red light district, Storyville, an area of the city zoned for prostitution. Sherrie Tucker writes: "Women piano players dominated the instrument at the very moment it joined the jazz ensemble."[4] Several female singers, including Esther Bigeou, Lizzie Miles (born Elizabeth Mary Landreaux), Edna Hicks (half sister of Lizzie Miles, born Edna Landreaux), Ma Rainey, Bessie Smith, and many others were crucial innovators in the art of blues singing and major contributors to the musical development of jazz in the first two decades of the 20th century.[5]

Singers

What today's listeners intuitively acknowledge as "jazz" singing, that is, the sound and array of techniques one hears in the voices of such contemporary singers as Diane Schuur, Dee Dee Bridgewater, and Jane Monheit (three of several singers interviewed in this book) is founded in pre-20th-century African-American spirituals, Tin Pan Alley repertoire, scat singing (with Louis Armstrong's vocal performance on the 1927 recording "Heebie Jeebies" being one of the earliest and most famous examples of this technique), and most definitely, traditional and classic blues. In a country where opportunities for African Americans were severely limited due to blatant prejudice, entrenched and legal institutional racism, including Jim Crow laws, and the implicit threat of violence, jazz singing grew beyond its roots to become a highly sophisticated and, for a time, popular and profitable American art form.

Lady Day, Ella, and Others

The 1930s heralded an unprecedented period of experimentation with the voice as an instrument, in both small ensemble and big band settings. So much of what we take for granted when it comes to musical phrasing, manipulation of tempo, and the interpretation of song lyrics in today's popular music is rooted in the groundbreaking efforts of singers, both male and female, who were popular at the time.

Eleanora Fagan. It's a name one might come across in the pages of a novel by Emily Brontë or Charles Dickens. Born in 1915, Fagan would take the stage name Billie Holiday and change the course of American music.

Bridgewater describes Holiday as ". . . a groundbreaking singer. Her style was extremely unique. Very avant-garde. She refused to go the way of other singers of her time. She was a vocalist who made it possible for singers like me to carve out a career for ourselves." Frank Sinatra, who readily acknowledged Holiday's influence on his own singing, put it simply: "With few exceptions, every major pop singer in the U.S. during her generation has been touched in some way by her genius. It is Billie Holiday who was, and still remains, the greatest single musical influence on me."[6] In addition to "standing up for her individuality" and making a career for herself against incredible odds, including segregation and racism, Holiday, in Bridgewater's words, "went down fighting."[7]

Born just a few years after Holiday, Ella Fitzgerald, known as the "First Lady of Song," turned scat singing into high art and enjoyed an extended career through the swing and later bebop years, and on into the 1970s and mid-1980s. She recorded over 200 albums, including several with trumpeter and fellow virtuoso of scat, Louis Armstrong, as well as several album-length programs of music by some of America's greatest composers, including Cole Porter, Duke Ellington, George and Ira Gershwin, Irving Berlin, and Rodgers and Hart.

For big band singers, the musicality of the voice and ability to sing "like a horn" were of equal if not higher importance to lyrical interpretation. Throughout the years of World War II and on into the 1950s, instrumentalists influenced singers and vice versa, and a new generation of singers, both white and black, including Anita O'Day, Peggy Lee, Sarah Vaughan, Dinah Washington, Beverly Kenney, June Christy, Abbey Lincoln, and many, many more, took the art of singing to newer and more daring heights.

Life for a female singer on the road could be tough. In a time where sexism was status quo, there were male bandleaders and musicians who were respectful of women, including the aforementioned Woody Herman. However, sexual harassment from less-enlightened colleagues was not uncommon, and it pushed many singers to toughen up. Regarding Vaughan, composer, arranger, and producer Quincy Jones writes in his autobiography, Q: "After all those years on the road with the 18 men of the (Billy) Eckstine band, Sassy (Vaughan) had learned to be one of the boys: she had to, like all the girl singers on the road, or her ass would have been grass."[8]

Mary Lou Williams

In this very brief history of jazz, pianist, arranger, composer, and writer Mary Lou Williams deserves a special mention. Her composed and recorded repertoire spans seven decades (Williams said on more than one occasion, "I played through all the eras.")[9] and her musical influence is still being felt in the 21st century.

Williams was born in Atlanta, Georgia, in 1910. Her mother played the organ in church and piano at home and taught her prodigiously gifted daughter to play spirituals, ragtime, and boogie-woogie. Shortly after her family relocated to Pittsburgh, Pennsylvania, Williams began playing professionally at the age of 7. By 1930, she was working full-time as a member of Andy Kirk's big band, contributing several distinctive arrangements and compositions. She also composed music for Benny Goodman, Earl Hines, and Tommy Dorsey, composed for Duke Ellington and became his staff arranger for a time, and contributed arrangements and compositions to Dizzy Gillespie's big band.

In 1943, Williams moved to Harlem's Sugar Hill section, and her apartment became a hub for musicians. During this time, in addition to writing and editing critical pieces about modern jazz, she mentored and promoted many young players, and unlike some of the musicians of her generation, Williams did not disdain the newly emerged form of jazz popularly known as bebop.

"The guys who originated it [bebop]," Williams wrote, "were as gifted as the creative musicians of the 30s and the eras that came before."[10]

Unlike jazz in its previous incarnations, bebop was not music for dancing; it was played at blisteringly fast tempos and demanded the players navigate and expound upon complex chord changes. When musicians played bebop, audiences were expected to *listen* and listen hard.

Many of the originators of this music, including pianists Thelonious Monk, Bud Powell, and trumpeter Dizzy Gillespie, regularly visited Williams' apartment for after-hours salons where a diverse collection of musicians, including Vaughan, singer Mel Tormé, and trumpeter Miles Davis, gathered to share, debate, and be inspired by each other's musical discoveries.[11]

Williams' original compositions include "The Zodiac Suite," a classically infused jazz suite with each movement named after a sign in the zodiac and dedicated to various friends and fellow musicians. The piece, arranged for a large ensemble, premiered on December 31, 1945, at New York City's Town Hall and was performed again at Carnegie Hall in 1946. In 1945, Moses "Moe" Asch recorded and released a version of the suite for piano, bass, and drums on his own Asch records.[12] In 1954, due to a combination of emotional and spiritual crises, Williams withdrew from music, playing and recording only sporadically. She reemerged at the urging of her spiritual mentors in 1957. Her later works, including the cantata *Black Christ of the Andes* (1963) and the mass *Mary Lou's Mass* (1970), reflected her renewed devotion to religious, charitable, and educational endeavors. In addition to recording and performing, Williams would teach as an artist-in-residence at Duke University from 1977 until her death in 1981.

Williams' influence on music was as pervasive as any of the men in her social and artistic circles. Her legacy continues to grow thanks to a body of jazz scholarship and writing, music festivals such as the Kennedy Center's "Mary Lou Williams Women in Jazz Festival" (recently renamed the "Mary Lou Williams Jazz Festival"), and musical tributes such as trumpeter Dave Douglas' album *Soul on Soul* (2000), which features four Williams compositions alongside several Douglas originals directly inspired by her music, and saxophonist Virginia Mayhew's critically acclaimed album *Mary Lou Williams: The Next 100 Years* (2012).

Before and After World War II

In 1938, *DownBeat* magazine published an article titled "Why Women Musicians Are Inferior," whose author, tellingly, chose to remain anonymous. In response, saxophonist and bandleader Peggy Gilbert, who founded and led some of the earliest "all-girl" jazz bands, wrote a scathing rebuttal that *Down-Beat* published in its April 1938 issue, albeit accompanied by the condescending headline: "How Can You Blow a Horn With a Brassiere?" Gilbert, who was already a strong advocate for female musicians, drew on her formidable experience both as a musician and bandleader to systematically dismantle *Down-Beat's* sexist assertions and dubious conclusions regarding musical competence and gender.

"I have a few girls in my band who could hold first chairs in the best men's bands if given the privilege," Gilbert wrote. "But what men's orchestras would consent to such an experiment? A great many men musicians have highly complimented my band, saying it was as good or better than their organizations. But if the question of actually giving up an opportunity to establish our equality arose, we should immediately be relegated to an inferior plane and given the form answer A: 'It's not being done.'"[13]

The years leading up to and through World War II saw a generation of innovative and influential female instrumentalists stake their place alongside female singers, as well as male instrumentalists. Bassist and guitarist Carol Kaye, who initially began her career playing in big bands and bebop groups before becoming a highly sought-after session musician, confirmed in an interview for the Rock and Roll Hall of Fame that "back in the 40s and 50s, there were a million women out there playing jazz with the men. The men back then *knew* that women could play."[14]

Throughout the 1940s, when jazz was a popular, though still not wholly respectable art form, women playing jazz drew reactions ranging from matter-of-fact acceptance to bemusement to outright hostility. In February 1942, a few months after the bombing of Pearl Harbor, *DownBeat* magazine published an op-ed piece by drummer Viola Smith titled "Give Girl Musicians a Break!" (a "break" meaning "employment"), in which Smith reaffirmed the existence of "hep girls who could sit in any jam session and hold their own." Smith believed women could "do our bit to keep up the morale of the country" if they were hired in the place of men who had been drafted to fight the war overseas. *DownBeat* readers responded with an avalanche of letters-to-the-editor to show either their support for or outrage at Smith's thesis.[15]

From 1941 to 1945, with so many men drafted into military service, job opportunities opened up for both white and black women, including women who played jazz. According to Smith, "When World War II broke out, female musicians started to be taken more seriously. They were finally given a chance."[16] Saxophonists Roz Cron, Vi Burnside, and Vi Redd; trumpeters Billie Rogers, Norma Carson, and Clora Bryant; trombonist Melba Liston; guitarist Mary Osborne (who Crothers describes in her interview for this book as "the missing link between Charlie Christian and all the guitarists who came after"); and pianist and vibes player Terry Pollard are just some of the amazing women instrumentalists who performed in both "all-girl" bands as well large and small ensembles of male and female musicians.

During this time, a small number of black women, including singer Lena Horne, appeared in major Hollywood films in classy roles devoid of racist stereotyping that defined nearly every single non-white actor in the early days of cinema. Pianist Dorothy Donegan, a protégé of Art Tatum, starred in the 1945 film *Sensations of 1945* and nearly stole the show from co-stars Cab Calloway and W.C. Fields. Pianist and singer Hazel Scott gained a great deal of attention upon appearing in several films, including the 1945 film *Rhapsody in Blue*, a biopic of composer George Gershwin, which showcased not only her stunning looks but the breathtaking range of her piano playing. Scott was also the first African-American woman to host a network television show, *The Hazel Scott Show*, which ran for just a few months in 1950 before being cancelled after Scott was accused of being a communist in the red-baiting publication *Red Channels*. The politically conscious Scott denied the charge and, after being called to testify before the House Un-American Activities Committee (HUAC), relocated to Paris to continue her musical career.[17]

For many artists in the U.S., including musicians, male and female, white and black, the decade after World War II and especially the years of "the second red scare," also named the "McCarthy era" after the notorious Senator Joseph McCarthy, was a time of persecution. Cold War politics, blacklists, and covert spying by the FBI created a collective sense of paranoia that enabled the government to persecute any person who questioned the status quo. Several musicians were called to testify before the HUAC, including the aforementioned Scott and Horne, Paul Robeson, Josh White, and Pete Seeger.

However, for American women, the war years were "also the era of Rosie the Riveter," a time for lobbying for equal rights for women and African Americans at home while a war to end fascism raged overseas.[18] Although the 1950s heralded an era of extreme cultural conservatism, the roots of activism and change were in place for what would become the second wave of the feminist movement as well as the civil rights movement, the gay liberation movement, and organized strikes and boycotts led by Cesar Chavez and the United Farm Workers, all of which would have a profound impact on the evolution of jazz.

Rock and Roll

I don't care who knows it,
I hate rock and roll!
—*Beverly Kenney, "I Hate Rock and Roll," 1958*[19]

In the post-war years, despite fewer opportunities to play due to the diminishing popularity of big bands, many women, both instrumentalists and vocalists, continued to find work and push jazz into unexplored territory, often in small ensembles that placed a greater emphasis on soloing and group interplay. Pianists Pat Moran, Lorraine Geller, Beryl Booker, the German émigré Jutta Hipp, and Toshiko Akiyoshi (who would form with husband and saxophonist Lew Tabackin the world-renowned big band, the Toshiko Akiyoshi Jazz Orchestra) are just some of the distinctive, post-war jazz musicians who were known, recorded, and appreciated in their time and still have dedicated followings today.

At the same time, rhythm and blues, alternately known as "rock and roll," depending upon the skin color and gender of the person singing and playing, became the favored dance music of both black and white teenagers. As with jazz, the contributions by female musicians to the development of rock and roll are typically ignored in most historical narratives.

Although the advent of rock and roll is usually traced back to a handful of 1950s recordings by such iconic male artists as Chuck Berry, Fats Domino, Little Richard, Jerry Lee Lewis, Bill Haley, and Elvis Presley, female artists, including Sister Rosetta Tharpe, Big Mama Thornton, and Ruth Brown, to name just a few, were just as crucial to the development of this new musical form that drew equally on blues, gospel, jazz, country, and Cajun music. Recordings such as Tharpe's "Strange Things Happening Every Day," Thornton's "Hound Dog," and Brown's "Mama, He Treats Your Daughter Mean," were as musically influential, if not more so, as Berry's "Maybeline" or Haley's "Rock Around the Clock."

Less than a decade after the release of these recordings, the emergence of three British rock and roll bands, the Beatles, the Kinks, and the Rolling Stones, each one heavily indebted to the blues and roots of black American rock and roll, heralded another musical and cultural transformation. Many young British and American women, inspired by the music and fashion of the British beat movement, formed their own all-female bands, including New York's Goldie and the Gingerbreads, Detroit's Pleasure Seekers, and the Liverpool-based quartet the Liverbirds, of whom Beatles guitarist and singer John Lennon famously quipped: "Girls with guitars? That'll never work!"[20]

In 1963, one year before the Beatles made their American television debut, the publication of Betty Friedan's book *The Feminine Mystique* ignited what we now recognize as the second wave of the women's movement. Friedan, who would found and become the first president of the National Organization for Women (NOW), described the depression and anxiety many college-educated women were experiencing in their prescribed roles as mothers and housekeepers.[21] But once again, change was in the air. Over the next two decades, the women's movement would gain momentum and influence and inspire the work of a new generation of female musicians across all genres, including jazz.

Women's Liberation Movement

I come from a generation that's naturally feminist. Our mothers were fighting for all kinds of women's rights in the 60s and the 70s, and we grew up with these iconic, feminist, musical heroes. Women of my generation are strong, and hopefully the ones that are coming after us are as well. — Jane Monheit to the author, 2012

Many of the women I interviewed for this book were completely matter-of-fact about their careers as musicians whose status is at least equal to that of men. Many play in ensembles made up of both men and women, or entirely women. This "naturally feminist" spirit is apparent in many of the interviews and speaks to how far society has come not only in its attitude toward women, but in the number of careers, musical or otherwise, women are able to imagine for themselves in their formative years.

That said, it might be hard for a person born after 1980 to imagine life as a woman in the U.S. before 1960 and the women's movement.

"Before the women's movement," says Crothers, "when I went to a club, it was like walking a gauntlet. It was just understood that if there was a woman on the premises, the men were going to hit on her. Now, this is called sexual harassment."

Many girls grew up in the 1950s and 1960s without ever seeing or knowing of a woman doctor, lawyer, police officer, professor, scientist, politician, or businesswoman. In many states, women could not go into business without their husband's permission or obtain credit without a male co-signer. Employers matter-of-factly discriminated against women when it came to hiring. In 1960, *Newsweek* magazine reported that 60 percent of women who enrolled in college dropped out before graduation. In response to this statistic, some college presidents touted their school's curriculum as preparation for female graduates "to be splendid wives and mothers."[22] This statistic would soon change as college campuses became literal battlegrounds where students protesting the Vietnam War and demanding equal rights for women and minorities clashed with police and members of the National Guard.

Strangely, when the women's movement emerged, many supposedly enlightened males involved in political activism rallied their troops with the promise of "free grass, free food, free women" to be enjoyed as bounty after "the Revolution." Poet, author, and feminist activist Robin Morgan's famous 1970 essay "Goodbye to All That" cited and decried the prediction by less-than-sensitive male soldiers in the ranks that "men will make the Revolution—and make their chicks." Morgan and plenty of other women involved in anti-war and equal rights causes found it ironic that their brothers-in-arms embraced the sexist attitudes that perpetuated the poverty and violence they sought to eradicate.[23]

Fortunately, the Revolution was televised, and the role of women in contemporary society continued to be reconsidered thanks to the momentum of the women's movement and to some truly innovative representation in Hollywood films, prime time television shows, and, of course, music.[24]

Abbey Lincoln, Dorothy Ashby, and Alice Coltrane

Throughout the 1960s, innovations in pop songwriting and recording technology pushed the genre of rock music into new, unexplored territory. This spirit of experimentation, an integral component to jazz, would fuel a new type of "fusion" that drew heavily on funk, psychedelic, and ethnic music from around the world. Toward the end of the 1960s and on into the 1970s, many jazz musicians, highly aware of what songs were being enjoyed by African Americans on the jukeboxes and radio stations across the country, as well as how those songs spoke to the social and political changes that were in the air, began crafting and recording a new style of jazz that went back to its original roots as a music designed to move your feet and shake your butt.

Trumpeter Miles Davis, who had played with saxophonist Charlie Parker in the formative years of bebop, led heavily amplified ensembles of electric guitars, electric basses, electric keyboards, drums, and African, Indian, and Latin American percussion into lengthy, collectively improvised performances, many produced by the legendary promoter Bill Graham, and blew the minds of young, mostly white audiences.[25] To this day, jazz musicians, historians, and educators are still debating the relative artistic value of this period of "electric Miles" Davis.

The 1960s also saw the emergence of several female jazz musicians whose influence continues to be heard in the music of today. Singer, composer, and actress Abbey Lincoln took her voice to its extremes on drummer Max Roach's landmark civil rights-themed 1960 recording, *We Insist! (Max Roach's Freedom Now Suite)*, which spoke directly to America's civil rights and black power movements. Beginning in the late 1950s, harpist Dorothy Ashby presented the harp as a lead instrument on a number of now heavily sampled jazz recordings (Pete Rock, Common, and Jay-Z have each sampled Ashby on their own recordings). Her compositions incorporated elements of soul, R&B, and psychedelic rock, as well as music of the Far East, as on her 1970 album with Richard Evans, *The Rubaiyat of Dorothy Ashby*, where Ashby plays the koto, a traditional Japanese stringed instrument, piano, and harp.

And the influence of pianist, organist, and harpist Alice Coltrane is arguably as pervasive as her husband John's, as her many recordings, including the 1970 classic album *Ptah, the El Daoud*, continue to be discovered and rediscovered by succeeding generations of jazz, R&B, rock, and hip-hop musicians. In her interview for this book, harpist Brandee Younger says of her college years: "You know how some people are obsessed with John Coltrane? That was *me* with Alice Coltrane." Younger, a musician with her own distinct approach to her instrument and unique compositional voice, performed at Alice Coltrane's memorial service with Alice and John's son saxophonist Ravi Coltrane, and has recorded several of Alice Coltrane's compositions.

Think Visual

The "iconic, feminist, musical heroes" Monheit speaks of in her interview for this book certainly include several female musicians outside of jazz who found their way into the popular consciousness thanks to a U.S. cable channel called MTV, the "M" standing for "music video."

Singer Pat Benatar's "You Better Run" was the second video MTV aired when the channel launched on August 1, 1981. The video featured Benatar, rocking a pixie haircut and leather pants, lip-synching the song's lyrics with conviction in front of an all-male band on what would become the quintessential set for many 80s-era music videos: an empty warehouse rehearsal space.

Some of the biggest-selling singles in the U.S. throughout the 1980s were songs of female empowerment performed by female singers who possessed a visual style that drew equal inspiration from the streets, classic Hollywood films, and the avant-garde. These top-charting artists included Madonna, Annie Lennox of Eurythmics, Cyndi Lauper, Teena Marie, Sinéad O'Connor, Janet Jackson, Jody Watley, and Gloria Estefan. Watley has said of the songs on her 1987 self-titled debut album: "I wanted a sense of strength to be conveyed . . . the woman as victorious, the survivor. . . ."[26] MTV's audience reveled in the visual cues of these now classic videos, many of which depicted liberation from the prescribed societal expectations of a woman's "place" in rock and roll and the world at large. As one half of the British electronic soul duo Eurythmics, Annie Lennox appeared in the band's videos as a leather-clad dominatrix, a wig-wearing femme fatale, and herself in male drag complete with facial stubble. Donna Summer, Tina Turner, and Aretha Franklin also starred in heavily rotated music videos that put African-American women into the consciousness of pop music culture.

The Grammy award-winning vocal quartet the Manhattan Transfer is a rare example of jazz artists who embraced the visual style of the times.

"That was part of the uniqueness of the Manhattan Transfer," says vocalist Cheryl Bentyne, who joined the quartet in 1978 and is interviewed in this book. "Here was this group sounding like an old 1930s big band ensemble, but looking insane. It was an interesting combination of the visual and the vocal."

Soon after Bentyne joined the quartet in 1978, they began to work with choreographer Toni Basil (who danced on the television show *Soul Train* and later worked with the Talking Heads) and a young Jean Paul Gaultier ("before Madonna got him") to create a visual look that was equally inspired by 1920s art deco, 1960s-era space-age fashion, and late 70s, early 80s British new wave.

Despite what in retrospect could be described as a time period of provocative experimentation in popular music with visual artistry, music, and gender, many musicians outside of pop music considered videos to be just another form of advertising that perpetuated an unhealthy emphasis on the visual (i.e., looks) as opposed to musical talent and artistic vision.

"There's a lot of sexualizing of women in this industry," says Monheit in her interview for this book, "and there's just no place for that in our genre."

Throughout her career, Monheit has cultivated what she herself describes as "a glamorous persona," but not because of pressure from a record label or manager.

"If that's who we are as people," says Monheit. "If we want to put on the sexy dress and the high heels, then hell yeah. But if somebody is telling us to do it and we don't want to, then absolutely not."

Although MTV as it was circa-1981 is no more, we are currently living in a time where it is generally expected that music, whether it's pop, jazz, or classical, be attached to and supported by some sort of visual component. YouTube continues to dominate as the number-one platform for consumption of music from all genres and eras, often uploaded by users ignorant (or ignoring) the penalties of copyright infringement (although recording labels do upload and manage artist uploads). If we aren't listening while watching some sort of visual presentation, music is often providing a sort of filmic underscore for work-related or leisurely activities.

The Growth of Jazz Education

During the 1960s, a time of cultural upheaval that included, in addition to student-led campus protests and strikes, a reassessment of college curricula, the number of jazz classes offered for credit by secondary schools, colleges, and universities increased dramatically. Between 1960 and 1970, the number of U.S. college jazz bands increased from 30 to 450, and between 1964 and 1974, the number of institutions offering jazz programs for college credit increased from 41 to 228.[27] Up until 1950, the majority of music educators in the U.S. were adamant in their refusal to consider including jazz in music curricula. Jazz musicians such as Donald Byrd, Billy Taylor, Nathan Davis, and Jackie Mc-Clean, who entered the field of academia as both highly respected musicians and incredible teachers, provided "a sense of legitimacy" to the emerging jazz programs of the time.[28]

Current bachelor's and master's degree programs in jazz studies typically include performance study on a major instrument, participation in an instrumental ensemble, core music courses, and a selection of jazz major courses that may include jazz improvisation, styles of jazz, and jazz arranging. As of September 2013, the Internet-based education website *Jazz in America*, developed by the Thelonious Monk Institute of Jazz, lists 291 colleges and universities offering degree programs that involve jazz. *DownBeat* magazine lists over 175 select jazz studies and jazz music programs in their 2013 "Where to Study: A Jazz Student Music Guide." The website for *JazzTimes* magazine provides a searchable database of over 2,000 "college jazz and music industry programs from around the world."

Jazz education is not only a relatively recent phenomenon, it's also big business.

Since the 1950s, the number of women enrolled in college has steadily increased to where today, in most wealthy countries, the number of women attending college outnumbers that of men. Here in the U.S., three women for every two men graduate from college, and 60 percent of master's degrees go to women.[29]

Interestingly, four of the 35 musicians I interview in this book, vocalists Diane Schuur, Dee Dee Bridgewater, Cheryl Bentyne, and bassist Jennifer Leitham, did not attend college or complete a college-level jazz degree program. (Bridgewater makes it very clear in her interview that she has absolutely no formal music training, and in fact, does not read music.)

Says Bridgewater: "I just grew up in a whole different era. . . . Back when I was growing up and later when I was a young adult, there were a lot of musicians who did not read music or have a formal musical education. For me, this seemed normal!"

Crothers attended the University of California to study music composition, but ended up leaving school in order to relocate to New York City to study improvisation privately with pianist Lennie Tristano. While attending the University of Miami, singer Carmen Lundy, also interviewed in this book, shifted her major from music performance with a concentration on classical voice to jazz, although at that time, "there was no curriculum for a jazz vocalist." Schuur, Bridgewater, Bentyne, Leitham, Crothers, and Lundy all grew up in a time when jazz education at the university level was still evolving and opportunities for paid employment as a professional jazz musician did not require a diploma.

In my experience, the definition of a "professional" musician varies dramatically, depending on whom you talk to, and measuring the level of one's own artistry according to a job title and salary is a self-defeating, potentially self-destructive exercise. There are also countless examples throughout history of amazing, forward-thinking musicians, in all genres of music, who held or lacked a college degree, but were unable to support themselves solely through their art and found other ways to pay the bills.

By pointing all of this out, I certainly do not mean to denigrate academia or jazz education programs, and this book is most definitely not an argument pro or con as to the value of a college education. But what is apparent to me upon transcribing and reading the interviews contained in this book is that there is no one single path a musician must take in order to discover and achieve her or his artistic potential.

2. New Forms, New Hybrids

In her interview for this book, Crothers speaks of a "jazz renaissance," and her belief that this music, a genre with such strong, foundational roots, is at present being reshaped and revitalized by its practitioners. But if, as Crothers contends, "we're moving," what does that mean exactly? Do these interviews reveal any heretofore unexplored musical developments?

I believe we are living in a time where an unprecedented number of new musical forms and hybrids are emerging through the efforts of women across the spectrum of jazz. These new forms and hybrids include music that combines jazz with musical styles from around the world, including, but not limited to, Indonesia, Brazil, Argentina, Haiti, and Israel; music that combines spontaneous or "free" improvisation with the skills required to interpret and improvise upon standard repertoire; and music that is, in the words of avant-garde composer John Zorn, "a bit of a freak,"[30] and draws on many influences and artistic mediums without being directly connected to any tradition.

Global Influences

Everything, music and all of the other arts, is becoming a melting pot. The challenge in a world that is more international is to be able to identify where things are coming from and not be superficial. — Malika Zarra to the author, 2013

There is, of course, plenty of precedent in the history of jazz for much of the music we hear today that embraces and creatively transforms musical genres and styles from across the globe. New Orleans pianist Jelly Roll Morton spoke of adding a "Spanish tinge," actually a tango (also known as "habanera") rhythm, to his playing "to get the right seasoning … for jazz."[31] And going back as far as 1917, Puerto Rican and Cuban musicians played alongside African-American musicians and helped to transform what was "New Orleans music" into new, but still danceable hybrids. In the mid-1940s, the great jazz trumpet player and bandleader Dizzy Gillespie and conga virtuoso and composer Chano Pozo introduced Cuban rhythms into the context of the American big band and recorded some of the very first examples of what we now call Afro-Cuban or Latin jazz. Many American jazz musicians and bands in the late 1960s and early 1970s drew heavily on the music of Brazil, India, and Morocco, to name just three sources for inspiration, while assimilating contemporary psychedelic rock and funk grooves, effects, and instrumentation.

Many of the musicians interviewed for this book relocated to the U.S. after initially studying music in their home countries, including Anat Cohen and Ayelet Rose Gottlieb (Israel), Eliane Elias (Brazil), Sofia Rei (Argentina), Malika Zarra (Morocco), Patrizia Scascitelli (Italy), and Val Jeanty (Haiti). These women, as well as many women born in the U.S., are creating a repertoire of work that speaks to their own ethnic heritage while embracing the music of many other cultures, cultures that no longer seem so disparate in an age of the Internet and globalization.

Cohen, a bandleader from Israel who plays saxophones and clarinet, an instrument associated with Jewish klezmer music, composes and performs music inspired by Brazilian, Cuban, and Colombian music, Dixieland, French chanson, and contemporary west African grooves. The American-born trumpet player Samantha Boshnack, who composes for her B'shnorkestra ensemble, draws from such diverse sources as traditional and contemporary Balkan folk music and Balinese gamelan. Jeanty, a DJ and percussionist who has recorded and performed live with such jazz legends as pianist Geri Allen, uses an array of old and new school electronic gear as well as hand drums to create a highly realized musical hybrid of hip-hop, contemporary electronica, free jazz, and the ritual rhythms of Haitian vodou.

Even with so much precedent, new forms of music continue to emerge in our century, and women musicians of all races, ethnicities, and ages are leading the way in the creation of a truly global and multicultural form of jazz.

Spontaneous Improvisation and Standard Tunes

For many years the jazz world was sort of divided into groups. For instance, there was a kind of division between the free improvisers and the jazz musicians who played tunes, as well as other divisions based on other considerations. But now we're moving into a new era. — Pianist Connie Crothers to the author, 2013

In her interview for this book, Crothers speaks so eloquently and passionately about the emergence of a new type of spontaneous improvisation, born out of a deep familiarity with playing composed or "standard" tunes, that I felt the subject warranted its own section under "New Forms, New Hybrids."

Free improvisation is a process of playing that does not begin with, and may not even utilize, common-practice musical building blocks such as chord progressions, discernable forms, or even a clearly stated time signature. Key centers may be implied, but often, tonality is ignored in favor of a kind of relentless forward motion of the music. Classic and contemporary recordings of free jazz may sound, to the uninitiated listener, chaotic, relentless, and even frightening, although this type of playing can also evoke a kind of quiet, prayerful, and devotional stasis.

Released in 1961, saxophonist Ornette Coleman's album *Free Jazz: A Collective Improvisation* was the first recording of a collectively improvised performance.

Performed by a double quartet of two drummers, two bassists, two reeds players (Coleman and Eric Dolphy), Don Cherry on pocket trumpet, and Freddie Hubbard on trumpet, the music lasted the entirety of side one and side two of the album.

This recording, along with saxophonist John Coltrane's large-ensemble album *Ascension* (released in 1966), saxophonist Albert Ayler's *Spiritual Unity* (1964), pianist Cecil Taylor's *Unit Structures* (1966), and saxophonist Peter Brötzmann's abrasive, almost punk-rock-sounding *Machine Gun* (released in 1968 and again in 1971) helped define what was then a new genre of freely improvised music. During this time, vocalist Maggie Nicols and pianist Irène Schweizer were just two among a growing pool of women musicians who embraced free improvisation in and outside the context of jazz.

This powerfully realized music, sometimes referred to by the writers at the time as "the new thing" and/or avant-garde, certainly has precedent in the collective improvising one hears on New Orleans trumpeter King Oliver's 1920s-era recordings, guitarist Django Reinhardt's 1937 recording "Improvisation #1," as well as two tracks, "Intuition" and "Digression," from pianist Lennie Tristano's 1949 album with saxophonist Wayne Marsh, *Intuition*. Crothers suggests that the first instance of free improvisation on a recording may be Louis Armstrong's solo trumpet introduction to his 1928 cut "West End Blues."

Crothers, a former student of Tristano, speaks eloquently and in great detail about a kind of free playing she calls "spontaneous improvisation" that is, in performance, guided initially by the melodic content of a standard song.

"The melody of the tune has the form," says Crothers. "If you internalize the melody of the tune, you don't have to count beats and bars ... and when you release your improvisation after that point, you can bring in anything."

Many of the interviewees in this book have and continue to embrace free improvisation in their music, including flutist Cheryl Pyle, violinist Mazz Swift, trumpeter Nicole Rampersaud, and pianist Roberta Piket, who describes in her interview her approach to freely improvising on various motives found in the Thelonious Monk composition "Monk's Dream." When it comes to describing the technique of free improvisation, Piket echoes Crothers' approach: "I think the first thing to do is really internalize the motive so you can play and express them organically. You can't be thinking about it like, 'Okay, now I'm going to play this motive. Now I'm going to play this motive. . . .' If you do that, it's going to sound really unmusical and stilted and awful."

This process of utilizing free improvisation to develop and explore new musical realms is another recurring theme in this collection of interviews and speaks to yet another way contemporary musicians are bridging "the roots of the form with the new possibilities of their own time."[32]

The Avant-Garde

I rarely write anything that swings in the real jazz sense of the word and I rarely play straight-ahead jazz.... I think in this day and age when we are all involved in so many kinds of music, playing all sorts of stuff all the time, you end up coming up with music that incorporates a lot of different things and can't be categorized.
—Samantha Boshnack to the author, 2013

The avant-garde as it relates to jazz certainly has its own history and canon and has arguably evolved over time to become a genre in and of itself that incorporates influences from all of the arts, not just music. This is the zone where more than a few of the musicians interviewed in this book operate and flourish, and where countless other women musicians continue to represent.

Two American musicians who have operated in this zone for many decades, Anthony Braxton and John Zorn, both saxophonists, both composers, and both with a thorough command and understanding of jazz, have each had a significant impact on more than a few of the musicians interviewed for this book. Trumpeter Nicole Rampersaud, violinist Jean Cook, and cellist Nioka Workman have each performed Braxton's music. (Rampersaud's interview includes a detailed description of her part in a performance of Braxton's "Composition #103 for Seven Choreographed and Costumed Trumpets.") Singers Sofia Rei, Ayelette Rose Gottlieb, and Malika Zarra are each members of the a cappella group Mycale, who arrange, contribute lyrics to, and perform the music from Zorn's *Book of Angels*. To take it a bit further, Boshnack has played with and acknowledged the support of Seattle-based keyboardist and composer Wayne Horovitz, who was a member of Zorn's groundbreaking band Naked City. The pluralistic spirit that informs the oeuvre of both Braxton and Zorn, where music is transformed into hybrid mediums that may include spoken word, physical movement, lighting, film, and even scents, is informing a great deal of the music being made by today's young musicians.

If it's a challenge to source the etymology of and then provide a concrete definition of jazz, accounting for the musical avant-garde doesn't make that job any easier. (Zorn himself has said he'd like to see avant-garde, experimental music "accepted as a genre in and of itself."[33]) In many of these interviews, the musicians offer some explanation to describe what it is they do and how it may or may not relate to "jazz" as a musical tradition and genre. What I hope comes across in these transcribed conversations is the joy and excitement each musician feels when exploring the inherent possibilities of the form.

3. New Business Models

I was a very rare artist in the 90s, to have that ability to produce my own albums. I decided my own music and my fate, my image, my everything. I controlled that. Not a record company.— Dee Dee Bridgewater to the author, 2013

When asked, each musician I interviewed for this book confirmed they are seeing more women than ever working in the music industry, and not only as musicians, but as recording engineers, managers, label owners, and publicists. This growing emergence of women in an industry that is almost unrecognizable when compared with what it was at the end of the 20th century, is significant, given what women bring to the proverbial table in times of upheaval and traumatic change.[34]

The business paradigms that since the earliest days of the music industry have destroyed the livelihood of artists are now being challenged and renegotiated by pop stars, such as Madonna and Beyoncé, as well as women musicians across the spectrum of jazz. Artist-run labels, crowdfunding, and new types of contracts with recording labels are just a few of the ways the artists interviewed in this book are taking control of the business of making music.

Artist-Run Labels

Anzic Records didn't start just because I wanted artistic freedom. It started because I wanted to have control over what happens to my albums.... The days where musicians just played music and didn't need to think about business are over.
—Anat Cohen to the author, 2013

All of the musicians I interviewed for this book are actively involved in recording, promoting, and selling their music. Several of the interviewees own or co-own independent record labels and/or production companies, including Anat Cohen (Anzic Records), Jane Ira Bloom (Outline Music), Dee Dee Bridgewater (DDB Productions, Inc.), and Carmen Lundy (Afrasia Productions), or manage distribution and sales of their music through their own websites and/or online platforms for selling CDs and downloads, such as CD Baby and Bandcamp.

In 1969, long before the advent of the Internet and MP3s, jazz vocalist Betty Carter took control of her music by creating a label she named Bet Car Records, which, in turn, inspired Bridgewater to start her own label and production company.

"I would go over to [Betty's] house and she would have her LPs lined up in the hallway [as] she was preparing to ship them out," says Bridgewater. "My biggest influence has been Betty Carter. Not because I tried to sound like her or imitate her ... but because I wanted that kind of freedom."[35]

As a member of a thriving, forward-thinking music community based in New Haven, Connecticut, in the mid-1970s, a community that included trombonist George Lewis, drummer Gerry Hemmingway, and bassist Mark Dresser, composer and soprano saxophonist Jane Ira Bloom was given the impetus to start her own record label and publishing company, Outline Music. Bloom points out in her interview for this book that the recording industry at the time "was in a real lull," meaning, if you were a creative but relatively unknown artist that "had music that was worth documenting," you had to learn how to record, package, and distribute your own album.

The independent music label New Artists Records began in 1982 after pianist Connie Crothers and drummer Max Roach recorded a series of spontaneously improvised duets. When no record company expressed interest in releasing the recordings, Crothers and Roach formed the label, which was later reconfigured to operate as a cooperative. Each musician on New Artists Records contributes to the operating expenses of the label and receives 100 percent of his or her album sales.

Since digital technology now allows audio and video recordings to be easily bootlegged and uploaded to the Internet, an overwhelming number of aural and visual examples of jazz performance, dating back to the turn of the century and on into the present day, are instantly accessible to both casual consumers and serious students of music. In her 2009 interview with the website *Solidarity*, Crothers describes the impact the Internet has had on smaller as well as "big record companies."

"This is a change in the technology of distribution," says Crothers, "and like other similar changes in technological history it will not be stopped. One conclusion is, inevitably, that recording is no longer a feasible way to make money."

However, in the same interview, Crothers acknowledges that there is a flip side to the less than artist-friendly aspects of the Internet.

"In a time when people bemoan the failure of jazz," says Crothers, "you can get the music of just about every jazz artist who ever lived and recorded. Having gone through a time in the 1960s when it was impossible to get records of even some giants like Charlie Parker, this seems like a renaissance to me."[36]

Crowdfunding

Crowdfunding has become an extremely popular method for musicians to raise funds for specific projects, such as the recording of a new album. With crowdfunding, a musician sets the funding goal for his or her project, and then uses an online platform such as Kickstarter or IndieGoGo to promote a fundraising campaign and facilitate monetary donations from fans to the project. Most campaigns offer a variety of "rewards" to donors, each based on the dollar amount of a donation. Crowdfunding platforms are typically for-profit businesses, and donations to a campaign are not tax-deductible. However, the New York-based art infrastructure organization Fractured Atlas, which offers fiscal sponsorship to artists without not-for-profit status, is partnered with IndieGoGo so that online crowdfunded donations to Fractured Atlas artist-members are tax-deductible.

Composer and big band leader Maria Schneider is one of the best-known jazz artists to successfully and repeatedly use crowdfunding, specifically the online platform ArtistShare, to finance the recording of several of her critically acclaimed albums. Among the interviewees in this book, trumpeter and composer Samantha Boshnack used Kickstarter to raise over $6,000 toward the recording of *Go to Orange* by her 15-member ensemble, B'Shnorkestra. Violinist Mazz Swift, bassist Jennifer Leitham, singer Ayelet Rose Gottlieb, and cellist Nioka Workman have each utilized crowdfunding platforms to fund their recording projects.

New Types of Contracts

In her interview for this book, drummer, composer, and producer Terri Lyne Carrington explains how a recording project with a strong concept or "angle," such as her Grammy Award-winning album *The Mosaic Project*, which features an all-female lineup of jazz, R&B, hip-hop, and Latin music artists, can help the process of securing a license deal with a record company.

In a license deal, the artist is expected to cover the costs of recording an album and deliver a finished product to the label. The artist then licenses out the rights to the recording for a finite period to a label, splitting any income that comes in from sales and licensing deals to television shows, commercials, and/or movies, before all rights revert back to the artist.[37]

Unlike the standard album deal, a license deal allows an artist to avoid being in debt to a label and retain the rights to their master recordings, rights that allow them to earn additional income so long as their music remains available and in print.[38] Many of the artists interviewed in this book have benefited from license deals, or what I call "hybrid" deals, which combine aspects of standard royalty, license, and manufacturing and distribution deals.

Musicians typically spend their formative years practicing and playing and honing their technique; this timeline of disciplined focus is crucial for any musician with aspirations of playing at the professional level. However, when it comes to building a career, a musician will be at a serious disadvantage if they do not also develop a basic understanding of the music business.

"For me it took, like, 20 years in before I was really seeing how involved I could be on [the business] side of things," says Carrington, who believes music business classes should be a mandatory part of a music conservatory's curriculum.

"Everybody has to know certain things," says Carrington. "It all should be talked about as early as possible."

4. Concerns About the Book's Title

One day, we won't need a book called Women in Jazz.
— *Mindi Abair to the author, 2012*

Every single musician I interviewed for this book has thanked me for doing a project that focuses specifically on the contributions of women to the art of jazz music. Several interviewees told me they were pleased to discover that such a book was being written. This is very humbling for me since my respect for musicians, regardless of what kind of music they play, is such that I do not take for granted the time a player grants to me to discuss their work and personal history. That may sound like a line, but it's not. Speaking now as a composer who is married to a classical singer and enjoys the friendship of several men and women who play, compose, and teach music, the day-to-day commitment of time, energy, and love required to produce art is not an abstract concept to me.

The project gained momentum very quickly. After my initial interview with Mindi Abair, who incidentally, does not identify herself as a "jazz" musician, although she has studied and played the music extensively throughout her musical life, I was able to quickly schedule conversations with Eliane Elias, Terri Lyne Carrington, and Jane Ira Bloom. Having the participation of musicians of this high of a caliber no doubt opened some doors for me as I contacted the publicists and managers of other female artists. However, there were a handful of musicians who turned down my request for an interview for this book, the main reason being the book's working title.

The working title of the book, *Women in Jazz*, struck a small number of musicians I approached as being out of date and even denigrating, considering the advances women in all industries have made in the 21st century. If women simply want to be considered as equals to their male counterparts in any industry, why single them out for a gender-specific book? If jazz is, as a [male] musician friend of mine put it, "the great equalizer," then isn't gender a non-issue? Either you can play or you can't, simple as that.

One well-known composer and bandleader I approached with my pitch said she was simply "burnt out" on participating in projects where the focus is on women. Another musician explained to me she does not define her creative work in terms of gender, genre, or skin color, and that participating in the project would only contribute to the regulation of her art. I should point out that the musicians who declined to be interviewed made it clear to me that their decision was a personal one and although they would not be participating, they looked forward to seeing such a book in print.

Speaking of gender, is there a place among "women in jazz" for a transgender man or woman? Does pianist and saxophonist Billy Tipton, born Dorothy Lucille Tipton in 1914, and who passed as a male both professionally and in private life, belong in a book called *Women in Jazz*? Tellingly, bassist Jennifer Leitham, born John Leitham, who is one of the finest jazz bass players in the world, thanked me at the end of her interview for focusing the majority of my questions on music instead of gender and including her in a book collection of conversations with so many inspiring women. The award-winning film *I Stand Corrected* (2012) documents Jennifer's transition from John to Jennifer, a transition she bravely made at a peak in her career and with the support of such high-profile musical colleagues as trumpeter Doc Severinsen and singer Mel Tormé.

I believe I understand and empathize, to the best of my ability as a male, with these concerns about the working title of this book. I believe debating the currency of the words "women" or for that matter "jazz" is healthy and stimulating. But the fact is, very few books in print about jazz make an attempt to comprehensively acknowledge the contributions women have made and continue to make to the music. Judy Chaikin's film *The Girls in the Band* is the only film I am aware of that, at the time of this writing, provides a comprehensive overview of women playing jazz in the U.S. from the late 1920s to the present day.[39]

There are a relatively small number of notable books that chronicle women musicians as trailblazers in the world of jazz, including Sherrie Tucker's *Swing Shift: "All-Girl" Bands of the 1940s*; Kristin A. McGee's *Some Liked It Hot*, which looks at all-girl bands from the 1920s through the 1950s; Linda Dahl's *Stormy Weather: The Music and Lives of a Century of Jazzwomen*; Janis Stockhouse's *Women Jazz Musicians: Conversations with 21 Musicians*; and Jan Leder's *Women in Jazz: A Discography of Instrumentalists, 1913-1968*. (Leder, who is also a flutist, composer, and lyricist, is one of the women interviewed in this book.) Leslie Gourse's 1996 book *Madame Jazz: Contemporary Women Instrumentalists* collects interviews with several young, contemporary female jazz musicians as well as women in the music business. There is also a growing catalog of academic writings on the subject of women in jazz.

However, male writers writing about the musical accomplishments of male musicians dominate the majority of jazz writing. A typical example is *Reading Jazz: A Gathering of Autobiography, Reportage, and Criticism from 1919 to Now*, compiled in 1996 by Robert Gottlieb, in which only 15 out of the 107 individual autobiographical excerpts, reportage, and critical essays are written by women or are about women in jazz.

So while some men and more than a few women believe a book about women in jazz is unnecessary, from my (male) perspective, I do not believe the book is going to do any musician a disservice, not from where I sit, and not at this point in history.

—Chris Becker

Dee Dee Bridgewater

The great jazz singer Billie Holiday possessed a certain genius at recasting the melodic, harmonic, rhythmic, and lyrical content of popular music. Dramatist, critic, and poet Amiri Baraka wrote that Holiday ". . . is never tied to 'the given,' either the form or the intended content,"[40] and describes her as "the poet of jazz singing."

Despite being described as a "keeper of tradition," Grammy and Tony Award-winning singer Dee Dee Bridgewater, like Holiday, has never been tied to "the given." She too is a poet, griot, and historian,[41] but she's also a hell of an entertainer.

"I used to say I came from the Sammy Davis, Jr. school of music," says Bridgewater. "Because when I was growing up, a lot of entertainers had to be able to do all of that, or they weren't considered a full entertainer."

Like the iconic singers she grew up watching on television, singers such as Judy Garland, Diahann Carroll, Frank Sinatra, and Elvis Presley, who reached millions of viewers on shows like the *Perry Como Show*, the *Ed Sullivan Show*, the *Lawrence Welk Show*, and the *Grand Ole Opry*, Bridgewater is a truly multifaceted artist, with a résumé that includes several theatrical and film roles. Bridgewater received a Tony Award for Best Featured Actress in a Musical for her role in *The Wiz* and a Laurence Olivier Award nomination for her immersive portrayal of Billie Holiday in Stephen Stahl's musical *Lady Day*.

To say Bridgewater is "theatrical" in performance is an understatement. In fact, I'd go further and describe what she does as something closer to channeling; Bridgewater establishes an almost psychic rapport with her audiences, all while directing her band with her voice, her eyes, and her body to create an experience more transcendent than mere "music theater."

In an earlier conversation, when I asked her about her singing "Strange Fruit," the 1939 song made famous by Holiday that describes, in graphic detail, the lynching of African Americans in the South, Bridgewater explained she let her audience dictate, in unspoken terms, whether or not to perform the song.

"I have to feel the audience," she explained, "and see if they want to go there with me."

There is great depth and variety to Bridgewater's recorded output, including tributes to singers Ella Fitzgerald and Holiday, pianist Horace Silver, and composer Kurt Weill, as well as *Red Earth: A Malian Journey*, a project recorded in Mali with musicians from Senegal, Guinea, and other parts of West Africa, that had a profound impact on her singing. Bridgewater cites the great jazz singer Betty Carter for inspiring her to start her own recording label (DDB Productions) in order to maintain control over her creative output and the

Dee Dee Bridgewater. Photo by Mark Higashino.

business of making art. Interestingly, like Bridgewater, several of the musicians interviewed in this book run their own record labels and handle much of their own PR and marketing.

"I decided my own music and my fate, my image, my everything," says Bridgewater. "You need to own it, baby."

....

When did you first begin playing a musical instrument?

I don't play any musical instruments. I've always sung my entire life. At the age of 7, I announced to my parents that when I grew up I was going to be an internationally known and very-well-respected jazz singer! And there you go. I predicted my future without even knowing it.

When I was a child, I thought everybody listened to jazz because there was so much jazz music playing in my home. Both of my parents loved jazz music. My mother was more into jazz singers, while my father [Matthew Garrett] was a trumpet player who had taught music back in Memphis, Tennessee, where I was born. I've always sung. Always.

After you made that announcement, did some kind of formal music instruction begin for you?

I've never had any formal musical training at all. None. I do not read music. I can't write music. I've just always relied on my ears.

You never had a voice instructor?

Well, I did work with a vocal coach. When I was with the Thad Jones/Mel Lewis Orchestra, I took a few lessons to learn how to breathe and project my voice.

After a tonsillectomy, when I was 26, 27, I had to take speech lessons and learn how to breathe again. I had enlarged tonsils up until that age and always had problems with laryngitis caused by infections in my tonsils. I had a very small wind passage for air to come through, and when my tonsils were removed, all of a sudden I had this huge passage for air. But I couldn't say words that started with "d" or "p" or "t." So, once again, I had to go to a vocal coach to learn how to breathe again with this open airway that had been so constricted all my life. But I've never had anyone work with me to teach me how to sing. Never.

Was some kind of music programming available to you in school?

No. I've never had any musical training.

When I was a teenager, I put together a vocal trio. We modeled ourselves after the first vocal trios that were signed to [the record label] Motown in Detroit. We called ourselves the Iridescents. I had a girlfriend who played piano, and she and I wrote songs together for the three of us to sing. But that's the closest I've come to any kind of training at all. I never had any kind of musical classes in school. Nothing. Zero.

As a young woman, who were some of your role models for singing?
My role models were drawn from people I heard on recordings. I was fascinated with a lot of different types of singers when I was young. My mother loved Johnny Mathis, so I heard a lot of Johnny Mathis and Harry Belafonte. I fell in love with Jimmy Scott. I was enamored with Nina Simone, and fascinated by her political stance and her pride in her African heritage. She was the first singer who made me think "maybe I have some African heritage."

My first big idol was Nancy Wilson. She just decorated my walls when I was a teenager. I liked Lena Horne—I just thought she was so beautiful along with Nancy Wilson. I thought Diahann Carroll was a very beautiful woman; she was doing more singing back in the 60s and 70s before her acting career really took off. My mother, sister, and I were big Aretha Franklin fans. We would go to Aretha Franklin concerts together when I was a teenager.

I listened to black radio stations, so I could know what was going on. When I was like 9, 10, there was a radio station broadcasting out of Memphis that I could pick up after midnight that played a lot of blues.

My mother swears that I could scat before I could speak. She said I could scat with Ella Fitzgerald when I was 10 months old. And there must be some truth to that because I have always been able to scat. I never had to learn to scat.

You grew up in what was a real golden age for music. All of these great women you named—it's amazing to think that their music was *the* popular culture.
We also had a lot of musical television programs back then. I loved to watch Judy Garland on her show when I was a little girl. I thought it was fascinating how she stood with her legs apart a little bit. And she could just belt out these songs. She really moved me.

I grew up in Flint, Michigan, which had a very large Polish community. We would go to little Polish restaurants to eat, and they would always have polka music. When I was little, I would watch the programs with Polish music. There was man who called himself Lawrence Welk who played Polish music on his television show.

I loved the *Grand Ole Opry*—that was a television show. I loved country and western music! [laughs]

We had the *Ed Sullivan Show*, the *Perry Como Show*, the *Bing Crosby Show*. We had Frank Sinatra, who was in movies and sang. We had Elvis Presley, who sang in movies as well. So we had music, you know?

When I was a teenager, I used to climb out of my window to sneak out and go and see James Brown. I got to meet him when I was in Paris. Every time he came to France, I would go and meet with him.

The only music I'm not so familiar with is classical. But I did a jazzy version of *Carmen*, the opera by Georges Bizet. So I listened to Maria Callas and … for me there's Maria Callas and then there's the rest of the opera world. She was unique in that she was so free in her interpretations. I've never heard anyone approach opera with that kind of freedom. I'm fairly close to Jessye Norman; we were both in Paris at the same time, and I'm a fan of Jessye's. I've worked with several opera singers, but growing up I didn't really have that exposure.

Acting and theater became a big part of your career. When you perform with your band, like Judy Garland, you're telling a story, with your body, with your face, with the way you lead the band. Was there any formal instruction for you in acting?
No, I've never taken acting classes. I never studied anything that I do.

I grew up watching old movie musicals. I loved the Ziegfeld Follies. I loved all of those beautiful numbers with women coming down stairs and being surrounded by men. I used to dream of doing that. I wanted to be like those people who sang and acted and danced!

I used to say I came from the Sammy Davis, Jr. school of music, because when I was growing up, a lot of entertainers had to be able to do all of that, or they weren't considered a full entertainer. I've always been very attracted to comedy, musicals, and drama. I can be such a drama queen myself in my personal life!

I'm a frustrated dancer. I did take dance classes when I was doing *The Wiz*, the first musical that I did. I was pigeon-toed, and I taught myself to walk like a dancer. Another woman who was inspiration for me was Isadora Duncan. As a child, I wanted to do interpretive dance and modern dance.

When I got my first role in *The Wiz*, I did come down the stairs, surrounded by men on both sides, and I was carried across the stage by the dancers.

Like Josephine Baker!
My great aunt Lottie Gee—she's on my father's side—was very instrumental in Josephine Baker's decision to go to Paris. She's mentioned in just about every book about Baker. She sang in Eubie Blake's production of *Shuffle Along*.

Many musicians I've interviewed, some for this book, learned to become a multifaceted artist not in a school, but on "the street."
I grew up in that era of doo-wop groups on the corner. This trio I mentioned, the Iridescents, we wore iridescent dresses that we made ourselves. Back when I was growing up, everybody sewed because we didn't have money. If we wanted new clothes we would have to get a pattern! We would make outfits to wear

to go to parties. I could whip up a dress in like, two hours, you know? With zipper and everything!

I just grew up in a whole different era. I always say my formal musical training came from being in the Thad Jones/Mel Lewis Orchestra for four years. Thad Jones was my biggest mentor. And all of those musicians in that band, they were like my musical fathers. I learned through working with people like Dizzy Gillespie, Clark Terry, Jerome Richardson, Roland Hanna, and Richard Davis. In my early 20s, I was singing with Sonny Rollins and Dexter Gordon. I worked with Max Roach, Pharoah Sanders, and Rahsaan Roland Kirk!

So I had a totally different upbringing. Back when I was growing up and later when I was a young adult, there were a lot of musicians who did not read music or have a formal musical education. For me, this seemed normal!

Jazz academia is a relatively new invention. What you were doing was going to college, getting your doctorate, your Ph.D., on the bandstand. Do you do master classes for young musicians?
Yes.

How do you approach those classes, given that your background is so different from the young musicians you're instructing?
I just share my experiences. I am able to show students how to breathe properly, how to be in the space, and how to be true to their instrument. I may hear a singer who says they want to do jazz, and when they start to sing, I may have to say, "I'm sorry, sweetie, you don't have a jazz voice. You should be doing such and such...."

I talk to students about the relationship between singers and musicians, how singers need to respect the musicians, how we are no better than the musicians, and that the musician is a singer's best friend. When I've worked with instrumentalists, I've taught them the importance of learning a song, learning the melody, and learning the lyric so they know how to better interpret the song when they're playing the song. I can talk to drummers about keeping time and to instrumentalists about how to put emotion into their playing.

I don't think that one necessarily has to have had a formal musical education background to be able to teach. I can talk, because I talk from experience.

Right!
And a lot of students come up to me and say, "Thank you so much. You have given us information that we don't get from our teachers."

And I'm starting to understand why, when musicians get older, you see them with young musicians. I am beginning to have a need to be with young musicians. I want to work with young people and try and help them along in their musical careers. I've produced a young trumpet player named Theo Croker. The trumpet is my favorite instrument, and I think of my voice as a trumpet. I've been talking to Theo and sharing with him things he needs to do with his instrument.

Are you seeing more women in the music industry these days? Not just musicians, but in the roles of producers, engineers, and publicists?
Absolutely. When I did my album *Dear Ella*, I had a female engineer. As I'm going across the country and doing master classes, yes, I am seeing more women working in production. And I think that's fabulous.

Singer Betty Carter had a big impact on you, correct?
How did I forget Betty Carter? When I first moved to New York in 1970 with [my first husband] Cecil [Bridgewater], I was Betty Carter's shadow. Any time she performed in New York, I was down front. I would get a table by myself—I didn't want to have to talk to anybody. I was just fascinated by Betty Carter. I wanted to sing with the same abandon. Betty was very physical in her singing. She could contort her body like nobody else! [laughs]

I would go over to her house, and she would have her LPs lined up in the hallway because she was preparing to ship them out.[42] So I said, "When I grow up, I want to be like Betty Carter. I want to produce my own albums. I want to have my own label." My biggest influence has been Betty Carter, not because I tried to sound like her or imitate her, but because she was totally unique. I wanted that kind of freedom, and I've got it!

When you say freedom, are you also talking about the freedom that comes when you have your own label and when you have control over certain aspects of the music business?
I've been producing myself since 1993. It has always irked me that when I would get album reviews, CD or album reviews, most writers would never mention that I had produced my record. I was a very rare artist in the 90s, to have that ability to produce my own albums. I decided my own music and my fate, my image, my everything. I controlled that. Not a record company.

When I give the record companies my albums, they are finished. I have recorded them and mixed them with whomever I have as my engineer. My guru has been Al Schmidt. Al Schmidt has done almost all of my CDs with the exception of two. I only master with Doug Sax. I have a graphic arts team that I work with out of France, because I started doing this in France. I do my own layouts, photo shoots, everything, the entire package. All the record companies have to do it press it and put it out.

Terri Lyne Carrington is someone else who is producing her own albums, like *The Mosaic Project* and *Money Jungle*.

Terri Lyne has always produced herself. Even when she did albums in the 80s, in the 90s, she always produced herself. I love Terri Lyne. Absolutely adore her.

I hope we see more and more of this happening with artists in all types of music, where artists take on this kind of control of their music.

This whole industry is changing. [coughs dramatically] I think eventually albums are going to be a thing of the past, with all the downloading and streaming and all of that. Sony has resuscitated OKeh records, and they are only interested in artists who are doing their own production, artists who will bring them an album produced from A to Z. One of the reasons they're giving me a distribution deal for my record label is because I'm going to give them a complete package. I will be at the helm of everything. I'll do the artwork, I'll do the whole thing.

I own all of my own albums. I own all of my masters. I lease them to the record company for a period of time. You need to own it, baby.

Terri Lyne Carrington

Drummer, composer, and producer Terri Lyne Carrington is one of the first musicians I interviewed for this book. In our conversation, she quotes composer Duke Ellington to help explain her relationship to jazz:

"I don't doubt my connection with it, because I don't look at it as a certain thing. It's creative music. Duke Ellington said jazz means 'freedom of expression.' And I think that everything that I do, for the most part, feels like jazz. As far as creative music and freedom of expression, like Duke Ellington said, there's no 'box' for that."

Her reply provided me with the first three words to the title of this book. Her early participation as an interviewee also opened some doors for me as I contacted other musicians around the country about this project. There's no question, Carrington commands a great deal of respect among the music community at large.

Born in 1965 in Medford, Massachusetts, Terri Lyne Carrington is part of a multi-generational musical family that includes her father, saxophonist Sonny Carrington, and grandfather, drummer Matt Carrington, who played with Fats Waller and Duke Ellington. Carrington was a child prodigy and began taking classes at Berklee College of Music under a full scholarship at the age of 11. In 1983, she moved to New York and became an in-demand musician, drumming for jazz luminaries Lester Bowie, James Moody, Pharoah Sanders,

Terri Lyne Carrington. Photo by Phil Farnsworth.

and many others. Her extensive résumé includes television gigs as the house drummer for the *Arsenio Hall Show* and Quincy Jones' late-night show *Vibe*, hosted by the comedian Sinbad. She has also toured extensively with pianist and composer Herbie Hancock.

In addition to being a virtuoso drummer, Carrington is a formidable producer, a role that allows her to bring together artists from all genres into her creative projects. I interviewed Carrington for this book not long after the release of her Grammy Award-winning album *The Mosaic Project*, a collection of tracks performed by some of the world's most highly respected female instrumentalists and singers, including Dee Dee Bridgewater, Carmen Lundy, Helen Sung, and Anat Cohen, who are also interviewed in this book. In the liner notes to *The Mosaic Project*, Carrington says the album "comments on historical, current, and appropriately feminine themes," and for listeners new to jazz, it is a wonderful, engaging, and profound introduction to this music.

....

When did you first begin studying music?
My grandfather was a drummer. He passed away before I was born. I guess my father was my first teacher.

At around age 9, I started taking private lessons at like a music shop. But I never, throughout my whole public-school time period, took music classes, except for violin, in third grade.

So at a young age, the drums were your main instrument?
It was always just the drums! I took piano lessons, but I guess I never really felt I was going to *play* the piano. I wanted to know music theory and things like that. But for the most part, it was just the drums.

At that age, before you were even a teenager, what kind of music were you listening to? And what kind of stuff were you playing on the drums?
Well, see my dad was a saxophone player too. I was into jazz because that was what he was into. But I was also listening to the popular music of the day because ... I was young! [laughs] I had friends! So I listened to people in the jazz world, Miles Davis, John Coltrane, and Michael Jackson, and Earth Wind & Fire as well.

And your family, as things got more serious, they were 100 percent behind this career choice that was forming for you at such a young age?
Oh, yeah! Yes, they were always supportive. Still are. My dad still plays a little bit, and my success was one of three generations.

So maybe it wasn't that unusual to have a musical prodigy in the house?

Well, not unusual for us! [laughs] I think you're very fortunate when you have a family that understands it and doesn't think music is something that should be a hobby. I wouldn't be the musician I am today without my dad and all of his knowledge.

You began at Berklee at the age of 11? Is that correct?
Yes. I was taking private lessons and jamming with ensembles. I didn't really attend real classes, mainly just private lessons on drums and piano.

Did you think back then, as a young woman, a young woman playing drums, you were cutting your path, doing something that had not necessarily been done before?
I think as a young person, no. As I've gotten older, I've been seeing myself more as a pioneer in a sense.

As a trained jazz musician, with a lot of experience playing live and touring, was the transition to playing on television weird?
No, because I always had respect for great artists in the R&B field and the pop field. And as a result of my television gigs, I ended up playing with a lot of those people, like James Brown, Whitney Houston, Rick James—all kinds of people. It was just fun for me. It wasn't like I was playing down to that music or those artists at all!

Did you end up shifting your focus as a musician as a result of the schedule demands of television?
Yes, but I think your focus should shift every time you work in and play another style. It wasn't about chops or anything like that. When I played jazz, which was a lot less during that time, I played better, because my approach was fresh. Because I had been away from it, I got better.

Was playing for Rick James different from playing for Herbie Hancock?
Yes. TV is a very different animal. You have to play in 30 seconds with such energy. It's not about a building; it's about getting to the point very quickly. When you're coming in and out of commercials, you have to sound good from the moment you hit the first stroke and absolutely have to have a certain level of energy.

When I play certain styles of jazz, it's more about telling a story, and starting something and building something into an experience for the listener.

But with TV shows, and maybe pop music in general, it's a little different. It's about really performing from that "one."[43] It's entertainment. So, maybe it's not as spontaneous. But I'm not saying it's not creative; that music is creative too!

As a drummer, I have as much respect for the groove aspect of music as I do the creative aspect. I always tell people, I always have the same great feeling from playing a gig with Bill Withers as I do from Herbie Hancock. The feeling is the same, though the experience is very different.

Your album *The Mosaic Project* brings together what you just described into one musical universe. From the first second, it just hits you and pulls you in. Is it more challenging these days to get a recording label behind a project like *The Mosaic Project*, a project that is so elaborate and involves so many musicians?

Well, yes. It's just more challenging in general, because the record labels are disintegrating. It's difficult to get interest for a product unless you have an "angle" and the label feels like they can sell that. Fortunately, *The Mosaic Project* had that, and did that.

I tend to make concept records anyway, you know what I mean? My next project is a cover of the album *Money Jungle*, the Duke Ellington album [with Max Roach on drums and Charles Mingus on bass]. This is a contemporary spin on that. I left a couple of songs as they were, but for the most part, I've rearranged everything with pianist Gerald Clayton and bassist Christian Mc-Bride. Trumpeter Clark Terry is a special guest, and I added some horns on some tracks, but it's basically a trio setting.

When a project is so focused conceptually, it's easier to get a label interested in it. *Money Jungle* is going to come out on Concord, but *The Mosaic Project* was a licensed project with Concord. It's not like I had a revolving record deal. So I have to come up with things that a label, whether it's Concord or another label, feels like they can sink their teeth into. I also have to finance each recording project myself, and then license it to the label.

Considering the state of the music industry, do you think it's as important for musicians to develop entrepreneurial and business skills along with their musical skills? Is that something you talk about with your students?

Yeah! I talk about it with my students all the time. I talk about it when I do clinics. I talk about it with other artists who are coming up.

It's a different time. For me it took, like, 20 years in before I was really seeing how involved I could be in the business side of things. Because of the time you spend honing your craft and playing, an understanding of the business happens in its own time. But if you can help a younger artist with some shortcuts, that's great.

Should the business of music be a part of music education in schools?

Yes. At Berklee, they have classes in music business, and you can even major in music business. But on a basic level, everybody has to know certain things. I think for a successful career in music, they should have mandatory music business classes from the very beginning. It should all be talked about as early as possible. I don't think you should have to major in music business to learn those things.

What's your relationship to jazz music? Do you look at jazz as having a beginning and a timeline? Where do you connect with it?
I don't doubt my connection with it, because I don't look at it as a certain thing. It's creative music. Duke Ellington said, "jazz means freedom of expression."[44] And I think that everything that I do, for the most part, feels like jazz. As far as creative music and freedom of expression, like Duke Ellington said, there's no "box" for that. In fact, Ellington said they stopped using the word "jazz" in 1943!

It's also like global music to me. When I look at Esperanza Spalding—I play on her last two records—I hear all kinds of influences in her music, from classical to Brazilian to pop to traditional jazz, you know? It's all in there! So that's global in a sense. The music is multidirectional.

Jane Ira Bloom

From the very beginning of this project, I reached out to a cross-section of musical innovators with the belief that each interview would contrast and complement the others in provocative and surprising ways. There are several thematic threads that connect these conversations, but each transcript has its own flavor, and is presented in the musician's unique voice. Speaking as a writer and a musician, the entire process of writing this book, from recording the interviews, to editing the transcribed conversations and attempting to capture the "voice" of the interviewee, felt very musical, as if everyone involved were collaborating to compose or improvise an extended statement.

Soprano saxophonist and composer Jane Ira Bloom has a penchant for musical experimentation and projects that mirror other artistic mediums (her six-movement suite *Chasing Paint*, inspired by painter Jackson Pollock and his gestures captured on canvas, comes to mind). This, along with her ability to cast a new light on old standards, as heard on her critically acclaimed, Grammy award-winning recording *Sixteen Sunsets*, brings a unique perspective to this project.

As a young piano student, and well before receiving her first formal instruction in composition in high school, Bloom learned music by playing the Great American Songbook *and* making up her own melodies.

"I didn't know what you called it," says Bloom, "that you called it 'improvising,' but . . . because of the way that I was learning music . . . the improvisation and the compositional awareness developed simultaneously. . . . Even to this day, you can hear how the two concepts are melded together in my music."

Since 1977, the year after she founded her record label and publishing company, Outline Music, Bloom has recorded and produced 15 albums (and counting) of her own music. She has also recorded for ENJA, CBS, Arabesque, and ArtistShare Records. Bloom holds degrees from Yale University and the Yale School of Music and is a professor at the School of Jazz at The New School. She has been described as an artist "beyond category" by writer Nat Hentoff, and not surprisingly, like many of the other musicians interviewed in this book, Bloom doesn't think of jazz as a box, but more a means of personal creative expression. However, the value Bloom places on the musical ideas she creates in the moment, be it on stage or in the recording studio, is a key component, maybe *the* key component, to not only defining what jazz is, but how she herself is connected to its history.

Says Bloom, "I value the musical decision-making that I make in the moment as a result of having studied and immersed myself in the Afro-American

Jane Ira Bloom. Photo by Johnny Moreno.

music tradition as well as many others ... I give improvisation as much credence in my musical thought as the ideas that I write down. ... That really is the heart of it."

When did you first begin playing a musical instrument?
I started taking piano lessons at age 4.

Did you start playing because your parents wanted you to take piano lessons, or were you drawn to the instrument?
I was drawn to it. At the time my mother was taking piano lessons ... from the moment I was aware of being self-aware, I knew that I loved musical instruments. I loved music and musical instruments. I just gravitated toward them, and I don't know why!

In your school, was there some kind of music program in place?

Yes, there was. At the elementary school level I remember they had this program, and these things don't even exist anymore, where they handed out a list of six or seven instruments to every student who went to school and said, "What instrument do you want to learn? Pick which one!" That was like, third grade.

Where in the country did you grow up?

Newton, Massachusetts.

Did the soprano saxophone come into your life around this time?

Later. Alto saxophone was the main saxophone that I began studying. I lived outside of Boston and by the time I was in ninth grade it was clear that I was getting serious about the saxophone. A friend of our family, who was a music educator, said, "The next step is for you to go meet Joe Viola." Joe was the head of woodwinds at the Berklee College of Music at the time and a legendary saxophone teacher. So at the age of 12 or 13 I began studying saxophone with him on a very serious level once a week. He was the one who introduced me to the soprano saxophone.

We began on alto but the soprano was his love. He used to always take it out when we were having lessons and when I heard him play, that's when I fell in love with the instrument.

It sounds like your parents were supportive of your love for music.

They were music appreciators. They were from New York City and had gone to hear people like Duke Ellington and Ella Fitzgerald when they were younger. Some of those records were in my house. But where music came from in my family nobody knew! [laughs] My studying music was an anomaly!

But of course they were supportive, with the music lessons and driving to rehearsals, absolutely.

You're also well known as a composer. When did you start writing music, and when did you get some kind of formal instruction?

Here's an interesting thing … when I began studying piano early on, I didn't study with a classical teacher. I was learning the instrument and playing classical music, but I was also learning the Great American Songbook from lead sheets and playing melodies with chord changes.

Very early on in my musical life I used to like to make things up. I didn't know what you called it, that you called it "improvising," but I used to like to invent melodies. And because of the way that I was learning music … the improvisation and the compositional awareness developed simultaneously.

My first music composition teacher was in high school. I was a junior in high school when I studied with a composition instructor by the name of Sally

Lutchens, who gave me my very first formal look at having musical ideas and writing them down. I guess I could credit her with opening up my mind to composition.

For me, music improvisation and composition always came from the same place. Even to this day, you can hear how the two concepts are melded together in my music. It comes from a way of thinking that started a long time ago.

[Saxophonist] Evan Parker said something along the lines of "composition is improvisation in slow motion." Does that make sense to you?
The rate of decision-making as an improviser is very quick, very spontaneous. But it also may be coming from a part of the brain that is less consciously aware, less reliant on the frontal part of the brain, the executive decision-making that you use as a composer. With improvisation there's something quite special about the quality of the spontaneity that's at the core of your thought.

So jazz was a part of your listening experience at a young age?
I wouldn't say jazz exactly ... maybe the Great American Songbook. The songs I was learning in those lead sheets were by composers like Rogers and Hart, Lerner and Lowe ... that's the music that I was exposed to early on.

With Joe Viola, did jazz repertoire and jazz musicianship become a part of what you were studying as well?
Absolutely. Even at the junior high school level, I played in the stage band and was exposed to some jazz repertoire.... There was a band director named Harry Morris, who introduced me to music that I had never heard before. It was a very exciting musical time. This was some of my earliest exposure to instrumental jazz.

How does the music you make now relate to jazz? What's your connection to jazz music's history?
Well, I think of it in the most primary way. I value the musical decision making that I make in the moment as a result of having studied and immersed myself in the Afro-American music tradition as well as many others.

But the thing that makes it so very intimately connected to some of the earliest players of that music is that I give value to what I think of musically in the moment. I give improvisation as much credence in my musical thought as the ideas that I write down, and that's a very important difference. That really is the heart of it.

We can talk about rhythm, and melody, and all those things, but at the heart of it is being an improviser. That's the best answer I can give you.

You're talking about not weighing improvisation against composition as if one is superior to the other. Some people think of these two things in hier-

archal terms. That they're separate, or even one requires less thought than the other. One is emotional and another more intellectual.

I would say that I improvise like a composer and I compose like an improviser. In other words, a lot of my compositional process mines improvisational material that I sometimes codify and a lot of the structural underpinning of many of the ideas that I improvise draws from knowledge of compositional flow and arc. So, the two are one for me.

Here's a quote from your bio. You're describing arriving in New York City and deciding to begin a recording label. You said, "I had the passion to be an improvising musician and figured that I had to be just as creative about how I improvised my career." I bring that up because I wonder if there really is a blueprint for any musician, when he or she leaves high school or college or whatever, who wants to play music but also has to figure out how to survive. You were also speaking, I think, of being a woman in a network that was mostly men.

You know that quote, or the meaning of the quote, actually dates to a time when I was at the end of my formal musical training. I was in New Haven in the mid 1970s and it was clear to me even then that for something to happen musically for me it was going to have to be self-initiated. I still can't actually tell you whether this was true for me because I was a woman or because of the way I thought about music.

You have to remember also that it was a time when the music industry was in a real lull. I mean even looking at what was going on in the recording industry then . . . nobody would call an unknown artist to make a record at the time. My trajectory was different. I didn't follow a traditional path in terms of choosing to apprentice with a well-known bandleader. I was writing original music and recording from the very beginning of my career dating back to New Haven, Connecticut, before I came to New York.

I guess just like that quote says, the passion was so strong that I thought, "Well, gotta do something!" [laughs]

I was very fortunate to be in a very vibrant music community in New Haven at that time. People have written about it now, they call it "the New Haven Renaissance." In the mid-70s there were a lot of very talented improvisers who all happened to be in New Haven at the same time. And from that community – Leo Smith was there, Anthony Davis, George Lewis, Gerry Hemmingway, Mark Helias, Mark Dresser, Ray Anderson (if I went through the list, it would really stagger your mind) – what I learned was that if you had music that was worth documenting, you learn to produce it yourself! Learn how to make your own record.

And so, we did! I didn't know how to do it and I asked a lot of questions and eventually figured out how to start a record company ... and in those days, it was not easy to do, to make an LP. It was hard and it was expensive and much more complicated than it is today but somehow you learned by doing. So that was the beginning of my story.

I remember hearing [composer] John Zorn give a talk where he described how hard it was back in the day to drag these heavy vinyl records to a gig. He was like, "You guys have it easy now!"
It wasn't just dragging them to the gigs; the thing was mailing those suckers! [laughs] In those days we had the New Music Distribution Service, but you still had to do all the mailing of those 12-inch monsters. Oh God, it was funny.

When you're teaching, this idea of improvising your own career, is that something you try to convey to your students?
You try. I don't think you can do it enough. Young musicians who have been in an institutional structure all their lives ... you have to help prepare them for how they will they handle themselves when all of that structure goes away. It eventually disappears and that's when you have to start drawing from an inner source, finding a way to navigate a path in music when the support system is no longer there.

That's an artistic life. As my friend, drummer Bobby Previte, says: "The life of an artist means you wake up every morning and you gotta have a new idea!" [laughs] And it's true! It's true. You wake up every morning and you invent your day!

And it can be scary!
Oh, sure!

What's helpful is that there are people who have taken this path ahead of you or are on the same path as you. . . . Just recognizing that you're not alone, that the artistic life is nothing new. Someone could point to you and say, "Well, here's how Jane Ira Bloom did it. . . ."
I think what other people glean from it when they look at other people's careers is the emotional underpinning of it, the perseverance, the patience, the timelines, the intangibles you go through in a lifelong journey as an artist. It's a journey. No question about it.

There's a very "hurry up" quality to our culture now, instant gratification that I think a lot of young people are raised with. So it's nice to give people this other perspective. Artists do a really good job of that.
Sometimes. When you're young, you're young. Sometimes you just have to do what you do! [laughs] But as you get older, you do get a little perspective, and all the notes that you played—you start chiseling away at a lot of them.

What are some positives and negatives about life as a musician in New York City today?

Well, if I look at it from the viewpoint of my students, there is so much activity going on. I mean, forget it, Manhattan is over. It's Brooklyn! There are so many places—a whole underground music world where young musicians are finding ways to play the music that is of their generation, of their time—their improvised music.

Do they make money? No. They just barely put it together. The realistic aspect of it is something everybody's got to figure out for themselves. You gotta live and it's expensive to live in a city like New York. Everybody's got to find their own way to do that and there isn't any one way to do it.

You wouldn't discourage a music student from coming to New York?

You have to have the passion. You have to have the passion to just want to be in the metabolism that is New York. I think that is special and unique and wonderful and rich. It is rich. And geography is everything. Everybody is nearby. The metabolism of the city creates its own energy. And if that's what you want, then that's what you'll do, and you'll find some way to do it. If it's not, you'll find another city to do it in, and it doesn't matter. [laughs]

Brandee Younger

In the hands of a great player, the idiomatic sound of the harp, a "classical" instrument that actually first appeared in ancient Mesopotamia and Egypt, can be as soulful as a saxophone, and certainly as soulful as a guitar, violin, or double bass, all string instruments commonly associated with jazz. With a background that includes years of intense classical training as well as mentorships and collaborations with some of the finest practitioners of jazz music, harpist Brandee Younger is recasting the role of her instrument as it is used in jazz and other musical forms, including classical, indie-rock, and hip-hop.

Dorothy Ashby, Adele Girard, Corky Hale, and Betty Glamann are just a few of the innovative, multifaceted harpists who are responsible for expanding the role of the harp in jazz. But it was harpist, pianist, and bandleader Alice Coltrane who first captured Younger's imagination.

"Around the time before I went to college [to study harp]," says Younger in her interview for this book, "my parents bought me an Alice Coltrane CD. The first track on the CD was her tune 'Blue Nile,' and I just loved it. I played it and I played it and I played it until the disc broke, and I had to get another one."

"You know how some people are obsessed with John Coltrane?" says Younger. "That was *me* with Alice Coltrane."

After earning her undergraduate degree in harp performance and music business at the Hartt School of Music and moving on into graduate studies at New York University, Younger was asked by Alice Coltrane's son [saxophonist] Ravi to perform with him at his mother's 2007 memorial service. That transformative experience, along with earlier mentorships with jazz masters such as bassist Nat Reeves, trombonist Steve Davis, and saxophonist Kenny Garrett, helped her to launch a career as one of New York City's most in-demand harpists. She also teaches harp, and in this interview, describes her earliest lessons on the instrument.

As a harpist, Younger possesses a truly unique and very personal sound that speaks to her classical training, feel for rhythm and grooves ("I'm from New York, so I'm a hip-hop baby," says Younger), and connection to the spiritual quality of this ancient instrument. She is also a formidable bandleader, and since this interview, has created a repertoire of original, moving compositions.

When did you first begin playing music?
My grandfather was a pianist. I didn't know him at all. And my aunt, my mom's sister, was a piano player. So there are some musicians in my family.

Brandee Younger. Photo by Erin Patrice O'Brien.

When I was young I was interested in music, but I went to a private school at some point that didn't offer music. So when I went to public school, I started to take flute lessons. I wanted to play clarinet, but asked for a flute, thinking it was a clarinet! When I got home and opened it up, I was like, "Oh! Okay...."

But you hung onto it?
I hung onto it for seven years.

So, not in private school, but in the public school you had some kind of music program?
Right.

Were you playing flute in a band or an orchestra?
I played in the elementary-school concert band. I didn't study privately, but we did get a 30-minute private-lesson teacher. And the band teacher happened to be a flutist.

Were you in New York?
Yes. New York. I'm from Long Island.

When did the harp come into your life?
Probably junior high school. I started to play and took private lessons.

There was a secretary in one of my parents' offices and she had just begun beginner-harp lessons. My parents thought that was cool and brought me to her house. And we played these harp duets. That's how I was introduced to the harp. And she suggested a teacher for me should I want to start playing harp. So my parents said, if they can afford it [a harp], let's try it.

Where does a family go to purchase a harp for a young person?
To purchase a harp, you go to one of the showrooms, there's one in New Jersey, there's one in Massachusetts. But usually, your teacher helps you out getting a harp. My teacher happened to have multiple harps, so we actually just rented one. Even a smaller harp is a big investment!

It sounds like your parents were very supportive of your musical studies.
Well, at that point they were thinking, "Well, it'll be an extracurricular activity for her to do if she wants to do it...." I'm sure they were thinking ahead to "let's increase her chances for a scholarship to college."

I was in sports. I ran track, I swam, I had a bunch of extracurricular activities anyway. And I got to that point where I liked sports but I was getting lazy. I didn't really want to get up for swimming practice or track. So when it came down to it, my parents said, "All right, something has to give. We can't afford all of this, what do you want to do?" And I thought, thinking I was going the easy route, "I'll stick with the harp, because I can sit down while I do it!" Uh-huh. [laughs] That's exactly what I said to myself!

What kind of repertoire were you playing? Was jazz a part of it?
Playing jazz had yet to come. Back then I was really just playing what comes in the method books. But I would get bored with the method book, and whatever my teacher told me to do. So to keep my interest up I'd come in to my harp lessons with cassette tapes of things I heard on the radio. I grew up listening to hip-hop, R&B, R. Kelly, [laughs] whatever was on the radio at the time. I'd come in with cassette tapes and would ask my teacher, bless her heart, to write the music out.

Your teacher was taking what you were listening to seriously and showing you how the music is broken down. I find that really interesting.
I still did what I was required to do, but she also let me do what I wanted. One of the things that my parents said later was, if she hadn't done that, maybe I wouldn't be playing today, which I think is accurate.

When you're little, and you're playing from the method book, and then you listen to the radio, and all your friends are singing what's on the radio, it's kind of weird!

Brandee Younger and a young fan. Photo by Erin Patrice O'Brien.

I don't remember what I was working on, but I remember just not being really *interested*. But what my teacher did for me kept me interested.

When did jazz become a part of your repertoire as a harpist?
College. Once I made it to high school, they took me off of flute and put me on trombone. Once I switched to a brass instrument, that was it, no more flute life!

Our high school marching band was modeled in the style of the historically black college marching bands, you know. Are you familiar with that style?

Sure!
Well, in marching band, we played Earth, Wind & Fire, Gap Band, George Clinton, in addition to the traditional marching band repertoire. But in jazz band, which was a separate group, our teacher, Cedric Lemmie, encouraged us to attend programs offered by Jazzmobile in Harlem[45] to learn more than what we were learning in school.

There was a period before college when I buckled down because my parents had told me, "Your sister is in college, but we can't afford to have you both in college. So you have to figure out how you're going to go to college." So I switched teachers to get prepared for auditions. I basically just learned a bunch of traditional harp repertoire at once. I played my auditions, and chose to attend the Hartt School of music after being offered a full-tuition scholarship.

When I was in college, I went to jazz master classes, I went to ensemble classes, I was very much immersed in the jazz department. The first person I met was Nat Reeves, the bassist, who would later become a mentor for me. When I got into school, he was very welcoming and encouraging.

I was very active in the jazz department, but would never really play. I would be there for concerts, master classes, sessions after gigs were over, you name it, I was there.

I had done some private gigs, me on harp and Nat playing bass, playing cocktail hours, stuff like that. When I was getting ready to leave school, Nat Reeves hooked me up with [saxophonist] Kenny Garrett. He was working on a project and I was just kicking myself, you know? If I had only embarrassed myself in jazz ensemble as a kid, playing with Garrett would be easier, [laughs] *much* easier!

I never had any trouble hearing and then understanding what was going on in jazz. But when you actually play jazz, it can be like, "Oops! I can't play that chord that fast, my pedals aren't ready! Whoops, missed it, and the song's over!"

When did you first hear the music of [harpist] Alice Coltrane?

Around the time before I went to college my parents bought me an Alice Coltrane CD; it was a compilation. The first track on the CD was her tune "Blue Nile" and I just loved it. I played it and I played it and I played it until the disc broke and I had to get another one.

You know how some people are obsessed with John Coltrane? That was *me* with Alice Coltrane. My college roommate's boyfriend would help me write letters to her, but I'd never actually send them.

When Alice Coltrane passed away in 2007, a memorial service was scheduled for her at St. John the Divine, and [saxophonist and Alice Coltrane's son] Ravi Coltrane called me to play that.

Wow!

That was something like the stars aligning, because I didn't know him! We may have had mutual acquaintances, but I didn't know that many people on the scene.

That's not the result of savvy networking. That's a spiritual thing.

Definitely. God just put this together. So I said, "Yeah! I can play! I can play! I'll be there! I'll be there!" I was nervous because there wasn't time for a rehearsal, we couldn't get together to figure this out. I was used to taking time to figure out what I was going play. I'm classically trained, you know? A *classical* person. Thank God I already knew her music. Her music was already in my ear. I had never played it, but I *knew* it. I had all the CDs. I had all the records.

You mean you never, when practicing the harp, said, "I'm just going to improvise an Alice Coltrane-esque introduction in the practice room and see what happens."

No. I'm classically trained. In my ear, I heard note for note. If I was going to do something, I was going to transcribe it note for note. I would think, "What notes did she play?"

Although her music is heavily improvised, I was taught that you transcribe people's solos in order to learn their style.

Ravi and I spoke before the memorial and he just briefly told me, "Well, this one tune is an E minor blues, and this other is a tune Charlie Haden wrote for my mom. . . ." So going into it, there was a lot of nerves involved. But also excitement! Because here I am about to play her music, and when I got there, it was way more serious than I expected it to be. I didn't know until I showed up that [bassist] Charlie Haden, [bassist] Cecil McBee, [bassist] Reggie Workman, [drummer] Jack DeJohnette, and [drummer] Rashied Ali—each one a master musician, were all going to be a part of the service!

That's amazing.

Yes.

But you were ready!

I was as ready as I was gonna get! So, the concert happens, and that opened doors to a lot more. I continued to work with Ravi after that. There was a series of Alice Coltrane tributes that I did with Ravi, [pianist] Geri Allen, Jack De-Johnette, and Charlie Haden, some festivals, major festivals, which opened up even more doors. I started to work with Reggie Workman a lot and I started to get more work for my own trio and myself.

What kind of music are you playing and exploring now? What's inspiring you now as a harpist and as a bandleader?

Always Alice Coltrane, always Dorothy Ashby, Ahmad Jamal, all the new indie artists out there, now. I also still listen to Top 40. Don't judge me. [laughs]

No judgment here!

This is music! If I like it, I like it. If I don't like it, I don't like it. There are pieces for orchestra that I hate and there are pieces for orchestra that I love, you know?

I'm from New York, so I'm a hip-hop baby. Hip-hop was born in New York. I can't deny that part of myself.

While doing all of these Alice Coltrane tributes, I learned a lot of John Coltrane's music with Reggie Workman and a lot of Alice Coltrane's music with Ravi. Then I did a gig with Ravi, Jack DeJohnette, Kenny Davis on bass, and me, and I had to learn a lot of repertoire that challenged the heck out of me. I would just learn these pieces, struggle through them, and play them on my own gigs. And that led me to start experimenting with writing my own tunes.

With the tune I wrote for Trayvon Martin,[46] "Awareness (He Has a Name)," I kind of knew what I wanted going into it, which is surprising to me. I wrote it when I was driving home from where I teach harp, I was sitting in traffic, as usual, and the news coverage was on about (Martin's murder), and the tune came to me. It just came to me. I wrote it out, the guys in my band loved it. It was easy to get them together to record it. They were all down for it.

Alisha Pattillo

If you stop a second and think about it, it makes total sense that Australian-born tenor saxophonist Alisha Pattillo, who is steeped in rock, R&B, soul, blues, and jazz, would be drawn to Texas. Texas is home to the big-toned saxophone sound made famous by Lone Star state players like Arnett Cobb, Don Wilkerson, David "Fathead" Newman, and Leroy "Hog" Cooper, as well as many other saxophonists, including Illinois Jacquet, who came up under the leadership of Houston-born trumpeter and bandleader Milt Larkin.

Pattillo, whose parents are both in the oil industry, grew up in Singapore. She remembers being "mesmerized" by the sight and sound of the tenor saxophone after hearing one played by a family friend. Her parents tried to placate her with a recorder, then a clarinet, before relenting and letting her begin private saxophone lessons at the age of 11. She went on to play in Singapore's blues and rock clubs as a teenager, below the radar of her parents. But her exposure to jazz would come later.

"In college I started listening to contemporary players like Joshua Redman and Chris Potter," Pattillo says. "I was kind of late checking out Charlie Parker, Lester Young ... that music didn't appeal to me until I was in my early 20s."

In Texas, jazz and the blues have always enjoyed a healthy, symbiotic relationship, with rock and roll, zydeco, mariachi, and even Eastern European polka music seeping into the mix to create a rhythmically compelling, very distinctive music that is as much about the heart as it is the head. That said, I'll go out on a limb and say you can hear a very Texan sensibility in Pattillo's jazz playing, which embraces elements of jump blues, rhythm and blues, and rock and roll. Her music, while sophisticated, hits you with a high degree of energy right from the "one" and doesn't let you go.

As you'll read in her interview, Pattillo's musical journey took her several places across the globe before she settled in the U.S. After living in eight different cities in five different countries, perhaps Pattillo has found her musical home.

When did you first start playing a musical instrument?
Does the recorder count?

Sure!
My mother was a receptionist at the elementary school I attended in Australia. Often I had to wait around for her to finish work, and I would go into the music

Alisha Pattillo. Photo by Pin Lim.

room and beat on drums, marimbas—anything else I could get my hands on. I guess that's where my interest in music was sparked.

We moved to Singapore when I was 7. I picked up the saxophone when I was 11 years old.

Why did your family move to Singapore?
Both of my parents worked for oil companies. After we moved to Singapore, my mother picked up a job in human resources with an oil company. We moved around a lot. So far, I've lived in eight different cities in five different countries.

What compelled you to pick up the saxophone?

We had a family friend who played the saxophone, and I was pretty mesmerized by the instrument even at the young age of 5. My parents first bought me a clarinet when I was 9, and then eventually, a saxophone.

It wasn't like I heard a particular recording or anything like that.

Did you start taking lessons?

I took private lessons in Singapore. My teacher's name was Miles [laughs] Tranter. He was a classroom music teacher at the international school I attended and was the first person to introduce me to jazz. I studied with him for about seven years.

When you were introduced to jazz, did other types of music seem less interesting?

Not really. I like all styles of music; I'm more song specific when it comes to what I find interesting. I remember as a teenager I listened to Sonny Stitt's *Verve Jazz Masters 50* album and *The Best of Blue Note* CD, but I really loved listening to bands like Tower of Power and Liquid Soul. When I went to university in Australia, I was introduced to saxophonists like Joshua Redman and Chris Potter, who blew my mind. I was drawn to more modern players and was kind of late in checking out the inventors of jazz, musicians like Duke Ellington, Charlie Parker, and Thelonious Monk. Their music didn't appeal to me until I was in my early 20s, but looking back, I think that had more to do with the sound quality of those early recordings. My saxophone teacher at university, Mark Spencer, was very influential in suggesting players to check out and listen to. Also, my good friend and fellow saxophonist Crystal Smith shared a lot of recordings with me. In fact, I think she gave me a copy of her hard drive!

The bio on your website reads: "Alisha Pattillo started playing saxophone at the age of 11. Five years later, she could be spotted playing in professional working bands in Singapore nightclubs and bars." So you were playing in bars at the age of 16? Is that correct?

[laughs] That's correct.

Isn't that unusual?

America is one of the few countries where the legal drinking age is 21. In Singapore, it's 18. I was 16 at the time, and most bar owners turned a blind eye. Those that knew how young I was were supportive of what I was trying to do.

I played in the Curtis King Band. The bandleader, Curtis King, was from Ohio. A senior at my high school was playing saxophone in the band, and when he graduated high school, he moved to Canada to attend college and recommended me as his replacement. I'd just turned 16. This band definitely gave me a taste of what it would be like to be a full-time musician. We had a lot of fun gigs.

How old were the other musicians in the Curtis King Band?
They were all over the age of 30.

There weren't a lot of saxophone players in Singapore at the time. I used to play four nights a week with the band. There is a bar in Singapore called the Crazy Elephant, and the owner also owned another bar nearby called the Voodoo Shack. We would play Monday and Wednesday at the Crazy Elephant and then Friday and Saturday at the Voodoo Shack.

What kind of music did the band play?
Mostly blues, but we played a bit of R&B as well, a little James Brown, some Jimi Hendrix, some Otis Redding. If we did any jazz it was blues-based jazz tunes like "Watermelon Man" or "Cold Duck Time."

Was your audience made up of Westerners or locals? Or both?
It was a mix. The clubs were located in an area of Singapore by the Singapore River called Clarke Quay. The area was filled with all of these old warehouses, since Singapore made its mark in the world by being a port. Over time, the port moved over to a more industrial location, and the warehouses were restored into bars, clubs, and restaurants for tourists. It's kind of a pedestrian mall, except for consumption as opposed to merchandise. There are a lot of hotels in the area as well. It's more Western than other parts of Singapore, but locals also hang out there.

So your parents were cool with you playing music in bars after hours?
My parents were living in Houston at this time. I remained in Singapore and was in boarding school for grades 11 and 12. Let's just say my parents weren't getting the full story. So, yeah, the plot thickens! [laughs]

Did playing in the clubs get you into trouble at school?
I got in trouble a few times. Teachers were noticing I was very tired in class. I'd sleep in and not make it to my morning classes because I didn't get back from a gig until two in the morning.

But at the time, I was so excited about playing in a band, I didn't really care about school. My grades were still good enough that they didn't raise any red flags for my parents. That was kind of the deal. As long as my grades weren't suffering, I could keep playing music.

Were your gigs a source of income? Did you make okay money for a 16-year-old playing music?
Not really. I was in it more for the experience than a source of income. I'd

make about 40 Singapore dollars a gig. The bandleader also let me sell CDs and gave me 50 percent of the sales. So, on my breaks, I would run around selling our CDs to all of the tourists. After CD sales, I would have more money than a 16-year-old could spend.

Musicians should get paid a living wage.
To be honest, at that time, when I was just 16 years old, I was probably worth about 40 dollars. [laughs]

Your bio also says you played in Vietnam in a blues and rock and roll band.
The lead singer and guitarist from another band I played with in Singapore moved to Vietnam. So that was my contact over there.

I graduated high school in Singapore in May. Singapore follows the Northern Hemisphere system of the school year beginning in August or September and running through May (or June). In Australia, because we're in the Southern Hemisphere and our summers and winters are flipped, the school year goes from January to December. So, after I graduated in May, I had nothing to do for the rest of the year while I waited for school to start up in Australia. My two choices were [to] go to America, where I wouldn't be able play in bars unless my mother came with me—and she had a full-time job—or go to Vietnam and get more experience playing music every other night with a band.

You went on to study music in Australia?
Yes. I received a Bachelor of Music in Jazz Saxophone and Education Preparation from the Queensland Conservatorium of Music in Brisbane, Australia.

Was the lifestyle at the Queensland Conservatorium of Music a shock after all of the experiences you had playing several nights a week in bars throughout Southeast Asia?
I had a hard time at first. I was the "foreigner"—even though I was Australian by birth. It was a humbling experience.

In Brisbane, there weren't a lot of opportunities to play. There were a lot of bars, but few bars that offered jazz or any sort of blues. Most of the clubs had rock bands or DJs. I went from playing four or five nights a week to having no gigs for three years unless they were associated with the university, doing a concert, or sometimes we'd do a gig in the pedestrian mall.

So to be honest, college was kind of a drag as far as being able to perform. That's why, when I graduated, I decided to come to America. Playing throughout Southeast Asia was cool, but at the end of the day, since there are so few musicians there, you can end up getting stuck in the same scene. It's not like you're going to be able to branch out. You can make a decent living, but I personally think America has so much more to offer.

Why did you decide to come to Houston after college?
My parents were living in Katy, which is located in the Houston metropolitan area. I moved over here in February 2007 on a one-year tourist visa just to check out the scene and see if this was a place where I wanted to live and work. I guess after all that traveling I wanted to settle down in one location for a while.

Houston has been good to me. I was able to begin playing in blues and top-40 bands almost immediately. I started going to jazz and blues jam sessions and got to sit in with some great musicians. Houston is a hub for great live music. Many talented musicians live here and play frequently, so I've found it to be a solid environment for a young player to listen, learn, and grow.

What compels you to choose a tune to add to your repertoire?
I would have to say the saxophone players I listen to have the greatest influence when adding a tune to my repertoire. I also like melodies I can turn into a groove. I do play standards, but modern groove tunes are the stuff I listen to and especially like.

In 2012, you recorded and released your first CD, *Along for the Ride*. Once you record a CD, what's the next step? What should musicians be ready to do after they've recorded an album they're happy with and want people to hear?
Recording and releasing my first CD was definitely a learning experience. I was originally going to put a demo together, however, everyone I spoke to about it on the scene suggested I just go ahead and record a full CD, seeing as how I would be paying for the studio time. Plus, with a CD, I would have a quality product to sell at shows and appear more professional when soliciting gigs.

After recording an album you're happy with, it's promo time! I was contacted by a few marketing agents to help promote my CD, but they were expensive, and I decided I would rather promote this first album on my own. I managed to get several reviews of my CD in local and national publications, which really helped get the word out, plus radio airplay in Europe and America. The Internet is a powerful tool, and getting your material out to as many online retailers as possible is definitely a good idea, but you are still largely accountable for getting traffic to those sites.

I am grateful to all those who spent the time to help promote my CD. I think it's a solid album, but every musician's aim should be to keep producing a better and better product. I guess it's up to the individual to decide if what they have created is worthy of investing a large sum of money to have it promoted.

My advice is to plan ahead. Many musicians are so focused on getting the album completed they don't think about the post-production world. However, the hard work begins once you have that product and need to find ways to market it. Being able to swap hats and jump over to the marketing realm is crucial if you decide to go the self-promotion route. But if marketing isn't your cup of tea, then make sure you include promotional costs into your overall production budget. What good is a great CD if nobody hears it?

This is a question musicians need to ask themselves: Do you want to pay someone to get your music played on radio shows and reviewed online or in magazines? A musician can do it alone, but it's so much work.

The main problem with doing it on your own is just not having the contacts. The time it takes to send your stuff off doesn't bother me, it's just that if the recipient doesn't know who you are, they may not even open up your package. That's the drag.

Do you compose music?

Composing is one of those things I need to focus on. I've been so focused on playing, teaching, and just being a professional gigging musician, that I've kind of put writing to the side. I am in the process of assembling a very basic home studio so I can have a place where I can put my ideas down and hear how they sound. Instead of writing it out, I'd rather play it and hear how it sounds. I can play a little piano and a little bass, enough to get an idea of how it would all come together. Hopefully my next album will have some originals on it.

What are some other goals you have for yourself as a player?

My goal right now is just to keep working on my craft. I continue to be exposed to new ideas, sounds, and tunes and sometimes it can be overwhelming to try and absorb the amount of material that is out there. By no means do I feel I've reached the top of where I want to be.

I love teaching and I strive to be a better teacher. Teaching has shown me ways to help myself comprehend things. When you have to suggest methods or ways to approach a certain passage, the metaphors and ideas I come up with for my students to help them learn can be applied to my own challenges.

Another goal is to release more music. I'm happy with my debut, *Along for the Ride,* but hopefully this is just the start of a long list of releases with my name on it.

Eliane Elias

Born and raised in the state capital of São Paulo, Brazil's most populated city, pianist, composer, and singer Eliane Elias began playing piano at the age of 7. Inspired by the jazz records her father would bring back from business trips to the U.S., she began transcribing and learning to play the music of some of the masters of her instrument, including Art Tatum, Bud Powell, and Oscar Peterson. By the time she was 15 years old, she was teaching piano and improvisation at São Paulo's renowned Centro Livre de Aprendizagem, the very school where she herself had studied and earned her degree. By the time she was 17, Elias was performing with her own trio throughout Brazil and South America.

To say that her passion for jazz at such a young age was unusual, even in a city as cosmopolitan as São Paulo, is an understatement.

"I was very different than the other kids," says Elias. "I had a very different way of looking at life and my interests still continue to be quite different now from most women."

Elias grew up in a nurturing, musical family. Her mother, a classical pianist, was especially supportive of her interest in music.

"(My mother) sought the best teachers and went after the best programs for me to learn and grow," says Elias. "(She) made her home a welcoming environment for me to practice, to receive musicians to rehearse, and to do whatever I felt I wanted to do with music."

In 1981, Elias made the decision to go to New York, the city where so many of the albums she grew up listening to were recorded. In 1982, she became a member of the acclaimed jazz fusion group, Steps Ahead, whose members at that time included vibraphonist Mike Mainieri, drummer Peter Erskine, bassist Eddie Gómez, and the late, great saxophonist, Michael Brecker. The group's self-titled 1983 album is considered a classic of its genre, and at least two of its tracks, Don Grolnick's "Pools" and Mainieri's "Islands," have become standards of contemporary jazz repertoire.

Throughout her performing and recording career, which includes over 20 albums of original compositions and standards, Elias has always played and sung the music of her native country. Her recent album, *Made in Brazil*, is an expansive, lushly arranged collection of original songs as well as classic repertoire by revered Brazilian composers, Roberto Menescal, Ary Barroso, and Antônio Carlos Jobim. While Elias's singing is much cooler and more plaintive than her piano playing, embracing the "soft Brazilian singer" sound made famous by Astrud Gilberto (whose 1964 recording of "The Girl From Ipanema" with saxophonist Stan Getz and guitarist João Gilberto was an international hit), Elias says both come "from the same source."

Eliane Elias. Photo by Tom LeGoff.

"I feel privileged to be able to do both, whether together or separately," says Elias. "The two performers in me are integrated; being the singer and the pianist makes a very personal statement."

When did you begin playing a musical instrument?
I started taking piano lessons when I was 7.

What kind of music were you being taught at that age?
I come from a musical family. My mother played classical piano. My grandmother, who lived with us, played guitar and was a composer. My formal music studies started with classical fundamentals and piano technique as applied through exercises and pieces to perform.

You fell in love with jazz at the age of 10 thanks to your family's portable record player. Where did the records come from?
My mother had a record collection and my father brought back records for me when he traveled to the U.S. on business. I expressed to my teacher my interest in learning what I was hearing on these records. He showed me the principles of notation, which are basically math and the sub-division of beats. I could hear and identify pitch already, and I have an excellent memory, so it was simply a matter of diligently dropping the needle repeatedly until I had transcribed what I was hearing. Then I played along, getting the fingering and nuances of the phrasing.

Jazz was played in the house very often on the home stereo system and the portable in the practice room, close to the piano, where I did my work.

By the time you were a teenager, you were already teaching piano and improvisation. Is that correct?
That is correct. I started teaching when I was 15 years old. I taught at the school I had attended, the Centro Livre de Aprendizagem. A couple years after that, I was performing all over São Paulo in different venues with my own trio. For three years, starting at age 17, I toured extensively in Brazil and South America with [singer, guitarist] Toquinho and the great poet and lyricist Vinicius de Moraes, one of the fathers of bossa nova and co-writer with [Antonio Carlos] Jobim on most of the classic Jobim songs. So things started very early.

Was this an unusual childhood in São Paulo?
Oh, very! I think anywhere! [laughs]

It reminds me of Mozart, or any young person with talent, who very quickly becomes not only a performer, but someone who teaches as well. It sounds like your parents were 100 percent behind your passion for music.
Well, the person who was really supportive, who noticed my talent from a young age, I mean besides my teachers, was my mother. The music comes from her side of the family. She created an environment for me to be able to try and do what I wanted to do with music. She sought the best teachers and went after the best programs for me to learn and grow, and made her home a welcoming environment for me to practice, to receive musicians to rehearse and to do whatever I felt I wanted to do with music. It was unusual. I was very different than the other kids. I had a very different way of looking at life and my interests still continue to be quite different now from most women.

So it was unusual for a young woman to be playing jazz in your part of the world?
Oh, it was absurdly unusual! My city, São Paulo, is the most cosmopolitan city in South America and one of the largest metropolises in the world, and still,

I mean, a little girl transcribing Art Tatum, Bud Powell, Oscar Peterson at the age of 10.... I think would be unusual, even in New York City.

It's wonderful you had access to such a great music education at that age.
I was very lucky, and you know, being born in São Paulo was a blessing. São Paulo is a very sophisticated city culturally. There, you have everything!

You decided to relocate to New York City again at a relatively young age of 21.
I moved to New York when I was 21. But I said I was going to do that at the age of 11! [laughs] It was a plan, you know? I wanted to be in New York, where most of the great players lived and worked.

Was that simply because New York was the hub for jazz music?
Yes! I'd look at my records and the liner notes read, "Recorded in New York," whether it was a studio in New York or a club, and I'd think, "This is the place I want to go to."

In practical terms, what brought you to New York? Were you going there to do more studying?
No, no. When I moved to New York, I chose the time when I felt ready as a professional musician. Earlier, I had two invitations from New York-based "artist management" companies who produced world tours, but I did not feel that the time was right or that the offers were compatible with my vision. When I ultimately made the move to New York, things happened quickly. Doors opened for me and within a few months I was playing with some of the greatest players on the scene, including [the band] Steps Ahead.

How would you describe your relationship to jazz standards?[47] You still play standards. You still interpret and sing them, right?
Yes.

That's not something you're going to stop doing.
No, of course not. I have very, very eclectic tastes, and I've always appreciated music when it's good music. It could be a pop song, a classical piece, a jazz standard, a folk song, whatever. Good is good.

You don't "date stamp" the material, and say, "This is the older stuff, and an older way of doing things."
Oh, no, no. I don't date music that way. That's not my criteria for choosing music. Music that speaks to me that has harmonic content, or rhythmic content, or melodic content, or words that speak to me, that's what I look for.

Early on in your career, you didn't speak English, and therefore didn't know the meaning of the lyrics to the jazz standards you heard. Is this correct?

Yes, that's correct. In those years, developing as a jazz pianist, I really wasn't paying attention to lyrics in English. On the other hand, I could sing all the lyrics to all the great songs I was hearing on the radio and television in Portuguese. And there were some great artists to hear singing the songs of the day. All the great bossa nova artists, Jobim, Elis Regina, João Gilberto, and the more contemporary music of Ivan Lins, Gilberto Gil, Caetano Veloso, Djavan, and Gonzaguinha. I heard and enjoyed so much music.

You sing standards, but you also play them as instrumentals. Can you talk about the difference between singing a standard versus playing and interpreting it as an instrumental?
I'm a pianist first, and many of my early recordings featured my playing and composing over my singing. Singing was a part of my music, but in a different capacity, mostly as a color, as wordless vocal lines, and the occasional lead vocal. That changed with the years and my voice started to take more and more a central role in my presentations, sharing the spotlight with my piano playing. A singer has to deliver a lyric and tell a story using words. Of course, both singing and playing involve all the other ingredients that are a part of making music, such as the feel, the rhythmic phrasing, the emotional content, the sound produced, etc.

When choosing a song to sing, I have to feel there is compatibility to my voice and my range and artistic sensibility. But playing the music, playing the melody on the piano, is different. It involves another set of criteria, which has more to do with the possibilities as an instrumentalist. As an instrumentalist, I have many more possibilities; a wider range of dynamics, speed when executing a line or phrase, and the ability to sound like a whole orchestra, with rhythm, harmony, and melody at my fingertips.

Singing offers certain other things, a different range of things that can be done and for me, the choice of repertoire goes beyond the American standards. It includes other genres plus all the Brazilian material, which is a part of my natural heritage. Arranging a song to sing using Brazilian rhythms is something that is very natural to me. For example, a song like "Light My Fire," I wouldn't record that as an instrumental. I love the song, but it doesn't quite fit the criteria of what I look for in instrumentals. But when I'm singing it, I love it! Singing it with the cool, sensual aspects of Brazilian jazz—it sounds great!

Do the lyrics of a song influence the way you play it as an instrumental?
To some degree. It really depends on the piece. I think it may be more true for ballads. But then, if you take a song, which was originally a ballad, and play it up-tempo as an instrumental, the lyrics at that point are of little or no consequence, because you are dealing strictly with line improvisation through harmony and rhythm.

But ultimately, I believe the way one sings and the way one plays comes from the same source. I feel privileged to be able to do both, whether together or separately. I think my singing is informed by my being an instrumentalist in terms of my phrasing and feel in time, as well as how I travel through harmony. I accompany "the singer" just the way I want to be accompanied; with the harmonic voicings, chordal choices, and tensions that enhance the emotional content of the lyric and/or the rhythmic feel of the phrase. The two performers in me are integrated; being the singer and the pianist makes a very personal statement. At this stage of my career I feel the most complete as an artist when I am doing both, singing and playing.

Val Jeanty

Any book that purports to speak accurately about the roots of jazz must acknowledge the role Afro-Caribbean culture played in its conception and evolution. For example, in the case of the Haitian religion Vodou, author Michael Ventura writes: "The question of how Haitian Voodoo [his spelling] came to the continental United States, and the question of why jazz originated in New Orleans, are in fact parts of the same question."[48]

Like Palo and Santeria in Cuba, and Candomblê and Umbanda in Brazil, Vodou represents a new world formulation of African religious practices, practices that include sacred drums and rhythms. Beginning in 1817, these rhythms found a public forum in New Orleans' Congo Square where, every Sunday afternoon, slaves were permitted to congregate, dance, and play music. To this day, Vodou, both as a religious practice and a musicological source, continues to have a pervasive influence on New Orleans' culture.

Haitian-born electronic artist and percussionist Val Jeanty began playing Vodou drums at the age of 5.

"I pretty much grew up in what we call 'lakou,'" explains Jeanty. "A lakou is just like a yard, and that is where all the ceremonies happen, all the prayers happen, all the drummers practice, all the singers practice, and all the dancers practice."

Now based in New York City, Jeanty uses an array of electronic instruments and controllers, as well as sacred hand drums, to create music that is poetic and multi-layered, combining Vodou's rhythms, rhythms that signify and call to its gods and goddesses, with modern electronica- and jazz-infused beats.

Given the breadth and complexities of Vodou's influence, even the most conscientious historians and anthropologists may confuse its practices with its misrepresentations in popular culture. For example, in her 1935 collection of African-American folklore, *Mules and Men*, Zora Neale Hurston uses the word "hoodoo" interchangeably with "voodoo" ("as pronounced by the whites") and inadvertently misaligns African- and Native American-based medicinal practices with the tools of religious worship. Such confusion continues to this day in souvenir shops across the southern U.S. where dolls, mojo bags, gris gris, powders, and charms are inaccurately branded and sold as accessories of Vodou worship. And I could write another book listing and describing American films and television shows that perpetuate ignorant and racist stereotypes about Vodou in the name of cheap thrills and gore.

However, there are several thoughtful, thoroughly researched books and film documentaries about Vodou, including Maya Deren's 1953 book, *Divine Horsemen: The Living Gods of Haiti* and film of the same title (shot between 1947

Val Jeanty. Photo by Richard Louissant.

and 1954), *Mama Lola: A Vodou Priestess in Brooklyn* by Karen McCarthy Brown, and Darius James and Oliver Hardt's recent documentary, *The United States of Hoodoo* [2012]. Jeanty is featured prominently in James and Hardt's film.

Jeanty's musical skills and sensitivity match that of any so-called "traditional" musician. Not surprisingly, in addition to performing and recording as a solo artist, she has collaborated with several highly respected musicians from the world of contemporary jazz, including Terri Lyne Carrington, Craig Taborn, Steve Coleman, and Geri Allen.

In her interview, Jeanty describes how sound, especially rhythms and specific frequencies, can compel a spiritual awakening in the listener, even if the listener is unaware of the historical origins of that sound. Her music often surprises even the most seasoned of jazz musicians.

"When I'm playing with a jazz musician," says Jeanty, "I'll play something, and they might say, 'You know, I heard you play some African stuff, and I really, really like that.' Yeah, yeah, yeah!" [laughs]

You were born and raised in Haiti?
Yes.

When did you relocate to New York City?
I came to New York in 1994 after high school. That's when I moved here to Brooklyn. I was in Miami, Florida, before that.

Why did you move to the U.S.?
At the time, when we moved to Miami in 1988, the whole political state of Haiti was just a mess. All the schools in Haiti were closed for quite a while, so my mom decided it was time for us to keep it moving. Jean-Claude Duvalier left Haiti in 1986[49] and we left two years after that.

As a young person, was moving to the U.S. a little scary for you?
Not really. It was mainly exciting. The U.S. is very enticing from the outside. I was always interested in video games and electronic music. All that stuff was here, so I was excited to come to the U.S. and see what it was all about.

The thing that was shocking was dealing with the reality that once you're here, you're not just a "foreigner," you're a Haitian. That was a culture shock. It was less about fear than just cultural differences. Miami at that time especially had those huge cultural differences. Haitians that came over on the boat would be discriminated against. If you were a Haitian at that time, let's just say you would just keep it quiet. [laughs]

Kids that I went to school with, in junior high and middle school, would say, "Oh, you're Haitian?" "Yeah, yeah, yeah! I'm Haitian!" "Wow. How come you're so light? Do you sleep in trees? Do you have AIDS?" For me, it was kind of funny, because I never really took it that serious, you know?

When did you first begin playing music?
I started playing Haitian drums at the age of 5. Before that I'm sure I was banging on things. I have an old photo of me in my crib just banging away. [laughs] My hands in that photo are all blurry from the movement. But yeah, 5 years old is when I said, "I have to do this every day!"

Are your parents musicians?
My mom teaches science and chemistry and my dad is an architect. We have a lot of artists in the family. We have some painters, and of course architecture is a whole different kind of art. As a musician, you are like an architect, but you're just working with sound.

You've said that you "see" sounds. Do you experience sound visually as well as with your ears?
[laughs] I thought once that everybody did. For me, sound is always very, very visual, and very visceral, and very connected to the spiritual aspect of things.

It's not just 3D or 4D. It's more like 10D. It's difficult to explain, because there are no words for a different kind of "eye." I could say, "the third eye" but beyond that, it's kind of hard to explain.

Is this experience you're talking about, experiencing music with a different kind of eye, is this an experience you had as a young person playing drums?
I have to kind of clarify it. The type of drums I'm working with are Vodou drums, not just ordinary drums. So we're talking about tapping into your source, tapping into your own consciousness, tapping into your ancestors, a whole lineage or a whole pattern or even a channel, if you want to take it that far. Vodou drumming has always been very much used for that purpose.

I think musicians who improvise have to tap into that source. You have to be connected. Whatever you want to call it, creativity, life force, colors, shapes, we can call it all kind of different things. For me, playing music was always about connecting to that source. There are so many different levels that we can channel and tap into. That's what Vodou music is. When you're playing it, you feel it. You go into these states, alpha states, beta states, which are similar to Buddhist chanting with its repetition. When you improvise, even when there's something repetitive, there's something that's not the same.

Was Vodou a part of your family's spiritual and religious practice?
Yes. I pretty much grew up in what we call "lakou." A lakou is just like a yard, and that is where all the ceremonies happen, all the prayers happen, all the drummers practice, all the singers practice, all the dancers practice. It's where all the food is cooked, so I was always there to eat and play drums! [laughs] If you play good, you get to eat! But at the same time, the lakou is very much like a connection that's sort of deeper than any one person that's there. You play your part within pieces that are connecting this machine that needs to move forward or whichever direction you want it to move.

I'm reminded of some of the musicians I interviewed who started out singing gospel music in the church. It's a very similar thing. Maybe their parents were involved with the church, a relative played organ, another relative was the music director...
Yes!

...and you had to be a part of this one way or another.

You mentioned video games. And I'm thinking Pac-Man, or am I going too far back?
I was born in 1974, so I remember the original Pong, which had the [sings] doot ... doot ... that Pong sound is so classic, you know? I loved that sound. It was actually soothing. I don't know if you remember, but there always used to be a

theme song that would fit with the video game. So you were forced to deal with that theme song. But if you think about it, it was all very theatrical. The themes would have different parts, including a breakdown. And if you won a game, you got to hear the whole theme, not just half of it! When I played Nintendo or Sega, I wondered, "How are they creating that music? Is it all electronics?"

When did you first begin exploring electronics? Did that happen in Haiti or did it happen later in the U.S.?
It happened here. In Haiti I didn't have any access to drum machines. I don't think they existed at that time. Maybe the old school Roger Linn [drum machine] did.

So when you got to the U.S., what were some of your first electronic tools for making music?
What really caught my interest were samplers and drum machines. I still wanted to play drums. I had a few congas and a few djembes in my house. But it was kind of hard to practice because I had just a little studio here in Brooklyn and you couldn't really play late at night after work. So I thought I should get some headphones and a little sampler. I started to get gigs, but realized I would have to take taxis with all of my drums to the gigs. So the decision to explore and play electronic instruments was a practical one.

A friend of mine named Masa had an MPC 2000 (a 64-track sampler, MIDI sequencer, and drum machine that allows you to play sounds by tapping pads). When I saw him playing it, I was like, "Wow! There are drums in each pad? And I can put this in my backpack?" So that did it. That just did it. I went out and got one.

Why were you in Brooklyn? Were you going to school?
My sister was at Pratt University. Every summer, before we moved from Haiti to Miami, we used to visit my uncle up in Harlem at 135th Street between Broadway and 8th Avenue. This was the time of break dancing, so it was very exciting. Actually, this was Pac-Man time, Qbert, Donkey Kong … so I kind of had a taste of that whole hip-hop culture. My brothers were into it, my cousins were into it, it was new and it was colorful and fun. For me, New York has always been an interesting place to be. More interesting than Miami, because Miami didn't have that energy. That's why I'm describing exactly where my uncle lived in Harlem so you can see. He lived not too far from the Apollo, so there was always something going on. Just going to the little bodega, if you can imagine, was like an adventure for me. I'd see people with Adidas suits on, things I would only get to see on MTV when we would sneak and watch it at night in Haiti. To me, New York was always a place where art is very, very free. When I was in high school, Florida was very segregated. Now it's completely

different than when I was growing up. I think people who improvise also live that kind of life, and it can be hard for them to try and fit into another type of structure. Sometimes, you need a lot more colors, and New York has a lot more colors, sounds, and opportunities. You get to meet so many different kinds of people. I would never have met [pianist] Geri Allen if I was in Florida. But at the time, I wasn't even thinking about that. I was just thinking about the vibe and the freedom.

A lot of this knowledge you're talking about, is it something that's self-taught?
The MPCs and all the machines that I work with, that's all self-taught. But when I moved to New York, I did a six-month internship as a sound engineer, because there are some toys that I can't afford. Like the SSL board! I want to smell it; I want to plug every single thing into it and hear what every single button does, you know? I just love it. I interned six months at the Cutting Room and a couple years at Sound on Sound studios. That's really how I got the opportunity to work with jazz musicians. I've worked with Geri Allen as a sound engineer and did a few records with her. As an engineer, you have to improvise with your ears to make things work.

In the videos I've seen of you performing, I'm seeing percussion technique as well as DJing technique. You're playing the wave drum over here while you're adjusting levels with your other arm.
But if you think about it, that's an engineer mixing a record. You have to sort of manage all of these tools in front of you.

It's also important to have a passion for these tools. That's why I did the internship with no pay whatsoever. I had to clean the studio's bathrooms—the first couple of months were not pretty at all. But the first chance I had to just take a peek at that SSL board, I was in there. I didn't care if I had to grab the trash and then bring it back to just quickly look at it. That kind of passion should go hand in hand with your art and the tools that you work with.

When did jazz music come into your musical life? Did you listen to jazz growing up in Haiti?
Back home we have Haitian jazz. I connect with jazz musicians because I improvise and I am working with that kind of language. Musicians like [saxophonist] Henry Threadgill and [saxophonist] Steve Coleman, they kind of "get it," and I connect with what they're doing too. When it comes to finding textures and harmonies that fit with say a [pianist] Geri Allen piece, if you can express that with a turntable or an air synth or say the Kaossilator like you would with a piano, there's the instant connection that happens. A lot of times, I have all of their charts, because I can read the music, even though I'm

not gonna play that F sharp or try to comp.[50] For me, it's always more about feel or a mood, that's a huge part of the language. Improvising is a language, and if you listen, you may hear something like a question, and you just have to answer! You *have* to answer. [laughs] And no one is going to stop and tell you, "Okay, when I say this you say this. . . ." It just happens. You kind of catch it or you don't. It's very, very simple.

I've seen performances where jazz musicians have a DJ onstage but they completely ignored the electronics. They filled up the space with their sound, with rhythms, and the DJ was trying to find a space in the music to be heard.
You do have different kinds of musicians. Certain people can hear it. Certain people have a kind of mindset. [Keyboardist] Craig Taborn is another person I work with who has that kind of mind. You can have a dialogue with these kinds of musicians and not step on anybody's toes. It's a fine balance. And yes, the people that I work with respect what I do. I think those days are over; those days where DJs aren't considered to be musicians.

The people that I work with, if they ask me to come in and do something, it's like, "Okay, she plays *this* part. . . ." It works when you have the right elements and everyone understands that each person has a part to play. It makes that machine work better, instead of people saying, "No, no, no! That's my part! No! That's my part!" [laughs] And then the machine just tumbles!

You've spoken about the spiritual aspect of sound and bridging that aspect with modern, electronic instruments. Can you talk a little bit about this?
This gets a little esoteric, because we're dealing with different layers of how you perceive sound. Some people hear it, they feel it, it touches them a certain way, or they don't feel it at all. When you're dealing with different perceptions, it gets a little tricky.

Basically, it's about frequency. The frequency is very much present in the sound, and that frequency is connected for sure to a specific thing, a specific deity, a specific energy source, a specific history, a specific legacy, a specific ancestor, a specific emotion, a specific memory in your mind, even one from a past life. So when you're talking about sounds in the background in my music and how those sounds capture you a certain way, that's exactly what they're supposed to do! It's supposed to let you experience different layers. At that point, you're not really trying to jump up and dance, you're trying to really peek in and say, "Whoa, what did I just see?" It's like something that you remember but you don't remember. It's forcing you to go into a deeper kind of level, as far as listening and experiencing the sound itself.

That's what basic spirituality is for me. If you can experience it and connect it to a source, a feeling, especially if it's something empowering. That's the type of stuff that I'm working with, especially with the Vodou culture. I'm trying to bring it to light and expose the beauty of it, because it's a beautiful culture. And it's not really exclusive. That's the thing I love to connect with. When I'm playing with a jazz musician, I'll play something and they might say, "You know, I heard you play some African stuff, and I really, really like that." Yeah, yeah, yeah! [laughs]

Just infusing those things in there to say, hey, we're all in this together. We're all part of this. This is our gift, this is our way of expressing or fighting or living. Feeling those layers that sometimes we're not allowed to feel. We're so busy waking up and thinking, "Okay, it's 9 to 5! I gotta pay the rent! I gotta pay the phone bill! And get on the phone and text, text, text, text, text!" So it's like you stop and you hear something. You think you hear it, but you didn't hear it, but you thought you heard it. You're forced right there to engage within your own layers in your own mind. [laughs] Which is sometimes very, very empowering, especially if everything else is exterior. Now you have a moment to bring it back into yourself.

Sometimes taking time to stop and listen is half the battle, to just slow down and breathe.
Yes! Breathe and connect, you know? You might not know what it is, but you feel it, and it feels good. And it's stopping you from that mundane or that plug or that matrix or whatever, you know? Breathe just a little bit before you gotta plug back into the 9 to 5 again, but for a *minute*, [laughs] you unplug!

Lenaé Harris

They teach you there's a boundary line to music. But, man, there's no boundary line to art. — Charlie Parker[51]

I first heard cellist, pianist, composer, and producer Lenaé Harris in concert as a member of the New York-based alternative funk collective Earthdriver. During the performance, Harris held her own as the sole cellist in a rock ensemble that included guitar, bass, and drums, three lead vocalists, a spoken word artist, *and* a DJ. Some time after that show, I invited Harris to play cello on a score I was composing for a dance company. As we began to collaborate, I quickly realized her range as an instrumentalist extended well beyond her powerful contributions to song-driven bands like Earthdriver.

Harris' musical training is rooted in Western European classical music. She started piano lessons at age 6, and began playing cello at age 11 as a member of her school's string orchestra. She connects her abilities as an improviser to her classical music studies.

"I spent a lot of time listening to the Romantic composers ..." says Harris, "and I think that may be why I'm able to pick up things in terms of improvising. Debussy is one of my top favorites, along with Rachmaninoff, Ravel, Liszt, and Beethoven, and many of the chords those composers used in their music you could arguably say are jazz chords."

Improvisation was once an integral part of classical music. Bach, Mozart, and Beethoven were well known in their time for their ability to improvise. Ornamentation (melodic elaboration around a single note) was an essential component to Gregorian chant, Baroque music, and Italian opera.

In her grandparents' home, Harris grew up hearing her grandfather play honky-tonk and boogie-woogie on the piano. The gospel music she experienced as a young woman in church services and revivals was another powerful source of musical inspiration.

"Gospel *is* jazz, in a sense," explains Harris. "One could argue it incorporates several elements found in jazz."

Currently living and working in New York City, Harris grew up on the South Side of Chicago in a single-parent home. The sense of independence she developed as a young woman is apparent in every musical venture she chooses to explore, be it classical, electronic, R&B, film scoring, or jazz. When Harris plays, she hears everything that is happening around her, and then makes her own statement.

Lenaé Harris. Photo by Craig Bailey/Perspective Photo.

When did you first start playing a musical instrument?
I started taking piano lessons at the age of 6. But there was always a piano at my grandparent's house. My grandfather played the harmonica, the piano, honky-tonk blues, and also sang. I was plunking around on their piano before I started taking lessons. My mother asked me one day, "Do you want to take lessons?" And I said, "Absolutely!" [laughs] There was no question about it! I loved the instrument.

I began my piano studies with Ryna Krysiak in Chicago. She was a Suzuki instructor but also came from the Russian school. She incorporated those methods to teach me music theory and to sight read really early in the game. Suzuki is all about learning by the ear.

When did the cello come into your life?
When I was 11. There was a string orchestra in my public school. The first time I heard the instrument, I fell in love with it. I asked the instructor how I could get into the orchestra. Before I actually got to play the cello, I ended up playing all of the other stringed instruments. I played a little violin, viola, bass, and then cello was assigned to me, and that's what I really wanted to play.

Many of the musicians I've interviewed have told me that their musical education began in a public school.
I'm still in touch with my elementary school. Unfortunately, they actually cut that particular music program. Last time I checked, they now have a drum instructor teaching djembe, and that's about it.

So you were lucky to be there at that time.
Yes. Because that's what started it all. That program, as well as attending the Merit School of Music, propelled me to where I am today.

When did you begin composing music?
I started composing things at an early age, maybe even as early as age 11, but I never wrote anything down. It actually wasn't until I was an undergraduate student that I really started working on a composition for piano I called *Turning Point*. That piece, the entire piece, had been in my head until I got to college. College is where I formally began studying composition.

I entered DePaul University in Chicago and majored in composition and cello performance. My early lessons were with Janet Misurell-Mitchell—a composer, flutist, and vocalist in American contemporary music, who really helped me out in the beginning stages. I also studied with George Flynn and Kurt Westberg.

As I was developing *Turning Point*, I had the opportunity to have a rough draft performed by the school's orchestra. Cliff Colnot was the conductor of the DePaul Symphony Orchestra at the time while I was a cellist in the orchestra. He is widely recognized not only as a conductor but also as an arranger and for his work in commercial jingles, two areas that also piqued my interest. So, I approached him about giving me advice on further developing the piece. During our meetings, he taught me more about orchestration since I wanted *Turning Point* to become a piece for piano and orchestra. Those lessons were invaluable to me as a budding composer.

It sounds like your family was supportive of your desire to study music. Is that accurate?

Yes, that's very accurate. Although, my mother always preached to me throughout my entire career about having something else to fall back on, which is something I am grateful for. But it's almost a blessing and a curse. [laughs] Because you never know. When you're a musician, it's often hard to pay your bills. And even though I have a job now, it's still hard to pay my bills.

But my family was 100 percent behind me because I was creative from the time I was a little child. At the age of 4 I was ready to play. You could see my soul wake up anytime I heard or was around music. Even just going to church services and revivals, that's where I woke up. Anytime I heard music, it was like I became a different child! [laughs]

When did you first start listening to jazz and jazz improvisation? I know jazz informs and is an important component to your music.

During my junior year of college, I started checking out jazz. A lot of my friends were a part of the school's jazz program, which was directed by Bob Lark. I really connected more with the jazz musicians than the classical musicians.

It was funny. I would go to orchestra practice, go to chamber ensemble, and then after that, go hang out with the jazz kids, and the camaraderie was there instantly, just in terms of being friendly!

There was one guitarist in particular that I started hanging out with, Mike Kunz, who started to open up my eyes and ears. He got me listening to [guitarist and composer] Pat Metheny, who I had only heard previously on smooth-jazz radio. Mike told me, "Your piano playing reminds me of [Pat Metheny's pianist] Lyle Mays . . ." and I was like, "What do you mean? I don't even play jazz." So he started exposing me to the whole relationship between Pat Metheny and Lyle Mays.

He had a copy of *The Real Book*,[52] and one day we were sitting in his dorm room and I started reading though it. I told him I didn't really understand all of the different chord symbols. I remember that for the first jazz piece I ever wrote as an undergraduate student, instead of writing jazz chord symbols like Abm9, I wrote out Roman numerals. [laughs] Like V of V, ii, IV, V, I . . . it was funny. I told Mike, "Well, this is what I was taught!" and he was like, "No, no. Back it up. . . ." [laughs] It just took me a while to get all this in my brain.

At DePaul, were you being exposed to music you'd never heard before?
Yes, definitely.

My mom had some jazz recordings at home, like Herbie Hancock, George Duke, Miles Davis, and John Coltrane. That world was always there, but was just so different to me. My world when I was growing up was classical music. I spent a lot of time listening to the Romantic composers specifically, and I think that may be why I'm able to pick up things in terms of improvising. Debussy is one of my top favorites, along with Rachmaninoff, Ravel, Liszt, and Beethoven, and many of the chords those composers used in their music you could arguably say are jazz chords.

While at DePaul, were you thinking about what kind of career you wanted after graduation? Did you have a specific career path in mind?
Well, when I started out playing both piano and cello, I imagined I'd be doing that. But once I started studying composition, I wanted to do film scoring. In my senior year, I started exploring film-scoring programs at other colleges.

But while I was an undergrad, I also went the business route. I got an internship with the Chicago Transit Authority's marketing and development team. Again, I wanted something to fall back on, and I went through an internship program that they offered to college students. Our team was successful in launching one of the country's first pilot programs of transit media for college students that encouraged students to get on public transit known as the U-Pass.

I was torn a little bit. Before I came to New York to go to grad school at New York University, I worked in an office 9 to 5.

Did you think film scoring and commercial work might be a way to make a living as a composer?
Yes. I was a big Alfred Hitchcock fan. As a composer, I'm very inspired by both Bernard Hermann (who scored Hitchcock's films) and John Williams (who scored "Star Wars" and the first three "Harry Potter" films). With film, your music can be heard by millions of viewers at once. And jingles were and still are the very fabric of commercials, and I have always thought I could compose that type of music as well.

So you came to New York to go to grad school, and you stayed!
Absolutely. In retrospect, I assumed after grad school that staying in New York City would be the best avenue for all that I had to offer. If there was a rock band, I wanted to be a part of that. If there was a classical chamber ensemble, I wanted to be a part of that. Even the arts management and business side of making music, I wanted to be a part of that and all the while continue playing cello and composing.

If I could have a piano in my apartment, I'd be playing more. I don't have any way of getting to a piano to practice after work. By the time I get off of work, the places I could go to practice are closed.

But there's nothing really keeping me here in New York City now, given the technology today. There aren't as many networking possibilities here as I had originally thought. It's a very transient place to be in. So I'm exploring where else I might go, maybe even to another country, where I know there's going to be an avenue for all of the styles of music that I have an interest in.

Who were your role models when you were a child or later when you were studying music in college?
My instructors, Ryna Krysiak [piano], Elizabeth Anderson [cello], and Cliff Colnot [conductor]. My technique and knowing how to really express what the composer wanted was a result of studying with all three of these instructors.

In 1988, I began attending an all-day Saturday music program at the Merit School of Music. I had instruction in theory, music history, conducting, piano, cello, and chamber ensembles. Merit was founded by the late Alice Pfaelzer and Emma Endres-Kount. It is a tuition-free conservatory dedicated to ensuring that Chicago-area children have the chance to experience and excel in music. I credit Alice Pfaelzer, Ann Monaco, Duffie Adelson, Elizabeth Anderson, Bernice Ransley, and a host of other instructors at Merit for encouraging me to excel in music.

And last but definitely not least, my late aunt Rosetta Coleman. My aunt played organ in our church, Liberty Baptist Church, as well as within the Catholic church. She played pipe organ and piano. She and my grandfather were the first people I witnessed, on a daily basis, playing the piano.

Although I didn't study gospel, my aunt really influenced my desire to improvise. Gospel *is* jazz, in a sense. One could argue it incorporates several elements found in jazz. Just being around my aunt and seeing her play made me want to play.

Did you sing in church?
I don't sing a lick! [laughs] I wasn't a gospel pianist either. But I was a part of the church, and a part of every church program under the sun.

What's it like for a creative musician now in New York City? Is it hard to find places to play and audiences who will listen?
Well, the good part is there are all kinds of opportunities here to perform any style of music you could possibly think of. If you're coming to New York City to study music, I would say that once you arrive, try to get to know as many musicians as you possibly can. Go to as many concerts as possible. And if you're

a classical or jazz musician, try to check out music that's the opposite of that. Make the effort to expose yourself to different genres.

Also, given the economic downturn, you need to have a plan in your back pocket. New York is one of the toughest places to live. It's not that you won't be able to live here, but at this point, your income probably won't supersede the expenses you incur on a daily basis. Speaking for myself—and I'm not speaking for anybody else—that is what has held me back from doing music as much as I want to do it. I'm from this old school where when I was a child, at the age of 10, I was doing weddings and getting paid. So when somebody comes to me and asks me to do a five-hour recording for free, it's just not worth it.

Having a back-up plan—I can't preach that enough. And make sure that back-up plan is also something that you could potentially enjoy should things not work out for you. Not everybody's gonna be a mega pop star, and that's completely okay! Find something else that you're extremely passionate about besides music to fill in the gaps when you need extra income.

I know that sounds weird, like, "Wait, isn't your passion music?" Yes, indeed it is. But that's why I get up in the morning and even go to work from 9 to 5. I want that 9 to 5 because I want to be able to feed the monster that I know resides within me.

Sofia Rei

Born and raised in Argentina, singer and composer Sofia Rei's musical journey is perhaps one of the most complex among the musicians in this book. It is a journey that directly informs her compositions, a focused and powerfully realized hybrid of South American styles, jazz, and other contemporary idioms, as well as her singing, which draws upon her classical training along with the idiomatic phrasing and articulation heard in jazz singing. Rei also embraces folkloric influences, especially the sound of Colombian, Peruvian, and Argentinean singers, a sound Rei describes as being "almost like a scream."

For Rei, her study of and time spent singing jazz had to be reconciled with her fascination with folkloric sources. Fortunately for Rei, after relocating from Boston, where she studied at the New England Conservatory of Music, to New York City, she found the mentorship and vocal instruction she needed to sing what she heard in her mind's ear.

"I figured out a way to come in and out of these different styles," says Rei, "and always come back to a center, a healthy sound that works as the middle ground for all these different things. And now I can combine them, and I do that a lot especially with my music and the different things that I do with my band."

Sofia Rei. Photo by Sandrine Lee.

In her interview, Rei speaks in great detail about the influence of jazz on her singing and the ways her band performs her music.

"With the music in general, it's always very interesting to me, this question: 'What is jazz?'" says Rei. "I'm doing music all in Spanish, with instruments that don't come from the United States. But jazz informs how I and each member of my band express ourselves and communicate with each other in a performance."

Rei belongs to a generation of musicians who have discovered ways to make seemingly disparate cultures and genres work and play together. On her recordings and onstage, drum machines groove with Colombian marimbas, an electric guitar strums along with a Paraguayan harp, and Rei's voice shifts between the milky textures of a cosmopolitan chanteuse to the sound of a controlled scream. The current evolution of jazz includes the emergence of new musical hybrids inspired by traditions from around the globe, and Rei, along with Anat Cohen, Ayelet Rose Gottlieb, and Malika Zarra, is leading this evolution.

What prompted you to move from Boston to New York City? Why not stay in Boston and continue playing music there?

Even before I moved to Boston from Buenos Aries, I really wanted to eventually have the experience of living in New York. When I finished school, I stayed in Boston about a year and a half. I was teaching; I had my octet; I was putting together the music for my first album, and I was working with a lot of different bands. But the Boston music scene is a very strange animal, because on the one hand you have a lot of amazing musicians there because of the music schools, the teachers, and the students. Berklee College of Music alone has more than 4,000 students. There's NEC, the Boston Conservatory ... and if you just combine the numbers, you have so many music students and so many great faculty in the city. But the music scene is really just sad. It's just sad. There's nothing going on. People don't go out to see live music.

I remember the struggle of creating places for my band to perform. Just going to art galleries and saying, "I have this project. Would you guys be interested in having music here? I can create a night based around a theme...." I even organized a vocal festival at a gallery there with another friend. I was really actively trying to create new spaces for the musicians to perform. But the live music thing really wasn't happening at all. And it was really frustrating.

I would still go to New York to check out the music and I really fell in love with the city. The first time I came to New York City I was 16 years old and I was stunned by the energy of it. And I'm a very high-energy type of person! Even when I lived in Buenos Aries, which is a crazy active city as well, I always liked the fast speed of things, you know? Of course it can get tiring sometimes. But New York has that speed. The city fits the way that I do things and the way that I move, you know? I love it! I really like that on any given night you can hear any kind of music in any borough in the city and there's just so many amazing musicians playing everywhere.

I am interested in a lot of different music scenes. It's not just that one thing that I like. If it was only jazz or if it was only folkloric music from Peru or if it was only avant-garde contemporary vocal music or whatever, maybe there'd be another place where I could also feed my need to hear and perform that kind of music. In New York, I can extend all these different arms and find really good musicians to work with in any of these genres. It's been really fantastic for me.

Before Boston, you studied music in Argentina. Is that correct?
Yes. I started studying music when I was about 4 and I really liked it. My parents realized I especially liked singing. So later on, I started working in different choirs.

My grandmother took me to an audition for the Buenos Aries opera house's children's choir, and I got in. I started working there four days a week when I was (I think) 9. That opera house, the Colón Theater, is a really beautiful theater and is considered to have one of the best acoustic halls. Singers from all over the world talk about it. There's something special about the acoustics.

At that young age, were you studying with a teacher?
Actually, it was a job. It's a strange thing. It was a job with the choir and you had to be there four times a week for rehearsals. On the weekends there would be concerts, sometimes trips to different places.

But it was really crazy, because I got placed in the soprano section, which was *completely* wrong for me, completely wrong. [laughs] I already knew how to read music, but they wouldn't teach you any technique, or sight-reading, or anything. They would just expect you to be able to do it, you know? It was really crazy.

And you were a kid! A young kid.
Oh my God, the director was completely insane. He would not let us bring any kind of music or notation paper or anything to the rehearsals because he wanted us to memorize everything. I remember the first rehearsal I walked in and it was, "Okay, Handel's *Messiah*! Here we go! Sopranos! [Imitates a piano playing an incredibly fast phrase of musical notes] Okay, sing that back!" That was it. You didn't get it, you were out, don't come back tomorrow! It was like really old school, hardcore classical music training, but in a bad way. [laughs]

Eventually, one year later, I got fired from the choir, because this director was expecting me, in the soprano section, to develop a very strong dramatic powerful voice and I had this very small stream of sound coming out of my mouth! Very in tune and everything, but I was in the wrong section. And I guess he couldn't tell that, so he fired me.

And getting fired was like the saddest moment in my life. My parents didn't know what to do with me, I was so depressed. Seriously depressed, and a kid. My parents were like, "What are we gonna do with this girl?"

I auditioned for another professional choir, the National Children's Choir, who sang in another amazing theater, the Cervantes Theater. And that was a really cool experience. In that choir they did work on [vocal] technique and solfège.[53] There was training for the kids who were a part of the choir, music theory, and a crazy amount of rehearsing, three hours a day, every day. And I lived really far away from the place!

And it was a job.
It was a job. They paid you a salary to do it. I was a state worker! [laughs] I don't know if there's an equivalent here in the U.S. of that type of organization. Basically, my salary and my position depended on the president and then the secretary of culture. These choirs belonged to the secretary of culture. They worked us as ambassadors for Argentine music for all over the world.

Later on I did high school, and that was the only period where I was not singing in any organization or anything. I just decided to just do my thing. I played drums for a while. Then I auditioned for the National Youth Choir and that again was my work for many years (until I moved to the U.S.) as an alto. Finally in the right place! [laughs]

So I sang a lot of classical music and I studied in the National Conservatory of Music back home in Buenos Aires. I got my bachelor's in classical voice. I did a lot of chamber music, opera, Renaissance music ... my background in music in Argentina is more in the classical music world.

Can you talk about your vocal technique? Have you kind of created your own hybrid technique as a singer, one that combines your classical training with jazz?
Yeah, actually. That's exactly what happened but without my thinking about it.

When I was at the New England Conservatory of Music, when I started singing jazz and other types of popular music, I was, for a period of two or three years, struggling between the two really badly. When you sing classical music you work specifically with your head voice. You're expected to develop a lot of volume and sing without a microphone for an audience of hundreds of people in a big theater. That's different than the kinds of needs you have if you sing jazz or Brazilian music or Argentine folkloric music. So while the classical technique informs and helps anything that you sing later on, any kind of style, there is a point where you really go a different direction to sing, say, tango or folkloric music. Because the type of resonance that folkloric music requires is very different from the one that you would use for singing, let's say, Renaissance music. So for a while, I struggled with these techniques.

But it got to a point where I couldn't move forward anymore because . . . when I moved to New York I was doing a lot of things. For instance, for a period of time I was working with Maria Schneider and her big band. And that kind of singing was a very light type of singing, where I would have to use all my range. Almost a three and a half octave range and blend with the horns with the band. I would have to really work on making my voice very light and very flexible. And then I would have to work with another band singing tango, which was completely in the other direction. [With tango] I would really have to push my chest voice all the way up, almost scream, you know? So it was a time of confusion.

But I figured out a way to come in and out of these different styles and always come back to a center, a healthy sound that works as the middle ground for all these different things. And now I can combine them, and I do that a lot, especially with my music and the different things that I do with my band. All these different things came together. I definitely use things that came from singing contemporary [classical] music, extended techniques, and the use of my voice as an instrument as well as to make noises and percussive sounds. And also to be able to control the amount of vibrato I want, to be able to control the type of resonance that I want, if I want something that's more brilliant and brassy and metallic, and stretch my chest voice to the very top the way a folkloric singer does.

What I find really fascinating about folkloric music, what you can hear all throughout South America, in Colombian music, Peruvian music, Argentine music, is this sound of the singers, it's almost like a scream in the high part of your range. But it still keeps the speaking quality of the voice. When you hear it, it never loses that. But it was hard for me to figure out how to do that in a way where I would be able to keep all the rest of it! A lot of singers who only sing folkloric music lose their ability to just go beyond certain notes of their range. They're kind of stretching a muscle every day in only one direction.

Now I can use all these techniques together without creating a problem in my voice. For many years, I was not so sure this would work out!

One person who really helped me with technique was a teacher here in New York who I started working with while I was in Boston. Her name is Jeannette LoVetri. She's really phenomenal. She's someone who really knows so much about the voice internally. It's like, she can hear you, see through your skull, and tell you exactly what's going on. She developed a very interesting method for all styles of popular music, Broadway, whatever, you name it, jazz, anything. A lot of fantastic singers study with her, including Theo Bleckman and Luciana Souza. She really helped me a lot.

The teacher I am working with now, Barbara Maier, is fantastic and she is also the teacher of a great Colombian folkloric singer Lucia Pulido. Barbara is able to understand how that music is sung and how to do it in a way where you're in control of it. And you can actually sing and do it without pushing your voice and be in control pitch-wise. So she really helped me a lot!

You sing original arrangements and original music. Was composing music that used these different techniques part of the learning process as well? Did you compose or arrange tunes that took advantage of your ability to sing in different ways?

Actually, I never wrote for my voice. I always wrote with a specific sonic idea in mind. For instance, when I had this octet, I was thinking of myself as another horn. I was not thinking, "Well, this is my range, what key would be best?" I never felt like that when writing or arranging. I don't. I should! [laughs] Sometimes I write music and say, "Oh, this is way too high for me. Why did I do this to myself?" or "This is too complicated!" But I don't think what would fit my instrument, I kind of think of a sonic idea, and I try to play it, and I try to sing it. When I write, I tape it, and I sing it, so eventually I'll know if I'll be able to do it!

With the octet, I did a lot of music where I was just the fourth horn in the band. I had a sextet back in Boston where I arranged the music of Astor Piazzolla, and we were doing all this instrumental music of his with a saxophonist.

You weren't singing lyrics.

No. No lyrics. We did add some compositions of Piazzolla that had lyrics. But in general, it was more instrumental music. So you challenge yourself range-wise and sound-wise. Because blending with other instruments requires other types of skills as opposed to blending with other voices. Vocal music for me is kind of second nature. I understand how it works. I worked so many years on blending in a vocal ensemble.

Can you tell me about Mycale, the vocal quartet that you're a part of that came together to work with composer John Zorn? [54]

Zorn sat down one summer and wrote over 300 tunes.

How does he do that? [laughs]

I know! But they do exist! I've seen them! Of course, it is a very minimalistic type of composing where you have maybe a melody line and a counterpoint line, maybe some chords in a section, like a small, very tiny lead sheet where you get the "head" of the song and some information. It could be maybe some chords, maybe three counterpoint lines in a section. And each of these song titles is the name of an angel.

Zorn had the idea of realizing these songs with an all-female vocal quartet. I knew Ayelet Rose Gottlieb from music school, and we reconnected when I was applying to this program at Carnegie Hall to do an "instant opera" with [vocalist] Bobby McFerrin. I told Ayelet about the program, and we both got into it. And it was really good to sing with her again. Ayelet was also working with Zorn, and when his proposition to form an all-female quartet came up, Ayelet sent him my name and information.

Each member of Mycale initially took three of Zorn's compositions and tried to come up with a text to sing that related to the angel named in the title. Each angel is actually the angel of something, the angel of fire, the angel of creation, the angel of fear. The name or the idea of the angel has triggered the selection of the texts we sing.

So each one of you has participated in shaping these songs.
Yes. And Zorn really liked what we did. I think he himself was surprised by the sound of our voices singing these songs. For instance, one of the other singers, Malika Zarra, brought a lot of amazing stuff from North African music. We're singing in Arabic, Hebrew, Spanish, and French. And the texts are also really interesting. It's a crazy mix of stuff. Just to sing in tune with three other people is so complicated! [laughs]

How has jazz influenced or inspired the compositions and arrangements you sing and perform with your band?
Let's divide it into two different things, the vocal thing and the music in general. In the vocal sound specifically, I think it has informed so much of my singing in the sense of textures and different types of articulations. In jazz singing, you will find the most amazing range of styles and ways to articulate sounds and words. All these different swoops and slurs and flips, you know? It's fantastic! It's so fascinating to me. It's something you will not find in classical music or in pop genres. Think of Billie Holiday. She had a very tiny range. But [her singing] is not about the range or a great throat for singing. It's about phrasing and articulation and how you connect to and land on a note. All that has informed my singing a lot. I look to a lot of jazz singers for that.

With the music in general, it's always very interesting to me, this question: "What is jazz? And do I fit into that category?" I'm doing music all in Spanish, with instruments that don't come from the United States. But jazz informs how I and each member of my band express ourselves and communicate with each other in a performance.

Yesterday we had a show at The Jazz Gallery, and sometimes when you put together a show, everything just goes as planned, and I don't have so much fun with that. I like it when we really take chances onstage. Taking chances and being open to whatever happens live, and being really in tune with each other in every moment of a performance. We each want to be able to react and interact. This is different than a pop band situation where things are so established, where there is this automatic pilot kind of thing going on. I can't relate to that.

Improvisation is very important in my music. And this can be done in any genre, not just jazz. You will find improvisation in cultures all over the world, but Americans have been really good at creating a system out of it and creating methods out of it. The kind of schooling you're going to have for improvisation in the States is definitely the best. That's why musicians from all over the world come to music schools like Berklee or NEC.

Through jazz I was able to become a better musician and develop my musical skills in different genres. It's music that is creative. It incorporates spontaneity in the live performance. And it's music that can be challenging for a person who just listens to super mainstream pop music. That may be a common thread between all the musicians you're interviewing for this book!

We're a little bit, all of us, a bunch of music nerds, right? We like the challenge. We don't expect to create music just to make money. We love the challenge, the music itself, and the creativity.

Ayelet Rose Gottlieb

Growing up in Jerusalem in a household filled with records, singer and composer Ayelet Rose Gottlieb was exposed to a dizzying array of musicians and musical styles at a very early age.

"My grandfather on my mom's side used to listen to the Jordanian radio station," says Gottlieb, "so I was exposed to traditional Middle Eastern music ... I listened to albums of classical guitar and Spanish guitar music from my dad's record collection, as well as Ella Fitzgerald, J.S. Bach, and Edith Piaf. And in my uncle's collection, I discovered Janis Joplin, Laurie Anderson, and Leonard Cohen."

Hearing such a diverse selection of music at home inspired Gottlieb to study a variety of musical styles and techniques. While studying classical flute in high school, she sang jazz standards and explored free improvisation. Gottlieb also began composing in her teens, incorporating elements from African, South American, and Arabic music, as well as modern and avant-garde jazz. She found opportunities to sing in clubs under the tutelage of American saxophonist and educator Arnie Lawrence. Arnie welcomed students of both Jewish and Arab backgrounds, and performed with them across Jerusalem and the West Bank.

"Arnie is really one of the main reasons why there are so many prominent

Ayelet Rose Gottlieb. Photo by Gem Salsberg.

Israeli jazz musicians today," says Gottlieb. "He gave us an onstage education in a place that wasn't an integral part of any scene."

Gottlieb relocated to the U.S. after receiving a scholarship to study at the New England Conservatory of Music. While at NEC, and later, after relocating to New York City, Gottlieb met several musicians who, like her, were open to applying a variety of styles and approaches to improvisation and composition.

"I really became more familiar with what was happening in the U.S. after I moved to Boston and later when I moved to New York.... Israel in the 90s was an amazing place to be, but it was great to discover there were other people out there in the world trying to do what I was trying to do."

Although Gottlieb has recorded jazz standards, her most recent albums feature her own songs, sung in Hebrew and English, with original lyrics as well as settings of texts by Jewish and Palestinian poets. For her most recent album, *Roadsides* (2013), Gottlieb draws upon her Jewish heritage, as well as her deep familiarity with Arabic poetry, music, and culture, to realize a song cycle that speaks to "our shared and universal experiences."

Not surprisingly, the gender and ethnic makeup of her bands is as diverse as her musical influences.

"I find diversity in a band to be very interesting and enriching and healthy for group dynamics," says Gottlieb. "It's always good to surround yourself with people who are not versions of what you are, but rather, who are different than you."

....

When did you first begin playing music or singing?
My father plays the guitar. He's very musical and taught me a lot. His father played clarinet and my uncle also plays music, so I always heard music growing up.

I started taking music classes for small children when I was around 3 years old. Later I started playing recorder and then the flute. I played classical flute from age 8 until the end of high school. But I was not born to be a classical musician. [laughs] I started experimenting with writing music and singing when I was around 14 years old. The two kind of came together. I went to Jerusalem's high school for the arts, and that's when I started discovering my own voice in music and focusing in on what I wanted to do.

I think it's a common experience for musicians, and artists in general, to know what you are before you fully become it. Music is something that chooses you from a very young age, and then the education follows.

You mentioned classical music. As a teenager, were you inspired to begin

composing music by listening to classical music? It sounds like you grew up hearing a lot of different kinds of music.

I did listen to and play a lot of classical music, but I also listened to a lot of other kinds of music. My uncle moved to Australia when I was a little girl, and he gave me his entire LP collection, which was maybe 1,000 records.

My father also had a huge record collection. In my room, I had a wall of LPs, and in my parents' living room, many more LPs. So early on, I was exposed to a lot of different kinds of music.

Growing up in Jerusalem, I heard many kinds of sounds. My grandfather on my mom's side used to listen to the Jordanian radio station, so I was exposed to traditional Middle Eastern music . . . I listened to albums of classical guitar and Spanish guitar music from my dad's record collection, as well as Ella Fitzgerald, J.S. Bach, and Edith Piaf. And in my uncle's collection, I discovered Janis Joplin, Laurie Anderson, and Leonard Cohen. [laughs] It was quite broad.

When I started collecting music on my own and developing my own tastes in music, I bought records from Africa, South America, Turkey—music from all over and all of which influenced my musical sensibility. Avant-garde jazz also became a part of my soundscape.

I actually got into improvising before knowing about the improv scene and the whole history behind it. When I discovered that there was this whole community of improvisers, it was, for me, a revelation. Because improvising was just something that came very naturally to me.

When you say "improvisation," are you talking about free improvisation as opposed to improvising over chord changes of a standard tune?

Both. When I was 16, Arnie Lawrence, who was one of the people who founded The New School for Jazz and Contemporary Music in New York, moved to Israel. He played with everyone, including Dizzy Gillespie, Charles Mingus, Liza Minnelli, and Billie Holiday. In the last 10 years of his life he lived in Israel, and I was lucky enough to be around at that time.

Arnie is really one of the main reasons why there are so many prominent Israeli jazz musicians today. He gave us an onstage education in a place that wasn't an integral part of any scene.

Performing with Arnie was an intense learning experience for me. We would play a lot of things, mostly jazz standards. But his approach was so open and his ears so big . . . improvising went beyond learning what scale goes on which chord. I don't think he was even thinking in those terms. It was all about using your ears, just diving in with a very open approach.

My friend and fellow vocalist Julia Feldman and I would explore free improvisation together, with no guidelines or forms. But, at the same time, I was learning hundreds of standards and improvising over them, too. I was also exploring possibilities within my own compositions, including extended, linear, and through-composed forms. That tied in with the Arabic music I listened to. Arabic music is very different from Western music in its forms. It doesn't go by A/A/B/A forms. The forms are longer and unravel in a more linear, "storytelling" way.

Shortly before I moved to Boston, I met pianist and composer Yitzhak Yedid; he's currently living in Australia and records a lot for the German record label Between the Lines. Yitzhak—I call him Itzki—introduced me to musicians who were working in the realm of improvised music. Because of him, I went on to attend the New England Conservatory of Music. He had studied there previously and introduced me to [pianist] Ran Blake and helped me get my scholarship to study there. That's where I discovered there was a whole world of people who were doing this thing that I was interested in doing.

So you came to the New England Conservatory of Music with a lot of knowledge about creative, improvised music in the U.S., as well as the music of Israel and other parts of the Middle East.

Yes, but I really became more familiar with what was happening in the U.S. after I moved to Boston and later when I moved to New York. I kept finding like-minded people, which was very exciting. Israel in the 90s was an amazing place to be, but it was great to discover there were other people out there in the world trying to do what I was trying to do.

When did you begin performing publicly as a singer? Either singing your own music or other people's songs?

Before Boston, when I performed with Arnie Lawrence in Jerusalem. He would also take us to the West Bank, Palestine, which, at that time, did not have the wall. We performed there and all over the country, which was a great experience. Parallel to singing mostly standards with Arnie, I started performing my own compositions in clubs in Israel. When I moved to Boston, I continued performing and really started to go deeper into my own music.

Did your family support your decision to pursue a career in music?

Absolutely. I feel very lucky about that. My family has been really supportive through all the ups and downs of being a musician.

When you graduated from school and went to New York City, how did you initially get by and survive in the city?

It's not easy!

Right! Given the kind of music you do, I'm assuming you didn't jump on a cruise ship and start singing pop songs. Did you teach? How did you pay the bills? If you don't mind me asking!

No! I don't mind at all. Before moving to Boston, I met Shahar, who is now my husband. We moved to Boston and New York City together and lived in some very small, very dumpy apartments. We lived *very* modestly. [laughs] I did a lot of babysitting in Boston. I'm still in touch with some of the kids I took care of.

Our first apartment in New York was located on Duke Ellington Boulevard. It was a tiny studio apartment, which for one person living alone would have been fine, with crooked floors and orange and blue walls. [laughs] The bed was raised and Shahar would work under it.

With the move to New York, I made the decision not to work, like you said, on a cruise ship. I avoided music "money" gigs so the music could stay pure. Instead, I taught Hebrew and tutored bar and bat mitzvah kids. I taught myself the tropes, which is the Jewish musical language for chanting the Torah and prayers, so I could tutor bar and bat mitzvah kids on how to read passages from the Torah. That was one of my jobs for about four or five years.

It was nice, because the tropes are a really fascinating musical language I had always been curious about. Those melodic phrases definitely found their way into my music. The melodies of the trope are implied by a series of little symbols embedded into the Hebrew text. You know how to chant the text according to those little drawings above and beneath it. Jews from different diaspora all have alternate melodies related to the same symbols. So it was a fascinating thing for me to learn regardless, and it was a good way to earn a living without interfering with my art.

Parallel to that, I also had several steady gigs in cafés and bars in Queens where I sang standards. Although the pay was horrible, it was a nice way to develop my chops, play with a variety of different musicians as I was putting together my band, and expand my repertoire. You need to know a lot of tunes to hold a weekly four-hour gig and not get bored with too much repetition!

It took a while before I found better-playing gigs, taught workshops, and gave private music lessons. I feel very lucky to be doing all that now.

What did your husband do for a living?
He is an animator. He has worked on films such as *Avatar* and *X-Men* doing animation and special effects.

Who are some American jazz singers that have influenced you?
I was listening to Ella Fitzgerald and Betty Carter before I knew that what I was hearing was jazz. These were just records I found and loved. I didn't think about genre, you know? Betty Carter is definitely one of my biggest influences. I also love Jeanne Lee, Jay Clayton, Norma Winstone, and of course Billie Holiday and Sarah Vaughan. Laurie Anderson, who is not a jazz singer, is a big influence on me. Many of my contemporaries are very inspiring, such as Kyoko Kitamura, Fay Victor, and Katie Bull, and my "sisters" in [the a cappella

quartet] Mycale: Sofia Rei, Malika Zarra, and Sara Serpa. Not quite American, but living in America though—but what is nationality anyways?

Honestly, the list is endless. There are so many great singers.

I wouldn't have thought of Laurie Anderson, but as soon as you mentioned her, it made sense. The connection to you seems to be her interest in other types of media and artistic expression.
Yes, as well as her approach to text. In recent years I also discovered her as an improviser. I didn't know so much about that angle in her work until I heard her play in a very open improvisational context, with Lou Reed and John Zorn. It was a great concert.

Like you, she's also very interested in language and poetry. Your album _Roadsides_ is a collection of very imaginative musical settings of both Israeli and Palestinian poetry. This is a naïve question, but here goes: Outside of music, is this a provocative combination, a combination that might surprise people given the politics of the Middle East?
I don't know if it's provocative. I hope it's evocative!

In the years leading up to the project, I was drawn to and setting to music words by Israeli poets I loved and grew up with. But when it came time to record, there was something lacking. Since the songs, as a set, seemed to be somewhat like a letter to the place I grew up in, I felt the need to include the voices of Palestinian poets as well, which became a very important part of this project. I found poetry that spoke to me and had been translated into Hebrew. Unfortunately, I don't speak Arabic. I didn't grow up knowing these poets and their work; it was a search I had to do on my own. Since then, I keep discovering more and more contemporary Palestinian poetry as well as fringier Israeli poetry that speaks to me, and the project continues to grow and develop.

The texts I chose for _Roadsides_ are thought-provoking, but they're not obviously political songs or something like that. They're just very human. The poems offer personal perspectives on small moments in life. I think art and music have a healing quality. Through art you can detangle politics and just look at the essence of a person or an experience and consider our shared and universal experiences. That's important to me.

You also see this in the _Roadsides_ band. It's not a homogenous band. It's a mixed group of people both in gender and in ethnicity, which is always what I prefer with any band I lead. I find diversity in a band to be very interesting and enriching and healthy for group dynamics. I think it's always good to surround yourself with people who are not versions of what you are, but rather, people who are different than you. There should be room for each band member to expand into new directions.

I don't hear your music as being contrived in the way it blends different kinds of ethnic music. It sounds much more organic than that.

It's a mix. For me, in both composition and arranging, there is a combination of very intuitive writing, in-the-moment inspiration, with well-thought-out structured writing. No matter what comes first, be it text, a melody, or a rhythm, my writing usually starts with a moment of inspiration. But then there's the part of the actual work—much heavier and more analytical, when I sit with it and try to make it more ... exact. When inspiration comes, it's not focused and not worked out. For me, the next step after that initial inspiration is trying to figure out, is this note necessary here or is it too much? Do I actually need this bar of music? Or does it need something that isn't there yet, like a counter rhythm or melody?

Some of my compositions are completely written out while others, especially those I write for my duo with pianist Anat Fort, may just be a sketch of a very basic melody or just the outline of a harmony, a simple guide for us to thicken in real time. We'll take the music wherever we want to in a live performance, because we have that kind of communication. I don't have to spell things out for her at this point.

But when I write for larger ensembles, I focus on the smaller details, just like a classical composer. I write out every part, every countermelody, dynamics, and so on.

When you first began composing music as a teenager, did you first hear the music in your head?

Yes, definitely. I was making up songs back to when I was just a child. My brother Michael is also a musician, a singer/songwriter, and a lot of our childhood games had to do with sound and music. Singing, playing, recording sounds. We would sample things from the television or outdoors and play what we had recorded on a double-cassette deck and manipulate these found sounds.

I started composing music because of a recurring dream that I had as a teenager. I would hear this massive orchestral piece and see these swirling colors that went along with it. And it made me crazy! [laughs] I wanted to be able to write down the music I was hearing in the dream, but I didn't have the tools. So, I started studying composition. But when I started writing music, the dream stopped.

I have this feeling that dream is going to come back to me on my deathbed! [laughs] That piece wrote itself in my head, and I didn't know how to take it out of there before it was gone.

Anat Cohen

From its very beginning, jazz, sometimes called "America's classical music," has drawn upon musical influences from around the globe. At the turn of the 20th century, dance music from Havana found its way into the syncopated rhythms of ragtime and the compositions of Jelly Roll Morton, Scott Joplin, and W. C. Handy. However, Cuban rhythms, each with its own clave pattern, were distinct from the triplet feel (or "swing") that was a defining characteristic of jazz. Trumpeter Dizzy Gillespie's 1947 collaborations with Cuban conga maestro Chano Pozo embraced these two distinct rhythmic approaches by layering "swung" and "straight" eighth notes to create the earliest recorded examples of Afro-Cuban jazz. In the decades after those first Afro-Cuban cuts, musicians continued to experiment with wild new hybrids of music that incorporated influences not only from Cuba and other South American countries, but from across Eastern Europe, the Middle East, Asia, Japan, and Indonesia.

And the debate as to what is or is not jazz continues! Even today, there are plenty of musicians who are quick to define jazz as "music that swings," period, end of story. Music that does not swing is "world music" or "fusion" or any other number of alternately named genres. Perhaps what is more important is, as Moroccan singer Malika Zarra says in her interview for this book, "to be able to identify where things are coming from, and not be superficial."

Israeli-born clarinetist and saxophonist Anat Cohen's earliest experiences playing jazz were in the Jaffa Music Conservatory's New Orleans band, playing clarinet parts and the written solos from arrangements of recordings by the Original Dixieland Jazz (also "Jass") band. In her interview, she describes how she fell "in love with the feeling of swing, which gave me so much joy and still gives me so much joy." She would eventually continue her studies in the U.S. at the Berklee College of Music where she met students from other countries who, like her, were studying American jazz, but were missing their native homes.

"(Students) from South America, they started missing home," says Cohen. "So they started to bring their folkloric elements into jazz. I started playing music for people who were writing music . . . that incorporated Brazilian, Argentinean, and Venezuelan rhythms. My rhythmic world just opened up because of that."

In performance and on recordings, Cohen plays tunes in a thoroughly syncopated, classic New Orleans style, such as her slow-drag take on "La Vie en Rose" from her album *Claroscuro*, as well as classic and newly composed music built on Brazilian, North African, and South American rhythms. Her latest recording, *Luminosa*, even includes an acoustic arrangement of electronic and

Anat Cohen. Photo by Jimmy Katz.

experimental hip-hop artist Flying Lotus' "Putty Boy Strut."

"Jazz is world music," says Cohen. "It's an American art form that started here, but it welcomes all of these influences."

Cohen welcomes these influences and, like many musicians interviewed in this book, is creating a truly global and multicultural form of jazz. And she's only just getting started....

When did you first begin playing a musical instrument?
I was 6.

Was it the clarinet?
It was just a keyboard.

When did the clarinet come into your musical life?
When I was about 12. I followed my older brother, Yuval. I was going to the music conservatory in our city of Tel Aviv. It's called the Jaffa Music Conservatory. My brother Yuval was already a saxophone student [at that conservatory], and one day my parents brought Avishai, my younger brother, and myself to the conservatory and said, "Okay. Pick an instrument."

I already knew about the clarinet. I had heard it before and liked the sound of it. I think they needed the clarinet in the band they had at the conservatory, so I was encouraged to pick the clarinet for my instrument. My younger brother picked the trumpet. He thought that since it only had three buttons it would be easy to play. [laughs]

Did you begin playing jazz in the conservatory?
When I was studying the keyboard at home, it was one of those "fashionable" Yamaha organs, as we didn't have a piano at home. I never really got into heavy classical repertoire. I learned songs instead. The kind of music my teacher brought to me to learn were [was] basically American standards and songs from musicals. I didn't realize until years later that learning those would come in handy! I said, "Wait a second, I played some of those when I was 8!" So that was my initial introduction to jazz.

My official encounter with jazz happened a couple years into my studies at the conservatory. I joined the conservatory's New Orleans band, and that's how I really started to get into jazz, by reading and playing clarinet parts and written solos from Original Dixieland Jazz Band arrangements and just falling in love with the feeling of swing, which gave me so much joy and *still* gives me so much joy.

Was this unusual for a young person growing up in Israel to be listening to and playing Dixieland music and jazz?
I don't know. The truth is that except for the people that were at the conservatory back then, I didn't know any other kids who played jazz. There weren't programs in schools where you could learn about it. There were no record stores in Israel where you could go and buy jazz records. You just shared records and cassettes of the music and whatever information your teachers and friends gave you. No Internet!

While you were at the conservatory, did you think about music as a career? Was a career in music the goal for you and your brothers?
You know, I never really asked my brothers that question. We are all very close in age. My older brother, Yuval, is a year and a half older than me, and my younger brother, Avishai, is just three years younger. So we were very close. From a very young age, we went to the same junior high school for the arts, the same high school for the arts, and the same conservatory. But there was never a point where we actually discussed the "career" part of making music. I think it just developed organically. It was never announced "this is what I want to do for a living."

Eventually, you made the decision to come to the U.S. to study music. Were you nervous about leaving your country to study jazz on a whole other level?
Yes and no. Again, I followed my older brother, Yuval, who got a scholarship to go to Boston's Berklee College of Music. I got a scholarship as well. We lived together along with a couple of other friends from Israel.

I had studied jazz in high school in a jazz program, so I was pretty accustomed to studying music. I studied all day long, in school and after school. Most of my friends played music as well, so it was just so natural. I wasn't worried about the music. I wanted to go and play jazz. I wanted to, you know, turn off the lights and play John Coltrane albums and just scream into my tenor saxophone, that's all I wanted to do every single day! [laughs]

I was worried about the language in a new country, but I wasn't worried about the music. I wanted to keep expanding my knowledge. It was all about growing as a musician and continuing my journey.

At Berklee, were you exposed to new ways of playing jazz music?
I think my whole affair with the music of South America started at Berklee College of Music. There were students at Berklee just like me, students from other countries who got scholarships to attend the school, and everybody had jazz as a common ground. Everybody wanted to further his or her knowledge about playing jazz. But then those people from South America, they started missing home. We all did! So they started to bring their folkloric elements into jazz. I started playing music for people who were writing music for large and small ensembles that incorporated Brazilian, Argentinean, and Venezuelan rhythms. My rhythmic world just opened up because of that.

Then of course there was my rediscovery of the clarinet, which came as a result of playing music from all of these different cultures.

Jazz has always been a very international music, and that's very evident in your music. You play everything from Artie Shaw to Milton Nascimento to South American music to Dixieland. But that's what jazz music is. Or at least, that's how I hear it.
That's how I look at it as well. Jazz is world music. It's an American art form that started here, but it welcomes all of these influences.

It's like, in the beginning I wanted to work on my American accent. When I speak, I say one phrase and people say, "You're from Israel!" All right. Cool. You can hear that. But I realized, there are enough people who speak with American accents, you know? I can keep my accent when it comes to the music.

Was saxophone your main instrument when you came to Berklee?
Yes. When I started playing jazz in high school, I put the clarinet aside, and picked up the tenor saxophone. For at least 10 years after I turned 16, I was mainly focused on the tenor saxophone.

I wanted to ask you about a few tracks from your album *Claroscuro*. The first composition I wanted to ask you about is "All Brothers." It opens with a piano part that sounds like a kalimba [African thumb piano] before going

into a free section for the whole band. I'm curious about the rhythms in this composition and the meaning behind its title.

Daniel Freedman, who plays drums in my band and on *Claroscuro*, wrote "All Brothers." He and I have been playing together for the past 10 years. The title "All Brothers" immediately grabbed me. When we perform it in concerts, I dedicate the song to everyone on the planet. I want to remind the audience that we are on this planet together. It's dedicated to all brothers and all sisters.

The rhythm in that composition is Moroccan. There's a beat in it that can work if you want to go all the way to folkloric Africa, but if you go to a dance club, you will hear the same kind of beat, just with more electronics. [laughs] There's something in the tempo that's very tribal. I connect to that.

For me, the free section where I scream into the soprano saxophone symbolizes the pain all over the planet. When we play that free section, sometimes it's long, sometimes it's short, but afterwards, there's a new groove and a new beginning, the optimism returns. That's how I look at the trajectory of the song.

The next composition I'm curious about is titled "As Rosas Não Falam." What does that title translate to in English?

It literally means "The Roses Do Not Speak." It's Portuguese.

This piece reminds me of Jewish music. There's a quality about it that reminds me of a song as a Jewish cantor might sing it. What's the origin of this composition? Where does it come from?

I want to comment about the cantorial sound you're describing. I wonder if it really is the piece of music that reminds you of Jewish music or if it is the way I play it.

Are you bringing something like that to your interpretation? Is that what I'm hearing?

It's a good question. First of all, the sound of the clarinet is associated so much with klezmer music. Clarinet has the ability to cry. The song is a sad song. The song is by a singer-songwriter from Brazil called Cartola [Angenor de Oliveira]. He wrote many beautiful old samba songs that are so pure. His songs always grab me.

If you listen to Cartola sing "The Roses Do Not Speak," I don't know if you're going to hear anything that sounds cantorial. That's what I'm saying. I don't think you would. But maybe the key, the tempo, and the way I shape the melody, the sound of the clarinet, maybe that's partially why it reminds you of Jewish music. I'm not sure, but maybe it's just the way I play it?

"As Rosas Não Falam" has a very moving lyric about a guy who misses his lover. He goes out to the garden to look for his lover and she's not there, and the roses remind him of her with the smell of love. It's a beautiful, beautiful lyric. You can definitely Google it and translate it into English.

When I played the melody, I was really trying to think of the lyric like I do with ballads and other songs where I feel the melody really represents the lyric of the song.

Do you believe it's important for an instrumentalist playing a song with lyrics to know what those lyrics are?
Absolutely. But sometimes it depends on what you want to do with the song. If you want to play a song, you better know what the song is about. Now, if you want to take a song and rearrange it, and give it your own flavor, you know, we instrumentalists can treat the melody in a different way. We can color it differently. We use the theme but we make it our own. In that case, maybe the lyrics are less crucial.

But if you keep the song simple, then all you need to do is present the words as the melody. Every melody has a meaning behind it. Our responsibility as instrumentalists is to connect that meaning to the notes, as well as to our emotions and our feelings. How do you play the word "love"? We have to find a way to color our sound with the meanings of words.

Speaking of melody, the third composition from your album I wanted to hear you talk about is Artie Shaw's "Nightmare." I'd almost call this a popular piece of music. It's a piece of music a lot of people have heard, but they may not know who wrote and recorded it. When did you first hear this composition?
Very recently. A couple years ago I got a call from people at ASCAP. They said, "Nat Hentoff [the jazz critic] is getting the Deems Taylor Award, and we would like you to come out and play this song 'Nightmare' at the award ceremony." The song was very important to Nat when he was a young man. When he was walking in the streets of Boston he heard "Nightmare," and the sound of the clarinet and that key, that minor key, just grabbed him and reminded him of his roots. There's something cantorial about the melody. So I transcribed the Artie Shaw part, brought my quartet to the ceremony, and we just played it. Unfortunately, Nat Hentoff didn't feel well and couldn't attend, but we still played it for him.

That is really how I got into that song. Playing it again and again, I was like, "Wow! This song is so powerful!"

I hadn't planned to record "Nightmare" for my album. But when [clarinetist] Paquito D'Rivera came into the studio, I thought it would be really cool to see if we could open it up and make the melody a two-clarinet part. Paquito had never played it with me, but we just tried it in the studio. On the recording, I'm playing the original Artie Shaw solo and Paquito is improvising and that's it, very simple and powerful. "Nightmare" has become one of my favorite songs to play with the band. We open our shows with the song. Although on the record, the song is pretty condensed, in performance it can become really extended, as much as the moment lets us.

You've released several records on your own label, Anzic Records. What would you tell a young musician who wants to start a record label? Where does one begin?

First of all, I can't say the name Anzic Records without saying the name Oded Lev-Ari, who co-owns the label and is the general manager of the label. He is really the brain behind Anzic Records. He and I started the label almost 10 years ago, back when most people were still recording for record labels. Independent labels were becoming the new model. What bothered me then was how little musicians wanted to be involved in the business side of making a record. Some musicians just wanted to document their music without caring who puts it out, and without caring if they ever see a dime from it or how much exposure the album gets.

Albums have always been a glimpse into what an artist is doing musically at the time of recording them. But it is important to pay attention to the connection between an album being released and the shows and touring period around the release time and to the connection with the PR promoting that release. It all has to work together.

Anzic Records didn't start just because I wanted artistic freedom. It started because I wanted to have control over what happens to my albums. I wanted to know how many albums are being printed and who is buying my albums and who finds out about them. I wanted to have the ability to connect the release of an album to when I'm going on tour. I wanted to understand how all these ingredients work together.

The days where musicians just played music and didn't need to think about business are over. Everything we do has a business proposition. But if you don't know how to do it yourself, you might want to partner up with somebody who has the ability to look at the bigger picture, someone who has a vision and a strategy.

The business thing can work organically with making music.

Absolutely. When partnering up, it doesn't have to be just with "business people."

Anzic Records is run by Oded Lev-Ari, who is a fabulous musician and a great thinker.

The artists on the label have their own ideas about business, and we always exchange ideas. When Anzic Records started, we believed that we'd make a bigger impact if we would put out a catalogue of music. [Pianist] Jason Lindner, my brother Avishai, saxophonist Joel Frahm, and many other artists have recorded albums for Anzic Records.

We're in an interesting time where everyone is sharing so much on Facebook, but I'm not sure how much people are sharing in their everyday lives, sharing experiences and knowledge and passing the torch to the person next to them. I think if people looked up from their computers they'd actually see people. Real people.

I was in Cleveland a couple months ago to talk to a group of high school students. I asked the kids, "Who in here has a Facebook account?" and everybody raised their hands. Then I said, "Okay, how many people in here get together with friends and play music?" and nobody raised their hands. How can you play jazz without being in the moment and communicating in the moment? This music is about feeling. It's about creating a feeling with the music. How can you study jazz without playing jazz?

We have to wait and see, Chris. We have to wait and see what happens to the music and if it can bring people together. I believe in music and its power. It has to bring us together. It has to.

Mazz Swift

From classical studies at the Juilliard School to exploring the outer strata of free improvisation, from shredding electric violin performances with Irish rock bands to television and streaming radio appearances with funk's prodigal son D'Angelo, the journey of violinist, singer, composer, and bandleader Mazz Swift has included many detours, with all roads leading to her own unique musical style she calls "MazzMuse." If we can agree that jazz means "freedom of expression," then Swift's musical ventures, taken together, reveal yet another provocative manifestation of that word.

Swift began studying classical violin at age 6, and was "dead serious" about music from the very beginning.

"My parents are huge music fans, especially classical music and jazz," says Swift. "I always liked the sound of the violin, and I asked my parents what that sound was. They told me, and I said, 'Okay, that's what I want to do!'"

Swift's early classical violin studies, and semesters at New York's well-known High School of Performing Arts (made even more famous thanks to the 1980 film *Fame*), led her to enroll at the Juilliard School. However, despite her love for classical repertoire, she decided to leave school and begin exploring traditional jazz and rock-inspired free improvisation, as well as a brand-new instrument, an electric violin called the Viper. Swift points to her joining

Mazz Swift. Photo by Nisha Sondhe.

the musical collective Burnt Sugar, led by guitarist and writer Greg Tate, as a major turning point for her as an improviser.

"In performance," says Swift, "Greg would set up this bed of sound, and then tell me to solo. So, I had all of this inspiration, all of the different sounds around me to really carry me and help me explore. I felt really free and that I could try anything in that situation."

Swift's recent album, *MazzMuse: The Band*, is perhaps her most personal musical statement. Produced by fellow musical polyglot, guitarist Vernon Reid, it features covers of songs by Annie Lennox and PJ Harvey, instrumentals inspired by both Irish reels and heavy metal, and Swift's original, highly personal songs. It's an unapologetic and emotionally raw recording that, not surprisingly, has Swift launching yet again into new musical territories while embracing her classical, jazz, and rock roots.

In the following interview Swift describes how she navigated her musical journey to become the musician and artist she is today.

....

When did you start playing a musical instrument?

Age 3 or 4 is when I sort of started banging on the piano. We had a piano in the house. My oldest sister had already been taking lessons. When I was that young, my family all knew I wanted to play the violin because I kept talking about it. But my parents didn't actually get me a fiddle until I was 6. They realized I was serious about it.

Were you inspired to play the violin after hearing or seeing somebody play that particular instrument?

My parents are huge music fans, especially classical music and jazz. I always liked the sound of the violin, and I asked my parents what that sound was. They told me, and I said, "Okay, that's what I want to do!"

So when you started on the violin at the age of 6, what kind of music did you play?

Really easy classical music. There are books that distill common classical themes into very, very simple pieces that are easy to play depending on your skill level. The music starts out with open strings, and you do that for a while, meaning, no fingering or anything like that, and then as you progress you learn to play short children's songs, like "Mary Had a Little Lamb."

Was there any kind of music programming in your school at that time?

I grew up in the projects in Long Island City. The public school there didn't really have a music program by the time I got there for third or fourth grade. My sisters before me had had music classes in the same school. They had recorders. I'll never forget that. I loved the recorder and I used to play their recorders and looked forward to the time where I would get my own recorder. But by the time I got there, they didn't have any recorders for students, and I was really disappointed. A music teacher would instead throw lyrics up on a screen using an overhead projector. You would copy that down, and then sing along to a recording. It was not a "music class" at all.

So when I asked for violin lessons, my parents found someone. I don't know how they found this person—I think she went to their church. She played cello, so my first teacher was a cellist. Then we got recommendations for other teachers as I progressed. I always had private teachers for the violin.

The teachers who had the most influence on me include Elisabeth Small, Shirley Givens, and Timothy Baker. I did the bulk of my training with Shirley. She comes from a good, strong line of pedagogues, and was a student of Ivan Galamian. Then I moved on to Timothy Baker, who taught me throughout high school and got me into the Juilliard School. Those are the three big teachers I had.

I was always serious about making music. I was dead serious about it from the very beginning.

And your parents were supportive?
Absolutely.

Can you tell me a little bit about the High School of Performing Arts? How would you describe it to someone who has never been there or is only aware of it through the movie *Fame*?
I felt like it was a pretty good school in general, although it was definitely focused on the arts. I know some of my classmates who were a little more serious about academics thought that the academics were not as strong as they could be. But I found I got what I needed.

Half my day was spent playing music, which I loved. I was in honors English, honors math, but then I also got to do chamber music, string orchestra, and full orchestra. The school also had a jazz program, but I hadn't considered playing jazz at that point.

I feel really lucky. That school is one of the biggest arguments for living in New York City or any city big enough to have a high school for the arts.

You went on to attend the Juilliard School, but you decided to leave. I imagine at the time that was a profound decision for you. What happened?
No one thing happened at Juilliard to make me feel like I needed to leave. I've always loved classical music and that was always my dream for a long, long time, just to be a classical solo violinist. But I felt that the teachers believed only a few people could really be at "the top." The general vibe of the place was,

"When you leave here, you're going to go into an orchestra. Even though your dream is to be a solo performer, that's probably not going to happen." I heard people say this a lot. I feel like that was partially particular to me, but it was also the general attitude, and I did not want to play in an orchestra! I actually really love playing in orchestras. But I always knew I wanted to be free to do whatever I wanted to do.

I know a lot of professional orchestra musicians have solo careers as well, but I felt like playing in an orchestra would mean being tied down, just like if you were playing a Broadway show. You can only do so much.

My issue was self-confidence, which is another reason I ended up leaving. My stage fright had increased. The older I got, the worse it got and the harder I was on myself. When it came to playing classical music, I could never perform at the level I wanted to perform at because I always got so nervous that I lost physical control. It was physically debilitating for me. A lot of that had to do with the competitive vibe of the school.

I was also a huge metal head. I was really into rock and heavy metal music. [laughs] I was into bands like Metallica, Anthrax, and Nirvana. I just sort of had this alternative head.

My boyfriend at the time had some Django Reinhardt and Stéphane Grappelli recordings. I heard that music, and really got into Stéphane Grappelli. And then I heard the Uptown String Quartet, and that just blew my mind because the quartet didn't just play jazz. They were doing spirituals—it was like *black music!* [laughs] You know what I mean? Although it's funny for me to say, "It wasn't just jazz, it was black music!" [laughs] The spirituals and the soulful kind of thing, but they also played modern music, new, angular sounds, and it all really appealed to me. I just got really interested in *that.* I thought, "This is something I'd really like to do!" These things made me think about music in a different way.

But there wasn't anyone I could really talk to in my school, like a counselor or a teacher, about playing that kind of music. There was just nobody there for that.

But somehow you started learning how to improvise.
What ended up happening was I decided to take a semester off to try and figure out how to "play jazz," quote unquote, but I had no idea how to do it. I didn't know who to talk to. So I went down to a music-union jam session. I wasn't particularly in love with the kind of jazz they were playing. It wasn't inspiring for me. And I was also intimidated, I guess because of the household I grew up in where jazz was respected as much as classical music. I thought I'd never be able to play it well and that I had a handicap because I sounded like a classical player. My musical accent, so to speak, was pretty classical. I just

literally stopped myself from trying, because every time I tried, I hated how I sounded.

I actually quit violin for about two years. During that time I decided to travel. I went to live on a commune in Texas where I was introduced to improvisational music. Nobody there was a jazz musician. They had kind of come from rock and folk backgrounds, and they were very interested in free expression. It was very edifying for me because I did have a lot of training but I also had a sense of music and how I wanted to play. Everything I did, the people at the commune were very encouraging, so that was a real turning point for me. I went from feeling like, "I can't do this ..." to having people really dig what I was playing and me feeling good about it.

When did looping technology come into your musical life?
That came much, much later. I got my first electric violin when I was still living on that farm and started messing around with pedals, like delay pedals, all the sound-processing pedals that electric guitarists use. But, I put the electric violin away for a while because I didn't like the sound. Much, much later I ended up on a gig with the violinist Mark Wood, who is the designer and maker of the electric violin I play now, the Viper. Mark loaned me the Viper for the gig, and I really liked it.

I started getting interested in Irish music, and began using the Viper in one of the Irish rock bands I was playing with. I had to think about it more like an electric guitar than an acoustic violin.

I began using the looper after the breakup of my band, Brazz Tree. I just wanted to make some kind of music by myself. At the time, I was a little bit turned off by collaboration or "running it by the committee," as I call it. So that's how I started writing and playing music with the looper.

In addition to playing music with the commune, joining [writer, guitarist] Greg Tate's band, Burnt Sugar, helped me to find out who I am as an improviser.

How did playing in Burnt Sugar help your improvising?
First of all, the conduction thing was really a brilliant idea.[55] Because then you could have this sort of organized chaos or organized improvisation. I think what Burnt Sugar did for me, aside from being a collection of killer musicians and just the best people, like a family, was just support. In performance, Greg would set up this bed of sound, and then tell me to solo. So, I had all of this inspiration, all of the different sounds around me to really carry me and help me explore. I felt really free and that I could try anything in that situation.

What facilitated your 2013 trip to Africa with the band Matuto?
It was a U.S. State Department-sponsored thing administered by a program

called American Music Abroad. American Music Abroad awards a musician or ensemble a grant that is matched by various American embassies to fund the trip.

There's an application process. You send in your paperwork on all the musicians. From that pool, they choose bands to go on to a second round, which is the actual musical audition. From there, we got chosen, but they don't tell you where you're going to go. You could end up anywhere in the world. Our bandleader, Clay Ross, had done this before, and knew if we said we'd like to go to Africa that there was a good chance they would send us to Africa. We each asked for that, and we got it. We were very lucky.

Was there any one thing that surprised you on that journey, a musical or cultural experience that surprised you either in a positive or negative way?
One thing that really surprised me, and it's a cultural thing, has to do with being a black American. The second day we were in Africa, we were in Mozambique, and we were taken to this morning TV show, kind of like *Good Morning America*. The host asked me, "So how does it feel to be in Africa?" and it was kind of this loaded question. He didn't ask the other musicians this, and we all knew he asked me because I'm black, you know? And I didn't have a response for him because I'd only just arrived. So I just said, "It's amazing!" [laughs] I didn't know what else to say! I just said, "I'm just keeping my mind open."

We did Mozambique for a week, then Côte d'Ivoire for a week, and all of these places blew my mind in different ways. We kept feeling like, "Wow. Mind can't be blown any further," and we'd end up in another country and it would be a totally different thing. Mind-blowing in another way.

Then we went to Ghana. Mozambique was . . . we all had this joke, sort of the "Florida" of Africa. Côte d'Ivoire was really intense and a little bit scary. They had that coup, and just a couple years before our visit, crazy civil unrest.[56] We were the first band they had brought into Côte d'Ivoire since that had happened. But Ghana just kind of felt like, I can't even describe it . . . like somehow really exciting and super cool.

The main language they speak in Ghana, aside from all the local languages, is English. That was sort of a relief. We did a radio show there, and people had been making comments to me as a black person, like, "Hey, how do you feel?" and I never knew how to respond. In Ghana, they do this greeting where they welcome you by shaking each person's hand and saying, "You are welcome." So they did this with us, going down the line saying, "You are welcome. You are welcome." But when the guy from the radio station got to me, he said, "Welcome home." And then he moved to the next person and said, "You are welcome." That was a real special moment for me. It just really hit me. I was really moved by it and touched. I thought, "Wow. This *is* home," and it went really deep.

I realized how I'd been feeling was something that I never thought mattered that much. Like I'd been missing something that I didn't know I'd been missing. Just to be around people that looked like me. It really made a difference. I know the rest of the musicians in the band, who are all guys and are all white, also felt completely welcome, so it wasn't like I was treated differently per se. But the feeling was really different. And that really surprised me. My reaction to it surprised me. I didn't realize how much I was missing this thing.

Was there a little more respect afforded to you as musicians in Africa?
Well, I feel like pretty much every other place I've been to in the world, including Africa, seems to have more respect for the arts in general. Which is very sad. That makes me very sad.

It sounds like the music you all played was very well received.
It was! It was really interesting. When you do something all the time, it's like nothing. But they were looking at us going, "This is so cool! What you do is so amazing!" And we're like, "This is nothing compared to you! It's not that big a deal!" [laughs] We felt really appreciated. Playing in Africa also gave me this real sense that we have so much to offer, particularly as American musicians. I think we often feel that the rest of the world has more color and is more interesting. Maybe it's because America is so young and so fucked up in so many ways. Somehow, the sense of value of what we do as American musicians, I got that sense from being there in Africa. That we do have a place in the world and the music that we make is very unique. Black music, which is American music, and includes folk, jazz, and soul, is really deep and really unique. I feel very lucky to have learned that lesson. I have so much more appreciation for what we do having gone there and come back.

Aurora Nealand

Some of the most important adult friends I have made in my lifetime (including my wife) are people I met when I lived in New Orleans, Louisiana. When I first landed in that city back in 1993 (via a 24-hour Greyhound bus ride from Columbus, Ohio—I don't recommend it!), I honestly felt as if I had stepped into another world, or perhaps another time. I witnessed my first jazz funeral my first week in the city. Not a staged parade for tourists, but the real deal, slowly making its way through the uptown neighborhood I was staying in toward Carrollton. When I stop to remember, I realize most of my fondest memories of New Orleans are of moments that took place late at night, in the dark, and involved music. Lots of music, including funk performed by young brass bands for packed clubs of sweaty dancers; contemporary, sometimes free-form music by incredible local musicians; DJs spinning house music, as well as the then-new jungle and trip-hop recordings that were coming out of England; rock and roll, opera, classical music—even music theater. In his book *The Year Before the Flood*, Ned Sublette writes that in New Orleans, "all times are present at once."[57] I know exactly what he means, and I'm not even a native.

In New Orleans, in the early years of the 20th century, women instrumentalists and singers were an active part of the city's musical community and important contributors to the musical development of jazz. New Orleans is a very feminine city. Writer Louise McKinney describes its geography accordingly: "... tucked into a turn of the Mississippi River ... putting her as it does at the bottom of the Mississippi's muddy overflow ... rich with dense, fertile soil ... this bottoming out, end-of-the-line location also places her in a deep psychic realm. It is the subconscious, the basement of the soul, where dark inexplicable alchemy occurs, often considered the root of creativity and expressly feminine."[58]

With all of the above in mind, I knew at the beginning of this project that not including a musician from New Orleans in a book subtitled "Interviews With Women in Jazz" would be a huge oversight. And given the fact that my goal with this book is not just to discuss where jazz has been but where it may be headed, New Orleans-based saxophonist and composer Aurora Nealand seemed like the perfect person to reach out to for an interview.

Nealand arrived in New Orleans after studying at the Oberlin Conservatory of Music and the L'École Internationale de Théâtre Jacques Lecoq in Paris, France. Not surprisingly, given her academic background, her creative work extends into the worlds of experimental theater and performance art, and freely amalgamates the music of New Orleans' past (the "traditional") with contemporary sounds, concepts, and spirit. Nealand leads the Royal Roses, a

Aurora Nealand. Photo by Melissa Cardona.

"non-traditional traditional jazz band" that is a part of a larger local scene of musicians digging into a style of pre-jazz jazz informed by collective improvisation and a desire to get listeners on their feet and dancing. She is also co-director of the Sound Observatory New Orleans (SONO), a performance lab and venue for local and visiting artists-in-residence.

Over the course of our interview, it became apparent to me that the pre-millennial New Orleans where I used to live and make music has changed and is changing. If "all times are present at once" in New Orleans, what I look forward to is how a creative tension between the traditional and the not-so-traditional will continue to shape and nurture the city's musical culture.

Before you relocated to New Orleans, had you played the kind of traditional jazz that you now play with your band, the Royal Roses?
I do remember listening to Preservation Hall Jazz Band[59] records when I was growing up in California, and I remember going to see that band when I was 12 or 13. They came through California and did some free concerts in Stern Grove Park in San Francisco. So that style had always been in my ear, and I really loved it. But it didn't really occur to me to try and play traditional jazz until I moved to New Orleans.

How did you learn to play this music? Did you check out recordings or talk to some of the older musicians about the history of the music?

I listened again to the Preservation Hall Jazz Band albums, which is interesting, because those recordings are from the 1960s and 1970s and the actual music they're playing dates back to the 1920s and 1930s. I didn't really scrutinize older, traditional jazz recordings until later. Most of what I listened to were recordings by current New Orleans groups, like the Preservation Hall Jazz Band, the Jazz Vipers, and the Hot Club of New Orleans. I would listen to those bands and try to learn melodies for the songs I now play with the Royal Roses.

I also started playing outdoors on Royal Street (in the French Quarter) and met other people my age with similar backgrounds that had moved down here because they were attracted to this music. I also went out to clubs to hear traditional jazz. This was before Frenchman Street became the crazy bar scene that it is now. When I first moved down here, you could go to the Spotted Cat and just sit down and listen to the band.

Around this time, I met Robert Snow's father, Sidney (a.k.a. Sid "Dr. Guitar" Snow). Robert is the bass player in the Jazz Vipers. His father, Sidney, is an amazing guitarist and bassist, and he's musically raised a *lot* of musicians here in town. He was in New Orleans during the 1960s, and played in all of the local soul and R&B bands and worked a little bit in the Motown scene. Sidney gave me my first traditional jazz gig in New Orleans, a five-hour gig playing with his band at the Market Café on Decatur Street. I was really nervous beforehand. One of the guys from the Jazz Vipers suggested I check out this book that's basically a fake book of vintage jazz songs. I knew how to read music, so I just thought, [scared voice] "Okay, I guess I'll just read the tunes on the gig." I'm sure I was not good; I'm pretty *positive* I was not good. But Sidney was very patient and kind. Like I said, these were five-hour gigs. You played five sets with ten-minute breaks. It was kind of intense, just jumping into it.

Whether you're playing out on Royal Street or at the Market Café, if you grab people's attention and they like what they hear, they tip you! So that influences the way you play, right?
Yes. Traditional jazz is very emotive music. All music is emotive, but this particular style is really tailored to feature individual voices and individual emotion and expression. I feel like I learned that very quickly. You need to tell a story with your solos.

How would you define "traditional jazz"? Is it Dixieland music? Is it "jazz" before this music became "jazz"?
I like to say the Royal Roses are a non-traditional traditional jazz band. I really equate traditional jazz with early New Orleans jazz. I know there's a lot of mixed views and feelings about the differences between traditional jazz and Dixieland, and some of that has to do with race and who was playing the music back then. But there is a certain sound I hear that makes me think, "Oh, that's

a Dixieland sound. . . ." It's a lighter, maybe even more European sound. I've also heard elders in the community speak about Dixieland in political terms. They consider "Dixieland" to be music white people adopted and made more Disneyland, for lack of a better description.

But the sound I hear as "traditional" jazz digs deeper into the music. It's more grounded. It hits you in the lower regions of the body, the stomach, loins, and legs. It's music that makes you dance.

There is something that happens to music as it's played in New Orleans. I have friends in New York who play traditional jazz who can play circles around most of us in New Orleans. But, there's something about the energy of the players here in New Orleans that is undeniably different. To me, that energy defines traditional jazz.

Were you in New Orleans when Hurricane Katrina hit? [60]
I first moved to New Orleans in November 2004. I had left New Orleans in June 2005 to go teach composition [in] the summer at a school in New Hampshire. Then Katrina hit, and instead of coming back to New Orleans, I went to live in Baltimore for a little while. But I came back to New Orleans in January 2006.

What brought you back to New Orleans so soon after the hurricane when so many musicians had left the city?
The spring before Katrina was when I met Sidney Snow and started playing at the Market Café, and there was something about the energy of playing with him that got in my bones and made me really excited to be in New Orleans. Before Katrina, I had planned to come back to New Orleans. I was actually driving back from New Hampshire when Katrina hit. In Baltimore, I studied composition and played music with a couple of people, but it wasn't the same. Baltimore is a beautiful city, but unlike New Orleans, music is not as socially integrated into the fabric of the city.

I was invited by the Panorama Brass Band to play the first Mardi Gras after Katrina. I'd only been living in New Orleans for nine months before Katrina. So it may sound funny, but I really felt homesick for New Orleans. I wanted to come back and do whatever I could for this place that was so magnetic to me. Being able to come back and play with the Panorama Brass Band was a really exciting way to reenter the community. That was my first Mardi Gras, and I got to experience it from the inside with the band. We played all three weeks of Mardi Gras, in Krewe du Vieux, and in a bunch of uptown and little neighborhood parades.

Going back to your earlier musical experiences, when did you begin formal composition studies? You studied composition at Oberlin, is that correct?
Oberlin has two separate schools, Oberlin College and the Oberlin Conserva-

tory of Music. The conservatory is directly across the street from all of the college buildings. I attended the college for about three years, but I was taking a bunch of music classes. I was extremely intimidated by the people who were at the conservatory. Growing up, I kind of dabbled in playing the piano and played the flute and oboe in the school band. I never had private lessons, but I was always very interested in music.

When I got to Oberlin, I realized I was never going to be an orchestral player. I didn't have the training or a natural ability for that. I never really thought I'd be a musical performer, but I was really drawn to music, so I just started taking music composition classes. My teacher didn't know I wasn't enrolled in the conservatory, but since I did well in the classes I took, I was able to transfer over to the conservatory to continue my composition studies. I also studied sound and art installation.

I also learned a lot about composition when I started teaching at this amazing school called the Walden School, which is a school for young composers. I observed how my colleagues taught, and that was a great education.

What kind of music were you composing during that time?
A lot of my influences were artists who switched from composing twelve-tone music to extremely tonal music. Composers like Arvo Pärt, who initially had a whole career as a twelve-tone, atonal composer, and then in his later years, began writing extremely beautiful diatonic music.

I was also listening to a lot of tape and instrument pieces, electronic music, and the musique concrète works of Edgard Varèse and Karlheinz Stockhausen. I never wrote symphonies outside of orchestration class. I wrote some string quartets, which was exciting, but they were more like exercises. I wrote pieces that were more like pieces for multimedia, veering toward a more collage-like style.

I think a lot of composers my age or younger have a cinematic approach to classical music because we experience it so much in movies as soundscapes. For me, that's been interesting to examine, as opposed to the old-school, strictly serial music of Schoenberg and Webern. I see a trend in composers my age of combining those more esoteric structures or processes with a more cinematic, tonal, and melodic style.

Did your studies at the L'École Internationale de Théâtre Jacques Lecoq in Paris come after Oberlin and the Walden School?
Yes. I stayed in Paris for a year. My last year at Oberlin, instead of doing a senior composition recital, I wrote this large-scale multimedia play, a kind of outdoor installation. I was inspired by the work of Laurie Anderson, Robert Wilson, Philip Glass, and John Zorn. I was very interested in that era of performance in New York in the 1980s. The piece was probably one of the best things

I've ever done, but I had no process for how to do it and nearly killed myself just trying to do *everything*. I was writing the music, writing the script, hanging these windows from these trees, sleeping four hours a night in the media lab where I was editing video.... Sometimes you look back at yourself and think, "That's really a lunatic phase you went through!"

Going to Jacques Lecoq stemmed out of these experiences. I really wanted to learn the process of how people create large-scale, multimedia works. I never really studied theater, but the forum of the stage as a meeting place for the intersection of sound, language, and movement really interests me.

In New Orleans, have you been able to pursue your interest in creating multimedia works?
A little bit. I didn't for quite a long time. I really kind of stepped away from it when I moved back to New Orleans.

I only did one year of the two-year program at Jacques Lecoq. Jacques Lecoq had died two years before I went to the school, so I think it was one of those things where when the head pedagogue passes, he takes a lot of the school with him. I felt like they were just teaching us to make performance art from 1970. It didn't feel relevant. They were teaching us to make this very stale work. And frankly, that's what a lot of Paris felt like to me. It felt very stuck in the past, and this can be a problem in New Orleans as well. Being a tourist city, it felt to me like Paris was resting on its laurels.

What's your impression of New Orleans post-Katrina? Is there potential for innovative, non-traditional music to develop and find an audience?
There are a lot of really interesting and amazing things going on in New Orleans right now. There is a resurgence of traditional jazz being played by young people, and the clubs are embracing that because tourists like the music. There's a new scene for the music and a new monetary incentive for the musicians to learn it. You can make a living playing this music. When I first moved down here, I listened to just the few traditional jazz bands I mentioned, Preservation Hall, the Jazz Vipers, and Hot Club. But now I can't even count how many young traditional jazz bands are out there playing. It's exciting, because in order for musicians to distinguish themselves, they have to go deeper into the tradition, in terms of different repertoire as well as their own level of musicianship. It's a very supportive community. But there's more competition, for lack of a better word.

But on the flip side, I do see this very dangerous commodification of culture happening, in particular with traditional jazz. The music can become just another tourist attraction. I've heard more than one musician say, "Man, I just feel like I played Disneyland."

When I talk to my friends who were heavily involved in the New Orleans music scene in the 1990s, who are more modern and play a more improvisational style of music, they tell me very few clubs are booking that kind of music now. The clubs are just following the dollars. These things go in waves, but the resurgence of traditional jazz is definitely pushing out a lot of other styles of music.

There is something to revering and really understanding a tradition in any field, to going in as an apprentice and learning from your elders and the masters. Like going to Preservation Hall and really watching and listening to [trumpeter] Wendell Brunious. When clarinetist Tommy Sancton was in town, I went and listened to him, and when his book *Song for My Fathers* came out, I got a copy and read it so quickly. It's so exciting to feed yourself from other people's experiences.

With my band, the Royal Roses, I'm really trying to learn the tradition well, but also bring the music into the 21st century and make it relevant. Sometimes that means we go into completely free improvisations, or our drummer goes into a drumbeat that's not a traditional New Orleans drumbeat. I'm not saying we shouldn't learn the tradition if that's what we're going to be drawing from. It's just dangerous when the music becomes a tourist commodity. I think this happened a little bit with the Mardi Gras Indians and the large exposure New Orleans got with the television show *Treme*. Now, I see men in Mardi Gras Indian suits walking around with buckets begging for money. That's what makes me sad, when the commodification leads to a detachment from the actual function of what made it what it was.

What has playing in New Orleans taught you as a musician?
A lot of things I bring to the musical table, even when I'm playing non-traditional music, are things I learned in New Orleans. I've learned about listening, melody, the spirit of energy, ensemble playing, what it means to be generous, and to be able to share the sonic space. Those are huge things I know I've learned from being in New Orleans.

But I do need to leave New Orleans every year in order to feed another side of myself that doesn't always get fed artistically here. However, the longer I stay here, the more I feel I am ready to try and bring some of those other styles of music to New Orleans.

Carmen Lundy

Singer, composer, multi-instrumentalist, and visual artist Carmen Lundy is one of the first musicians I interviewed for this project. At the end of our conversation, after I turned off the digital recorder, I mentioned that I was stuck on trying to come up with a title for the book, and that *Women in Jazz* just wasn't going to cut it. She told me she believed the title of the book would come out of one of the interviews, that somebody was going to say *something* and it would be apparent that *that* was the perfect title. Of course, she was right. The title would come from my interview with drummer and composer Terri Lyne Carrington, who quoted Duke Ellington's definition of jazz as "freedom of expression." The complete title came together via a brainstorming session with writer and musician Michael Veal, and I made a mental note I would have to tell Carmen that her prediction had come true.

I am not surprised Lundy has a gift for clairvoyance. Many musicians do. There is an otherworldly, sometimes visionary quality to Lundy's lyrics and music, as well as the production that surrounds her distinctive voice. On her track "Requiem for Kathryn" from her 2009 album *Solamente*, a self-produced album of "demos" on which Lundy plays every instrument, her sparse, wordless vocal somehow speaks to both the sadness and hope for deliverance that comes when someone close to you has passed.

Lundy's formal musical education began at the University of Miami in the early 1970s, a time when jazz instruction in a college or university setting was a relatively rare thing. But despite not having a prescribed, well-worn academic path placed before her, it is apparent from this interview that Lundy always had a vision for herself and for her future as a musical artist.

"I don't know if it's fortunate or unfortunate for me to find that there's this definition of a jazz singer as 'someone who sings songs from another time,'" says Lundy. "It's similar to what we've done with the classical singer, where what defines you is the repertoire of another century."

Lundy describes herself as "multi-repertoire," a description that's more than accurate when considering the breadth of her artistry and musical résumé. She composes much of the repertoire she sings, and at the time of this writing, has written or co-written over 80 songs. She also composes and produces music for film and television, has acted on stage, is a visual artist, and conducts jazz clinics for singers and instrumentalists across the country. Lundy certainly fits the mold of a traditional jazz singer, but at the same time manages to upend any and all definitions of that term.

Carmen Lundy. Photo by Victor Dlamini.

When did you first begin playing a musical instrument?

I think I began playing an instrument around the age of 4. I grew up in a family in Miami where every house had a piano—which wasn't so unusual.

I remember this day very vividly: I came in from whatever—kindergarten?—to stay at my grandparents' while my parents were at work. And I went straight to the piano and I started to do whatever! I remember getting a spanking and being told to just go home! "Go home!" you know? [laughs] So I have this vivid memory of shaking up everybody in the house, because I would just not leave that piano alone!

I was in love with the instrument. My aunt played piano for the choir and for the gospel group my mother sang in, the Apostolic Singers, in Miami. So my first real introduction to the instrument was through my aunt, who played gospel piano and still does to this very day. All of my initial chords and my understanding [of music] came from that gospel thing. Strong left hand, the inverted triads—all that stuff.

My mother arranged for me to get piano lessons when I was around the age of 6. My brother [Curtis Lundy] was taking drum lessons at the age of 5.

I pretty much stayed with [the piano] until I realized how everybody would get so excited when my mother sang! I thought, "Okay, I wanna do that!"

If I was a good girl, I got to watch my mother's group rehearse. That was when I started to notice that one singer had a certain part that the other singer didn't have. When I understood that there were harmonies, I think that's when I said, "Oh, that's how that goes!" And it wouldn't be the melody, but the middle part that would be more interesting to me.

I thought if I would learn that middle part, then maybe one day they would let me sing in their group. They never did! [laughs] But that's beside the point.

I think I was around the age of 10 or 11 when the church I was attending started a junior choir. So now you got all the daughters of all the singers in the gospel group with my mother leading.... We were all now of age to start the junior choir.

And I was terribly interested in doing everything but the lead! I just loved the whole idea of being the harmony, you know, to be a supporting voice. It seemed to be a little more challenging than just singing the melody that everybody already knew. To really support the melody was more interesting to me.

And as that junior choir began to go into different churches, do more special events, I kind of stepped out and thought that I could possibly also be a soloist. So somewhere between the age of 11 and 12 I knew, that was it! That was it.

It struck me as you were describing hearing those inner voices, how that very much describes the ear of an arranger or the ear of a composer. When you think back to those early days, do you think that maybe you were not only becoming the singer that you are today but the composer as well?
I don't know. That's a great question. No one's ever asked me that question. I don't know if the composer in me, if that seed was planted that early on. I don't know! It's a great question, it really is!

I'd have to say that as far as discovering that there was a potential composer in me, [that happened] when I was in college, and had switched my major from the opera side to jazz. There were requirements: composition, arranging, and improvisation, and being a jazz major, I had to take those courses. The composition teacher I had and the way that teacher introduced me to composition had a lot to do with it.

The musicians who played in my bands at that time were also an influence. They were writing their own tunes, and they'd say, "Carmen, I've got this tune, and it goes like this. There are no words. All you have to do is sing this melody along with the guitar line." Okay, no problem! Singing my classmates' and colleagues' tunes allowed me to hear *me*, you know? I got to be the one to introduce the composition. So there was something intriguing about that!

You started at the University of Miami as a classical voice major and then switched to studying jazz. Did the university have a Jazz Studies program in place then?
Absolutely, but not for jazz vocalists. Jerry Coker was the head of the jazz department. Jerry was a tenor player—a monster player, and a great master teacher.

But why did you initially begin with classical and opera?
I think what happened was, when I entered the University of Miami as a music major, you had two choices as a singer. One was you could choose education, of course, or, you could choose a performance major. I chose a performance major, because I wasn't interested in just being a teacher at that time. I wanted to be a performer. The performance major for vocalists was strictly a classical program— period. End of the story. I went into that program totally optimistic, totally into it. The Italian arias, the whole anthology, that's what I did.

The private voice lessons were where I began to learn the whole mastery and technique of all that voice production. The way to kind of sustain the voice over a career or a lifetime—all those things began there.

And my friend David Roitstein, who introduced me to jazz in high school, he went into the jazz department. Prior to both of our entries into the University of Miami, we put a little group together. David played Fender Rhodes piano, and we did these little gigs. I sang lead and played percussion. So when we got to the University of Miami, David went upstairs to the jazz department, and I was downstairs in the classical department.

I did that for my first semester, but then in the second semester there was an elective called Jazz Vocal 101, or something like that. And it was like a little ensemble, like a vocalise thing, where you would think of Lambert, Hendricks and Ross, the Swingle Singers, all of those kinds of vocal arrangements. So I took that class, because it just seemed like a nice balance to the classical stuff. And I was so deeply immersed in my musical life by then, I just wanted everything I could get my hands on.

I think it was that little bit of flexibility that I felt when I was singing in that jazz ensemble, and also being asked to sing some of the songs David was writing with some of his friends upstairs.... I discovered I had an affinity for jazz, particularly with my gospel background.

I went to the head of the vocal department and asked to change my major to jazz. But at that time, there was no curriculum for a jazz vocalist. So I stayed with the chamber singers for a while, maintained the private voice lessons, the classical lessons, and in addition to those courses, took on the full curriculum for a jazz major.

Once you began studying jazz, did you have some catching up to do?
That's a good question too! What happened was, David introduced me to jazz by playing me [saxophonist] Cannonball Adderley's albums, later Cannonball like *The Happy People*. I discovered the *Kind of Blue* album when I was baby-sitting for a Jamaican family. I was just looking through their album collection, pulled that out and said, "Oh, this is the guy Dave was talking about. Miles Davis!" So that's when I really heard Cannonball Adderley in that series, you know, the 1950s. This was in the 1970s, and Herbie Hancock's *Fat Albert Rotunda* was one of the first Herbie albums I ever heard. David was listening to Bill Evans' *Waltz for Debby*.... He pretty much introduced me to these artists.

One requirement [at college] was to go home, pick a solo, and transcribe the solo. [laughs] What? I remember my first transcription, but I first had to ask what 'transcribe' means! [laughs] That first year when I was in this jazz program, I would think, "Oh my God! What is a minor seventh again?" I got that in high school, but I really didn't pay attention to it! And I was playing it all the time on the piano, but didn't know what it was.

A lot of things were happening. I think the first time that I transcribed something, was the first time I actually applied a series of notes to a staff, but not as a composer. And that was a really interesting thing to do. Because it made you listen over and over and over again, and you had to put that down on paper so you could submit it as a complete transcription.

I chose an Ella Fitzgerald solo. I had an album called *Ella & Duke at the Côte D'Azur*. She sings and scats some amazing choruses on "It Don't Mean a Thing." That was my first transcription.

And then of course, I totally walked away from the whole vocal thing, and just got really deep into listening and transcribing a lot of Freddie Hubbard's stuff and everybody else's. The classmates upstairs, Hiram Bullock, Pat Metheny, Mark Egan, Danny Gottlieb, Curtis Lundy, Bruce Hornsby, Steve Williams, Bobby Watson, Will Lee, and so many other classmates of mine, we were each learning the next thing from [each] other. I think Chick Corea's *Light as a Feather* was all the rage then, Stanley Clarke, the Return to Forever group.... I think [the 1970s] was really the last great productive era for jazz. Personally, I think that's when you got a lot of innovation that we don't have on the same scale nowadays.

The best part was, I was gigging all the time. I would come to school during the day and I would perform six nights a week for the entire time I went to the University of Miami, which was almost five years.

This was a period of time where the music was uncompromising, and yet it was very much created for the public ear. Would you agree with that?

Yeah, that's an excellent way of describing that era. But I figure it was also that whole youthful thing. You're discovering, defiant, you're carving out your own niche and discovering who you are, as well as all these people who are not your grandparents' age, not your parents' age, who are all doing amazing things.

Miles Davis was our hero. When he started to incorporate *Bitches Brew* and all the electronic sounds in his music, it was like, "Okay! We're good to go!"

Do you do clinics where you work with young vocalists?

Oh yes, for a long time now. And musicians as well. Not just singers.

As part of your instruction for young singers, do you encourage them to compose music?

Yes. [The emphasis on] composing is the result of spending the last 12 years or so at the Kennedy Center in D.C., representing Betty Carter's Jazz Ahead program, along with other faculty. It was Betty's request to continue to press upon the students the value of writing their own music.

As people, we're more alike sometimes than we want to believe we are. Particularly when it comes to how you render the truth in a melody with or without words. I know for a fact that I decided to sing more original music when I got to New York. I was doing all the gigs and singing all the standards and club dates, doing my great arrangements of Ellington tunes, Mancini tunes, and everybody else. Everybody knew them and loved them, "Isn't she great?"

And I just realized, being in New York from the late 1970s and into the early 1990s, living there, developing my craft, honing in on it and establishing a reputation as a musician as well as a singer, I realized Betty Carter was around the corner, Sarah Vaughn was down in the Village, and Carmen McCrae had just returned from a world tour, so who would want to hear me, you know? What makes *me* so special? The greats are here! So what do I do? What's going to distinguish me from them? I'm not going to build a career singing Ella Fitzgerald solos, it's not gonna happen!

I realized that to distinguish myself, I should sing songs that come from *my* time, of *my* experience, and not so much of what has somehow come to be called "The Great American Songbook." So as a composer, I started to stick my neck out even a little bit farther by singing new songs. Just like Billie Holiday did when she introduced songs that didn't exist before her. "God Bless the Child," "Billie's Blues," and so many others, you know? "Don't Explain," "Fine and Mellow," "Lover Man"—these are songs Billie Holiday brought to us.

I just kind of went with that. It felt right. And now after having over 80 published songs of my own—I've collaborated of course, from time to time—that's quite a body of work in this particular genre of music, you know?

I don't know if it's fortunate or unfortunate for me to find that there's this definition of a jazz singer as "someone who sings songs from another time." Jazz singer: "Somebody who scats!" It's similar to what we've done with the classical singer, where what defines you is the repertoire of another century.

I find that this has made for a unique kind of distinction among my peers. I hope that at the end of the day, someone will recognize the contribution that I've made not only to keeping the bar high for jazz vocalizing, but also that I've given some of the young people behind me, including some of the artists who have covered my tunes, something else to say!

I feel at this point in my career, it would be nice to be allowed to be a jazz singer who is multi-repertoire! [laughs] You know what I mean?

Yes!

I'm not sure if people are ready to recognize me for that. And it's okay, you know?

At the end of the day, it's about listening to your own voice, and being true to yourself. And hopefully there is an audience that will support you. Just go put it out there. Somebody will be willing to listen!

It's so interesting to me that I can go in with a body of original compositions to countries where the [English] language is barely spoken, and convey something truthful and authentic in the music that we are playing. It's interesting how the world can be receptive to what we're doing, and yet, up the street, and around the corner from where we live, they're not. It's a funny thing!

Helen Sung

The piano may not be the first instrument most people associate with Texas. But in the early 1900s it wasn't unusual to find a piano in homes of both poor and wealthy families throughout the state, where several immigrant communities absorbed Spanish, Mexican, Cajun, German, East European, and African-American musical idioms. Along with the guitar, pianos were played in sharecropping communities, the popular musical styles of the day being "rags" (or "ragtime") and "slow blues." Classical and popular music would be played from sheet music, note for note, but when the grownups weren't around, improvisation would inevitably happen. Brothers George and Hersal Thomas and later Moon Mullican ("King of the Hillbilly Pianists") are a few of the Texan-born pianists who helped to develop if not outright invent the rhythmic concepts, bass lines, and melodic phrasing that infused pre-1950s rock and roll and jazz.

Houston-born pianist and composer Helen Sung did not grow up playing blues, boogie-woogie, rock and roll, or anything else close to jazz. But in her last year as an undergraduate classical piano performance major at the University of Texas at Austin, she attended a concert by New Orleans pianist and singer Harry Connick Jr., and was deeply inspired by what she heard.

"Classical music never affected me like that," says Sung of that concert in her interview. "There was an irresistible passion and energy in (Connick's) playing. And the fact that he was improvising blew me away, because classical musicians are all about the written notes."

In the years after that concert, Sung would go on to study with some of the masters of jazz at the Thelonious Monk Institute of Jazz Performance. In 1999, she was a semi-finalist in the institute's Jazz Piano Competition, and in 2007, won the Kennedy Center's Mary Lou Williams Jazz Piano Competition. Sung has played with several jazz masters, including Wayne Shorter, Ron Carter, and Clark Terry, and appears on Terri Lyne Carrington's 2001 Grammy-winning album, *The Mosaic Project*. Sung has also released several highly praised albums, including *Anthem for a New Day*, which incorporates her classical training with jazz in what she describes as an "organic and integrated way."

Several of the musicians interviewed in this book studied and seriously considered a career as a classical musician before making a shift to playing jazz, but Sung's transition is one of the most dramatic. In her interview, she speaks candidly about the challenges she faced in mastering its language.

"All I knew is that I wanted to find out more about this music," says Sung. "I wanted to be able to really play it, but not as a classical player who could fake it

Helen Sung. Photo by Kat Villacorta.

because she had the chops, you know? I wanted to be authentic, genuine. I felt jazz was a music that had to be respected and honored in that way."

....

Was the piano the very first instrument you played?

Yes. When I was 2 or 3 years old, I used to carry around a little electronic keyboard under my arm. It had about 12 keys. I started formal lessons on both piano and violin at age 5.

Were you drawn to the sound of these two particular instruments or did your parents direct you to them?

I don't really remember because I was so young when I started. I do remember I really loved that little keyboard. I don't think that keyboard was mine initially but it *became* mine. [laughs] My mom says she remembers hearing me play melodies I heard off of the radio and TV.

My parents were not musical; it's not like they played music in the house or anything like that. They definitely didn't have plans for me to be a musician. It was more like "let's give her something to do," and piano and violin were instruments they knew about.

There was an experience I remember from kindergarten that might speak to my choice to be a musician. I had just started playing the violin and I was in a group class. Suddenly I had this feeling of recognition, like, "Oh! I know this!" [laughs] The feeling wasn't specific to the violin; it had more to do with the act of playing and hearing music. I still remember that feeling. It's something I've never forgotten.

Your earlier music studies, before high school, was it all classical music?

It was all classical music. I didn't play a note of jazz.

Later you continued studying classical piano at the High School for the Performing and Visual Arts (HSPVA) in Houston, Texas, is that correct?

Yes, and what I can't believe is that even though I was there for four years and right across the hall from the jazz room, I never had a single musical interaction with any jazz students.

At that point, were your parents thinking you were getting serious about a career as a musician?

I think they were watching me with growing concern because they wanted me to be a doctor, or pursue a more traditional career.

The momentum toward a musical career had been building up since elementary school, because both my elementary school and middle schools had very strong magnet arts programs. Since I had been doing so much music, that momentum just carried me through to HSPVA.

We lived in a neighborhood that's zoned to Bellaire High School, which is one of the top high schools in Houston. People would move into the neighborhood (or pretend to live there) just so their kids could attend Bellaire, so everybody thought I was insane to go to HSPVA instead.

I was also taking private piano lessons with a hard-line classical teacher from the Soviet Union, who was trained in the Russian school. I started studying with her when I was 9 until I graduated high school. She was a great teacher, but very controlling. I remember her saying more than once that classical music was the only "real" music, the only music worth listening to. I felt so guilty whenever I would listen to pop music with my friends because she exerted such a strong influence over me. That was one of my few acts of rebellion as a teenager of Chinese heritage, where you revere your teachers and they are *never* wrong! [laughs]

When I was in college, I remember my dad mailing me articles about music majors in college who became very successful businessmen or lawyers or whatever. It was difficult for my parents to see me choose a profession so foreign to them. My dad is a retired civil engineer and my mom is a retired nurse. They didn't know any people who were self-employed or any musicians who performed for a living. The only people they knew who were musicians were teachers. I used to get so mad when they would tell me, "I guess you can always teach." I remember thinking, "Gosh, I'm practicing so much, I want to play!" But I had no role models to point to and say, "See? *They're* playing music for a living."

At the University of Texas at Austin, you attended a concert by [pianist, singer, bandleader] Harry Connick, Jr. and his big band, and his performance had a profound impact on you as a pianist.
Yes. I think that was during my senior year at UT where I was studying classical piano performance.

Can you describe what Harry was doing at the piano that was so different from what you were doing at the piano?
There was this vividness and life in the rhythm and the music. I thought, [excitedly] "How come no one ever told me about this?!" Classical music never affected me like that. There was an irresistible passion and energy in his playing. Like, ferocious. He was playing stride like Professor Longhair, really percussive and just going for it, you know? I had always been taught that you never bang. You want to make a beautiful sound, a beautiful line with the legato; that's the classical thing.

And the fact that he was improvising blew me away, because classical musicians are all about the written notes, about interpreting down to the finest indication what the composer means. That's a totally different paradigm.

It occurred to me when you mentioned stride and Professor Longhair that you were seeing and hearing piano technique you'd never seen or heard before, like, "I didn't know you could do *that* at the piano!"
I didn't know it existed!

You shifted gears and took as many jazz courses that were available to you while continuing to study classical piano, almost as if you were a double major.

In retrospect, it all sounds so neat and easy, but it really wasn't. It wasn't like I had a grand plan. It was an incremental, day-by-day kind of thing. I was almost done with my classical degree, and I still thought I was going to do the classical track. All I knew is that I wanted to find out more about this music [jazz]. I wanted to be able to really play it, but not as a classical player who could fake it because she had the chops, you know? I wanted to be authentic, genuine. I felt jazz was a music that had to be respected and honored in that way.

I took whatever jazz classes UT offered. And I was lucky, because at that time, jazz curriculum at the university level was still being formulated. It wasn't as established as it is now. There weren't that many jazz majors, and because there were so few students, I was able to do things I wasn't ready to do, like play in the big band and combos, etc. [laughs] Which was really good for me. I was basically thrown into the deep end.

Were you the only woman taking jazz courses at UT at that time?
No, but there were very few. I remember two female students studying jazz trumpet, both graduate students.

How did you go about checking out pianists and becoming familiar with jazz?
I began with recordings and books. I remember reading as many books as I could, and I was lucky enough to find some really good books at the beginning. There was one called *Meet Me at Jim and Andy's: Jazz Musicians and Their World* [by Gene Lees] that included interviews with several great pianists and instrumentalists. And I'd go to the library at UT to check out records. I didn't have a method, so my listening was all over the place. I remember hearing everything from Bill Evans, Keith Jarrett, Chick Corea, Herbie Hancock, and Anthony Braxton to Sun Ra, Cecil Taylor, and Fats Waller.

Playing in the UT jazz orchestra introduced me to the classic big band repertoire, folks like Count Basie, Sammy Nestico, Thad Jones, and Mel Lewis, as well as more contemporary stuff. Like I said, it was the deep end! [laughs] It was a real patchwork of experiences.

I also begged the UT jazz piano professor for lessons, and started going out to hear live jazz around town.

You said "patchwork" and I thought of the word "holistic" to instead describe your learning at this time.
No, there were things that were missing, so I wouldn't describe my education as "holistic." I would say instead … mishmash. Maybe. [laughs]

By the time I was getting ready to leave Texas for the Monk Institute in Boston, I felt like I could kind of "get by" on most stuff, except for bebop. When I played bebop, it didn't sound good, it didn't feel right, it was hard, and I hadn't been able to find someone who could teach me how to get better at it. That was one missing thing I worked so hard on while studying at the Monk Institute. Bebop is so foundational to the music. For me, it's foundational to the language and to the understanding of jazz.

While at UT, were there musicians you could go out and hear who were playing jazz? Were there jam sessions you could go to?
I did a little bit of that. But I mainly played with and listened to the community I had at school. There really weren't a lot of places in Austin to go to hear jazz. As far as any jam sessions . . . there was one session in town that I went to, and I remember being really scared. Heck, I was scared in class too! [laughs] Scared to improvise, embarrassed to sound bad—I was learning a whole new language, a whole new aesthetic while I was trying to finish my classical stuff. Looking back, I can't believe I made it through all of that!

Did your ability to improvise at the piano develop more once you got to the Monk Institute?
I studied improvisation at UT, but what the Monk Institute did was force me to build a really honest foundation, to really deal with the traditional foundation of the language. [Pianist] Barry Harris, he was instrumental in that. He unpacked the bebop language for me, and I'm so grateful to him for that. I had to work so hard, having started jazz so late, and I continue to do so because I believe learning is something that never really ends. You just get to higher and higher levels.

When you were improvising in those formative years, was there a leap that you had to make from playing things you knew would work to instead playing something you heard, where the playing is a more intuitive thing?
I was trying to learn a language. The great saxophonist Jimmy Heath, who was one of our first teachers at the Monk Institute, said something about this. He said, first you have to imitate, then you assimilate, and then you begin to innovate. In my experience, those three things are ongoing and happening all at the same time. Even today, I'm always trying to deepen and expand and improve my improvising.

At the beginning, it's like a baby learning to talk, which is a lot of imitation, right? As babies learn enough words and which words go together, they start to carry on conversations. That's assimilation. But then you go to school to learn how to spell, use grammar, read and write, and that's when you begin developing your own way of talking based on your personality. Going forward, you learn new and bigger words. You read different types of literature and see how different people use language.

That leap that you're talking about . . . except for that moment I heard Harry Connick, Jr., I can't really recall a moment where I felt like lightning had struck! It's just a daily, incremental thing. It never ends. To me, that's one of the most frustrating and wonderful things about being an artist.

Defining jazz can be tricky, and it's something I'm attempting to do in the introduction for this book. A friend of mine, a fine jazz guitarist, describes jazz as "a process." I thought of that while you were describing this ongoing process of imitation, assimilation, and innovation.

I would also add that it is music that originated from African-American culture. I think it's a huge blessing that something as amazing and timeless as jazz, that beautiful art like this came out of the ugliest part of this nation's history. That's a testament to the human spirit, to not give up, to not give in, to always fight for the good and the beautiful.

When I first moved to New York, I learned a lot playing with vocalists in these African-American social clubs in New Jersey and Long Island. It was such an interesting experience, because I would be the only Chinese person, the only non-African-American person in the club. Watching these folks interact and socialize helped me to understand this music even more. Every culture has its own cool, unique characteristics and qualities that I believe come through in their artistic expression, so those gigs were also a valuable part of my education.

Did your familiarity with the classical repertoire help at all with your improvising?

No. I feel like I shelved that for a long time. But now, I'm really grateful for that experience, not just with the piano, but with the violin too. Those years of studying classical music exposed me to so many different kinds of musical forms, textures, and orchestrations. That's why I'm really excited about my new album, *Anthem for a New Day*. I'm combining my classical background with jazz in an organic and integrated way.

How did you go about teaching your musicians the music we hear on *Anthem for a New Day*? I see music charts with notated parts in the album's booklet. Did the musicians learn the music in the studio or over a longer period of time leading up to the recording?

It was a combination. I had been working with these musicians, in different configurations, for the past two or three years, and I'd been workshopping some of the music on gigs.

Just because the musicians have never seen the music before doesn't mean it'll be a disaster. And just because you've been playing a piece of music for a while, doesn't mean it's going to come together in the recording studio.

I chose these musicians, first of all, because I love the way they play as well as the way they play my music and what they bring to it. They're also able to put up with me. [laughs] I really appreciated them hanging in there with me during the recording of *Anthem*. The process can be uncomfortable, and I wasn't always able to verbalize what I wanted. I appreciated their intuition, openness, and flexibility.

You produced *Anthem for a New Day* and licensed it to the Concord Music label. But what does that mean exactly, to produce and then license your album?
It's very simple. One records an album and then works out an agreement with another party (in my case, Concord Records), who will manufacture and distribute the finished product. I own the legal rights to the master recording, but I permit Concord to have those rights to manage for a certain length of time.

Is this a new way of doing business with the music industry? Something musicians should know how to do?
I think it's been a common practice, especially with the smaller independent labels. Before *Anthem*, I'd only been dealing with independent labels. I think it's an indication of how much things have changed that the "majors" are also doing this now.

We spoke about your parents earlier. What do they think of your music now? Have they changed their minds a little bit about this career path you've taken?
I don't know if they'll ever truly understand my fascination with music, but I think they do see that I love what I'm doing.

Being a musician is not an easy life by any means. I remember when I first moved to New York, I was feeling overwhelmed. I didn't have any gigs, I was just scraping by, trying to find pianos to practice on, and I'd ask myself, "What am I doing? Why am I doing this?" And this answer came to me, which is "because I love this music."

Nicole Rampersaud

About halfway through the course of this project, I got a call from a friend, trumpeter Lewis "Flip" Barnes. Flip is a member of the critically acclaimed William Parker Quartet, and is equally at home playing in free, avant-garde contexts as he is in the worlds of rock, funk, and modern jazz. He suggested I interview a few musicians he had performed with in recent years, if only to further expand the larger conversation about jazz that was taking place in what has ended up being 37 separate interviews.

To be blunt, for more than a few musicians in this book, the word "jazz" falls short when it comes to describing a genre or style of music Duke Ellington famously described as "freedom of expression." Trumpeter and composer Nicole Rampersaud is one of the musicians Flip suggested, and her interview provides yet another fascinating perspective on what it means to play jazz in the 21st century.

Rampersaud came to the trumpet at the age of 8, playing in bands in public school. Although she became skilled enough to play lead in big bands in high school and later at the University of Toronto [UT], she describes herself in those years as being "frustrated" with her playing.

"I was improvising, but not really happy with the improvising I was doing," says Rampersaud. "Everything I had been taught came from the bebop tradition. I love bebop, but bebop never really spoke to me in the way it resonated and spoke to a lot of my peers at the time."

A fateful encounter in UT's music library with saxophonist Ornette Coleman's 1959 album *The Shape of Jazz to Come*, and a move to Boston to study at the New England Conservatory of Music, enabled her to expand upon her already strong musical foundation by exploring new challenging and experimental modes of composition and improvisation. Her assured technique and tone and rapid-fire musical imagination led her to collaborate with and perform the music of Django Bates, Joe Morris, Bob Moses, Evan Parker, and Anthony Braxton. (In her interview, Rampersaud provides an inside look at performing Braxton's "Composition #103 for Seven Choreographed and Costumed Trumpets," which requires the performers to wear masks and execute a series of choreographed movements while playing.) She can be heard blurring the lines between composition and improvisation with the Shaw/Rampersaud Project, co-led with saxophonist Evan Shaw, and the bizarre yet thoroughly mesmerizing improvising trio c_RL, with fellow explorers Allison Cameron on amplified objects and electronics and Germaine Liu on percussion. For these musicians, jazz is but one component that inspires their musical output.

Nicole Rampersaud. Photo by Taurian Veerapen.

"I didn't grow up listening to jazz," says Rampersaud, "but I love jazz. I love all kinds of music. When I'm sitting down to write music, some of it's sort of jazzy and comes from the jazz tradition, and some of it is coming out rock or ambient or alternative music. For me, all influences inform the creative process...."

When did you first begin playing a musical instrument?

I was 8 when I started playing in public-school bands. I was a very timid kid growing up, so I never tried out for anything like sports or other extracurricular activities until finally, at the insistence of my then grade four teacher, I tried out for the school band. You had to choose what instruments you wanted to play, and being a timid child and petrified of making mistakes, I wanted to pick an instrument that seemed easy to put together and didn't have huge variables in terms of buttons and what have you. I saw the trumpet and how it was easy to put together, the mouthpiece goes into the horn, and it's only got three buttons, so I thought, "It can't be that hard!" [laughs] Little did I know what I was getting myself into!

Did you immediately enjoy playing the trumpet or was it something you gradually came to enjoy?

I enjoyed it. It was fun. I kept playing through public school and middle school. But high school is where I said, "Okay, this [the trumpet] is it. This is my voice."

What kind of music were you playing in school? And were you playing music outside of school, music that you didn't get a chance to play in your school's programs?

In school it was definitely the band arrangements of the classics or movie soundtracks of the day, like *Jurassic Park*. My very first band concert, we played a band arrangement of Michael Jackson's song "Beat It," and that was fun.

I grew up in modest means. My mother was very much living paycheck to paycheck, so I didn't really have exposure to any music performances outside of school. I didn't really take music lessons until I was in a university. I didn't really start playing outside of the school programs until high school.

While you were in school, were you exposed to jazz or any other kind of improvised music?

In public school not so much. In middle school, we didn't have a jazz band, but some of the teachers told me, "If you're really interested and really passionate about the trumpet, you should check out jazz." I was given the names of some musicians to check out: Louis Armstrong, Bix Beiderbecke, even Chet Baker, but not Miles Davis, oddly enough. In retrospect I find that odd that he never came up in middle school.

I would go to record stores and pick up "Louis Armstrong's Greatest Hits" and those types of compilations that you'd see for five or 10 bucks. But while in middle school, I was still very much on my own, and jazz was very peripheral.

Did you end up going to a music conservatory after high school?

Yes. In high school I really got into jazz. I played in the school's jazz band, and that's when I fell in love with the trumpet and decided that playing it was what I wanted to do. After high school, I auditioned for and got into the University of Toronto's jazz program.

Did you first begin improvising on the trumpet when you were in high school?

Not until my last year in high school. Again, that fear of making mistakes and screwing up was still prevalent for me in high school. The way I fell into jazz and playing in jazz bands was I sort of had a natural ability to play lead trumpet parts in arrangements. The University of Toronto offered me a scholarship based on my ability to play lead. And it wasn't until my last year in high school that I started to get into improvising.

How did you get from playing lead in big bands to free improvising?

At the University of Toronto, I was in a big band again. I was improvising, but not really happy with the improvising I was doing. Everything I had been taught came from the bebop tradition. I love bebop, but bebop never really spoke to me in the way it resonated and spoke to a lot of my peers at the time. So I got really frustrated playing without really knowing why. I would work on these exercises, the *Charlie Parker Omnibook*, the Clifford Brown book,[61] and I would transcribe solos. I did an okay job, but I wasn't really into it.

I remember going to the music library and finding an Ornette Coleman record, *The Shape of Jazz to Come*, with Don Cherry on cornet. For some reason, that record spoke to me. I didn't really know why, but the music intrigued me. I guess if I had to whittle it down to a moment, it would be that moment at the library and that Ornette Coleman record.

Did you find you had to seek out new musical peers and new teachers who could help you play this kind of music?

Yeah, I definitely didn't find that at U of T. And it's no fault of anybody really. I'm thankful for the musical foundation that I got as an undergrad. But it wasn't until I moved to Boston to attend the New England Conservatory of Music [NEC] that I found myself among like-minded people with similar values. It just kind of happened naturally. I found myself among people who wanted to explore. I got to study with Bob Moses. I met Joe Morris while I was there. I studied with Joe Maneri in his microtonal class, which was also very eye-opening and beyond enriching. Words can't describe the impact that his course had on me.

Here's a quote from the composer and saxophonist John Zorn: "The term 'jazz,' per se, is meaningless to me in a certain way. Musicians don't think in terms of boxes. I know what jazz music is. I studied it. I love it. But when I sit down and make music, a lot of things come together. And sometimes it falls a little bit toward the classical side, sometimes it falls a little bit towards the jazz, sometimes it falls toward rock . . . but no matter which way it falls, it's always a little bit of a freak. It's something unique, it's something different, it's something out of my heart. It's not connected with those traditions." Can you relate to that quote?

Totally. That's my thinking in a nutshell, really. I didn't grow up listening to jazz, but I love jazz. I love all kinds of music. When I'm sitting down to write music, some of it's sort of jazzy and comes from the jazz tradition, and some of it is coming out rock or ambient or alternative music. For me, all influences inform the creative process, so I can definitely relate to that quote.

You've performed music by the composer Anthony Braxton, including his

"Composition #103 for Seven Choreographed and Costumed Trumpets."
Can you talk a little bit about that piece? What was it like? What did you
have to do?

"Composition #103" is a 45-minute piece, 45 minutes of written material. There
are pages upon pages upon pages of material, and when you look at the material, it's actually not that difficult, at least compared to other compositions
I've played by Braxton. Braxton's "Ghost Trance" music, for example, is just
page after page of notated music with no rests, with different rhythmic values,
like quintuplets, septuplets, varying tempos, and all based on an inner sense
of time and rhythm. So I was expecting something like that. "Composition
#103" definitely has some of those elements, but the written stuff itself was as
straightforward as you're gonna get with Anthony Braxton. [laughs]

The piece is for seven trumpets, and I am one of the seven. And if I were to
read my part down I could play it, no problem. But when you put my part together with six other people's parts, you discover that there's a lot of hockets.[62]
Playing hockets requires a lot of coordination among the musicians. That's
where the challenge comes in, to be completely in sync with six other trumpet
players and all of us having the same sense of time.

There are also different physical movements. At the top of each page, before
the beginning of a new section of music, there's an illustration of what pose
you're supposed to take. For example, one pose might be me looking straight
up with my horn pointed up. Another pose would be me bent forward with my
horn facing the back of me. So that becomes a challenge, because you're trying
to read music, and if you're bent forward, with your horn pointed backwards,
you can't really read music. So you have to memorize some of these passages
while keeping coordinated with six other people and keeping these hockets
happening. [laughs]

The composition requires lots of mute changes. There was one particular
section where Anthony had us switching mutes for just about every phrase,
which meant we had to have our mutes basically strapped onto a belt and attached to a string so you could pull them up easily.

The final twist, which we didn't actually get to rehearse before our public
performance, was the costumes. Anthony had these amazing costumes designed by one of his friends, sort of like a poncho and a Zorro mask for your
eyes, which cut off your peripheral vision so you couldn't see side to side. You
could only see the music that's in front of you.

We played the piece twice, the first time in New York City, the second in
Philadelphia, and since it was the same group of trumpet players, that was
an even better performance. Everything lined up better, we were used to the
masks and the poses as well. It was great, great fun.

Did you begin studying composition at the New England Conservatory of Music, or were you exploring writing music before then?

I started writing seriously in my third year at the University of Toronto. I got to spend a lot of time with Phil Nimmons, who is a wonderful, wonderful big band composer in Canada. He's kind of a national treasure, in that regard. I learned a lot from him. He really sort of ignited that fire in me.

Did your composition studies include incorporating improvised elements into written compositions?

I started doing that while at U of T. That was very much following the traditional jazz structure of you've got a head, and then you have a solo for 15 minutes, and then play the head out, right? [laughs]

Right. Why a solo? Why are we having everyone take a solo? Is there some unwritten rule? You can think more creatively about soloing, like what Anthony Braxton does. He's taking improvisation and composing with it.

Exactly. It wasn't until I got to NEC that I really started to think in those terms, where improvising became an integral part of the overall piece. Whereas before, I was just following a very long written tradition where the "head" or melody is just a launching pad for people to solo for choruses upon choruses to show off their virtuosity.

For me, one informs the other. My composing informs my improvising, and vice versa. They're not mutually exclusive.

Are you based in Toronto?

Yes. I love Toronto. I find I can pretty much do whatever I want in the sense that I can play any type of music. I can play in a traditional calypso band for a few weeks and have an amazing time, and after each gig, later that night, go and play completely freely improvised music. I love all types of music.

The music scene in Toronto is very vibrant. The city definitely has the same challenges of many other cities. I would say trying to find venues that are sympathetic to host ensembles that aren't going to be playing bebop or Top 40 or what have you is the biggest challenge.

A lot of your experience as a musician is on you. You can't wait for people to come knock on your door. You've got to make those experiences happen. That means putting in the work to find out where like-minded people are going to hear or play music and going to those shows and asking them to play. It also means contacting venues and asking them if they'll host you for a night.

The onus is so much on the individual that I think if you just find a city that aligns with your values and where you feel you can do something of value, then it's the right place to be.

Sharel Cassity

Musicians born after the 1966 founding of the National Organization of Women (NOW) and what I would call the second wave of the women's rights movement have a unique perspective on what it means to be a "woman" who plays jazz. While many of the younger musicians I interviewed for this book readily acknowledge the fact that jazz is commonly perceived as a male-dominated musical art form, most came up studying and playing music with both men and women, and share the belief that as long as you can play, you will be accepted by your musical peers.

But I wonder what changes we may see a decade or two from now, as this younger generation of musicians continues to explore their options for a financially stable career in music. Being a musician is tough, no matter if you are a man or a woman, but women have yet to benefit from equal representation in jazz academia (i.e., teaching positions at colleges and universities) or onstage at jazz festivals across the country. Promotional channels for this music, including publications like *DownBeat* and *JAZZIZ Magazine*, still favor coverage of men over women musicians.

That said, it is refreshing to meet, hear, and speak to younger musicians who seem nearly unfazed by the gender divide, and are instead focused on and committed to the regimen that is required to make incredible music. Saxophonist, composer, and bandleader Sharel Cassity is one of those musicians.

"I heard Branford Marsalis say once that jazz musicians are magicians," says Cassity. "That's what we're supposed to do for audiences.... Whether it's from a more cerebral place or a celebratory place, we're supposed to bring magic, and if we're not doing that, it's not jazz."

At a very early age, Cassity was a serious student of classical saxophone (as well as piano), and performed on gigs with her father, a pianist, playing the melodies to jazz and blues standards while her father did all the soloing. She traces her decision to study and play jazz to a mix tape a friend gave her when she was just 14 that included music by Miles Davis, Cannonball Adderley, Count Basie, and Charlie Parker.

"... [T]he music on that tape really hit me," says Cassity. "That was when I said, okay, I don't want to be a classical saxophonist anymore. I have to chase this."

Cassity would go on to pursue a master's degree at the Juilliard School on full scholarship, receive recognition and awards for her playing and composing, and perform alongside such musicians as Christian McBride, Roy Hargrove, James Moody, Anat Cohen, Monty Alexander, Ingrid Jensen, and Sherrie Maricle (as a member of the DIVA Jazz Orchestra). Cassity has appeared

Sharel Cassity. Photo by Gulnara Khamatova.

on several recordings, playing alto and soprano saxophone and flute, and released three of her own, including *Relentless*, which received a four-star rating in *DownBeat*. Her compositions for her small and larger ensembles draw heavily on the traditional, "straight-ahead" vernacular that this new generation of musicians has embraced, even as they push the music into the future.

"What I'm really doing is coming out of the [jazz] tradition," says Cassity, "but playing modern. It's just like how we use words today. We don't speak the same way we spoke 100 years ago, but we use a lot of the same words, and we each use them differently, depending on where we're from and our experiences."

When did you first begin playing a musical instrument?
I began playing piano at age 6. I got my first alto when I was 9.

What drew you to the piano initially?
My grandma had taught both my dad and my aunt piano, and my aunt was a concert pianist. My dad had his doctorate in piano and is a music therapist. So a love for the piano ran in the family. My grandma gave me and my cousins our first piano lessons. After my parents divorced, my mom continued taking me to lessons throughout my childhood. I loved it. I would practice non-stop. I wanted to be a concert pianist until I was about 10 or 11 years old, but the saxophone kind of ruined that. [laughs]

How did the saxophone come into your life?
I had seen my dad play with his organ trio, which was saxophone, Hammond B-3, and drums, and I really loved the sound of the instrument. But I didn't think about playing the saxophone at first. I instead told my mother I wanted to play the flute, and she said, "You don't want to play the flute. I can't see you playing the flute!" I said, "Really?" She said, "You're gonna look funny trying to jam out on the flute. What about the sax?" and I thought, "Yeah!" So then I started begging for a saxophone, and the next Christmas, my dad got me one.

That's a progressive family. They didn't tell you that girls play the flute and guys play these other instruments. It sounds like they were very supportive of you playing music.
They were! At the time though, what I was playing was all classical music. My mom took me to lessons and supported any style I chose. My dad and his side of the family wanted me to play classical music, and they did support me, until I wanted to play jazz. Only then did I start to hear that "the road was no place for a girl." They hoped I'd grow out of it. When I was about 10, my dad asked my teacher to try to tell me how hard life on the road was. My teacher told me, "You have to sleep on buses, change in bathrooms, and wear polyester uniforms. Now, does that sound like fun?" and I eagerly replied, "YEAH!"

How old were you when you became interested in playing jazz?
My dad always had records, and he listened to Charlie Parker, John Coltrane, Bill Evans, Jimmy Smith—all kinds of jazz since I can remember. For fun, he would write out melodies for me to learn, bebop melodies, "Stella by Starlight," "Blue Rondo à la Turk," some blues heads. When I was 11, we would actually go and play little restaurants and nursing homes in town, and once we played at IAJE [the International Association for Jazz Education]. I would play the melodies and he would do all the soloing. I didn't know it then but I loved that feeling.

When I was 14, a friend of mine gave me a mix tape of Count Basie and

Miles Davis and Cannonball Adderley. Bird [Charlie Parker] was on that tape too. And for some reason, the music on that tape really hit me. That was when I said, "Okay, I don't want to be a classical saxophonist anymore. I have to chase this. That's it." From that point on it was like I'd been bitten, and I had to do it.

You grew up in Oklahoma?
I moved around the States a lot until the sixth grade. From then on, I lived in Oklahoma.

What was the music program like in your school?
It was pretty interesting. I went to Yukon High School, a public school, with a little less than 500 students. The school had a pretty good band program because it had a pretty good football program. Football funds the music. If you wanted to play in the jazz band, it was mandatory that you play in the concert band and marching band, so I played in all three. I played clarinet, flute, and piccolo in the concert band just to get my doubles up,[63] and I played saxophone in the jazz band. The jazz band at the time was one of the two top state bands.

There are times I wish I'd opted to go to a private school or an arts high school like the Dallas Arts High School when I had the chance. But I'd moved around my whole life, and this was the first time I had friends, including friends in the band. So I just decided to stay at Yukon.

Throughout high school, I studied classical saxophone with a retired saxophonist and professor, Dr. Jack Sisson, who was a protégé of Eugene Rousseau. Rousseau was a disciple of Marcel Mule, and Mule was the founder of the French school of classical saxophone. Studying those fundamentals so early was really good for me.

At the same time, you were getting some experience playing jazz as well?
I was in the Yukon High School jazz band, which was led by Wayne Coon, which often won state championships. I also had attended the Berklee Summer Performance Program and a couple of other camps. By my senior year, I had taken enough AP courses to be eligible to take a college course, so I was able to play in the jazz ensemble at the University of Oklahoma [UCO], which had players who were much more advanced. I traveled to play in that band three days a week.

Were there places you could go to and hear jazz?
There were a small handful of local musicians who were very good, and would always let me sit in. I remember going with my friends—who were a little older than me and could drive—to Kansas City, St. Louis, and Dallas. We would drive for hours to hear artists like Kenny Garrett or Joe Lovano. My senior year in high school, UCO had Phil Woods as a guest clinician with their big band, and that had a large effect on me.

Where did you go to school after high school?

I spent three years at the University of Central Oklahoma because they gave me a full scholarship, and I could stay near my younger brothers. I hadn't even thought about going east. I auditioned at North Texas, and they gave me a full scholarship for classical saxophone. But when I asked if I could play in the jazz ensemble, they wouldn't guarantee that as a possibility. UCO gave me a full scholarship to study and play jazz, but after studying there for three years, I was just kind of ready to get out of Oklahoma and find more music.

I ended up moving to Boston to live with my aunt in 1999. I was supposed to go to the New England Conservatory of Music, but my scholarship fell through because I was still a dependent. By the next spring, I had relocated to New York City. Two years after that, I applied to The New School to finish my bachelor's degree.

It's funny. I was raised with the idea that you didn't have to go to school to learn how to play. And technically you don't. But in this day and age, there isn't a scene with great sessions like there used to be. The most accessible way to learn from the masters, collaborate with your peers, and live in New York is through school music programs now.

Were there other women studying jazz at The New School?

Yeah! Renee Cruz [bass] and Vanessa Cruz [drums] were there. We were close friends. Another good friend, Meilana Gillard, was playing tenor. Lakecia Benjamin [alto] was there. There were a lot of female international musicians at the school, like pianists Katia Toobool and Yayoi Ikawa, as well as lot of vocalists.

So it wasn't like you were the only woman there?

No, but you know what's funny is ... when I was growing up, I don't remember thinking there are no women in jazz. It was either I could hang with the musicians who could play or not. If I wasn't good enough, I either knew better than to play or other players made it clear that I should sit out. If I was good enough, they would call me. I wasn't thinking in terms of "women in jazz;" I hadn't even heard that term.

I remember shortly after I had moved to New York, I was at the jazz club Smalls, and a person there thought that I was this German alto player, Karolina Strassmayer, who used to be in the DIVA Jazz Orchestra. Someone thought I was her and thought I was lying when I said I wasn't. This person told me, "It's so great to see women in jazz...." And all of a sudden, people were addressing me as a "woman in jazz" and asking how it felt to be a woman in jazz. I was completely new to that.

You went to Juilliard after The New School, is that correct?

Sharel Cassity (far right). Kansas State, 1994. Photographer unknown.

Yes. After I finished at The New School I applied to Juilliard. If you were accepted, you received a full scholarship. And it was great. I loved Juilliard.

Were you studying classical and jazz there?

I was in the jazz program, but to get the master's degree, you had to take some fundamental classical courses. But I wasn't studying classical saxophone. It was mostly centered around jazz performance, and I studied under Victor Goines for both years.

In college, did you take any music-business courses?

At Juilliard, I took a music-business course, but it was mostly geared toward pop music and music that already made a lot of money, so I had a hard time applying it to what I was doing and what the next steps of my career should be. I learned about the business mostly from just being around friends who were business savvy. While at Juilliard, [trombonist] Michael Dease told me, "You really need to put out an album," and I said, "Why? I'm not ready. . . ." But he insisted, "You're ready," and helped me figure out how to do it.

When it came to the teachers at Juilliard, like any school, some were fantastic and some weren't. The environment and workload could be very intense, and everyone found their own way to thrive. But many of the students stuck together, and we learned a lot from each other. A lot of us used each other on our recordings. Also, the program encouraged students to have a camaraderie, which was good.

This term "post-bop" gets thrown around a lot by music writers. I saw it over and over again when I was researching you for this interview, but I don't know what "post-bop" actually means. So how would you describe your playing? Can you talk about the language or musical materials that you use?

What I'm really doing is coming out of the tradition, but playing modern. It's just like how we use words today. We don't speak the way we spoke 100 years ago, but we use a lot of the same words, and we each use them differently, depending on where we're from and our experiences.

When I think of post-bop, I think of it as what players like Woody Shaw, Joe Henderson, and Freddie Hubbard were doing after bebop. This term "post-bop" being used now is really funny, because everything since 1960 that swings and uses bebop harmony is post-bop! That's a huge range, a term being used very broadly. Most great modern players of the jazz tradition know bebop, post-bop, and all the styles that came after thoroughly. Maybe we don't have a label for all the new styles of jazz that happened in the last 30 years, but there were some major innovations made that seem to be overlooked by jazz writers. Calling a modern player like Brad Mehldau or Marcus Strickland "post-bop" to me is limiting what they actually sound like, when what they are doing is very fresh. Post-bop happened 50 years ago. But then someone like pianist Robert Glasper doesn't get labeled as "post-bop," and people then say he's "not jazz." Sometimes you can't win. Everyone has something different to contribute and I think that's beautiful. There's enough room for it all, even if it's not categorized with a word to validate it. This opens a big can of worms that I don't think the industry wants to address, because they *really* love saying "post-bop." [laughs] But that's okay. I'm happy to be a part of it.

Who are some of the saxophonists that inspired you in the way they used this language, these words, in their playing?

There's so many. Some of my modern favorites are Kenny Garrett, Antonio Hart, Jimmy Heath, Steve Wilson, Vincent Herring, Gary Bartz, Myron Walden, Jaleel Shaw, Greg Osby, Dick Oatts, Joe Lovano. I love Eric Alexander, Marcus Strickland, Jimmy Greene, of course Branford Marsalis.

What is it about these players that you love? Is it more of a poetic thing? Like the way somebody speaks to you?

These players have digested the musical language so thoroughly and in such a meaningful way. I think a lot of people digest the language and it's not meaningful. They just "know it." These guys know what the language originally meant, who played it and how they played it, so they can actually take it and do something with it that is meaningful and original.

Each of the players I named, their playing is honest. They've really worked to hone and craft their art to a very high level. They all have blues in their playing and lots of rhythm, which is kind of going by the wayside lately. I feel that these days, jazz is often either very esoteric, and played only for other musicians, which is not a good progression for the survival of the music, or it's instrumental pop music. Both approaches are missing the core of what jazz is and what makes it great.

Is jazz music for listening or for dancing?
I think it can be for both. Either way, it has to reach people, you know?

If I'm listening to something and it's not hitting me, but I can describe to you all the techniques the player is using and why it's amazing, that's not . . . right. There's something wrong with that.

I heard Branford Marsalis say once that jazz musicians are magicians. When I go and hear him live in concert, it is like he's a magician. I hear him play something and think, "Man, how did he do that?" It's not until you go home and dissect a recording that you figure out how he did it. That's what we're supposed to do to for audiences. Bring magic! Whether it's from a more cerebral place or a celebratory place, we're supposed to bring magic, and if we're not doing that, it's not jazz.

To make magic you have to have the technical facility on your instrument, but you also have to have the desire and ability to speak to people. That's something I hear in your recordings.
Thank you.

Day to day, what's life like for a musician in New York City?
All I've ever really wanted was to play music. I've never wanted the house, the kids, the car, you know? That was never my dream. Year after year, things have continued to get better, I'm playing with more and more bands I've always wanted to play with.

When it comes to a daily routine, I wake up, I practice, I go to the gym, I write, I do whatever I have to do that relates to business, and then I usually have to go to a rehearsal, gig, or a session. I've been having sessions at my apartment, and I've learned that nowadays, that's a much more efficient way of playing. You can have whoever you want come over and you can play for hours. If you go out to a club to a session, you can end up waiting until 1:30 or 2 in the morning just to play one tune! I also travel a lot, by car, bus, and plane, and end up practicing a lot in hotel rooms or wherever I can find. I try to keep the same routine on the road as off but it can get tricky.

A lot of musicians complain about not working enough, or not making enough money. And I've had thoughts where I've wondered, what if I had a steady job? There are people my age who have houses by now. But you can't think about that. Other people's "normal" is not *our* normal. I chose this life. Maybe I could have been a surgeon or something and made a lot of money. But whenever I meet the surgeons and the dentists and the doctors, they say, "Wow! You're a musician! It must be wonderful to get to travel to so many places and play music!"

I always have to remember, not everyone can have everything. This is what I chose to do, and it's what I work on, continually, every day. Don't get me wrong, I would love to find a teaching position or gig that provided a little more income. That would be really nice. Or maybe my band will become successful? Who knows? I believe everyone deserving will at some point have the opportunity to make more money. But for now, my goal is just to be happy and create as much as I can.

When a non-musician meets a musician and gets excited, I think it's because they've met somebody who loves what they're doing.
Yeah. I do love what I'm doing. It's a lot of hard work like anything else, and I think that when people meet someone playing music, they have the impression that it's all talent and not a lot of work.

How do your parents feel about your music now? You said they initially weren't crazy about your decision to pursue jazz.
My mom is starting to become a jazz lover. My mom is all for me, she's behind me 100 percent, especially now that she's seen what I do and the great community I'm a part of. I couldn't ask for more. My dad loves jazz, but he loves the old stuff. [laughs]

I think my whole family is proud of me, but many of them are sort of holding their breath. They all love hearing my stories, but I think they're still thinking, in the back of their minds, "Okay, when can I relax? When is she going to be okay?" When really, I'm fine!

Jacqui Sutton

When it comes to realizing one's musical potential, a musician must cut his or her own path. The journey is never straightforward and certainly doesn't unfold within the prescribed timeline of a four-year degree program. Interestingly, across all artistic disciplines, coming into one's own is commonly described as "finding your own voice."

The beginning of singer Jacqui Sutton's musical journey can be traced back to the 1960s when she, along with her siblings and mother ("newly single, and pregnant with her sixth child"[64]), relocated from Orlando, Florida, to Rochester, New York. At the end of the final decade of what author Isabel Wilkerson calls "America's great migration,"[65] over six million black citizens had relocated from the South to northern and western states. The 1969 Supreme Court decision *Alexander v. Holmes County Board of Education* ruled "school districts must immediately terminate dual school systems based on race and operate only unitary school systems."[66]

Integration also found its way into popular music, in bands like Sly and the Family Stone, or the influence of the Beatles' track "Eleanor Rigby" on Stevie Wonder's "Village Ghetto Land" from his conceptual masterpiece *Songs in the Key of Life*. And like the Fab Four from Liverpool, Sutton explains that during this time, "I found myself drawn to experiences that were the opposite of my own."[67] You can hear what she's talking about on her first album, *Billie and Dolly*, a tribute to two of her favorite singers and biggest influences, Billie Holiday and Dolly Parton. Her second album, *Notes From the Frontier: A Musical Journey* (That word again!), expands her repertoire to include Appalachian songs, classical composition, and jazz standards in inventive musical settings Sutton describes as "a stylistic mash-up of jazz, bluegrass, and orchestral/chamber music."[68] Sutton's singing is similarly multifaceted and sits comfortably in an ensemble that forgoes traditional jazz instrumentation to include banjo, cello, and hand percussion.

In addition to being just fun to listen to, Sutton's conceptual approach to music making is part of a continuum of jazz as once described by the great Jelly Roll Morton as a music that uses ideas drawn from operas, symphonies, and overtures.[69] Add Appalachian ballads, country music, and rural blues to that list and you get an idea of what Sutton and her band, the Frontier Jazz Orchestra, are able to pull off on record and in live performance. Finding one's voice can mean finding the threads that tie together seemingly disparate influences in a way that transcends modern-day pastiche and resonates with a similarly diverse cross-section of listeners.

Jacqui Sutton. Photo by Richard Tomcala.

Here's a quote from you I got from your biography. I'm taking it out of context. "In many ways, I feel grateful that I've discovered my voice now rather than when I was in my 20s. All those years languishing in oblivion forced me to respond to music in a more mature way." Can you talk to me a little more about discovering your voice now as opposed to when you were in your 20s or right out of high school?

While I was going through it, I was incredibly frustrated. I didn't think I would ever be a singer or put something together like the Frontier Jazz Orchestra.

With the exception of studying flute as a kid—I had a very short career on the flute in elementary school—I didn't study music. I didn't study in high school, I didn't study in college. I didn't really start to study until I was like 23 or 24.

I have a low speaking voice. I auditioned for this vocal jazz ensemble called Jazz Mouth and I got in; I don't know how! I still to this day don't know how

Molly Holm cast me in that jazz ensemble. But she said, "Okay, now you gotta study!" So I did, but I kept getting miscast as an alto, because of my speaking voice and because I didn't know any better. I was always trying to sing as an alto, and doing that gave me a lot of bad habits.

So after about 10 years of studying, I moved to New York in my mid-30s and found a voice teacher who said, "You are a soprano. Now we don't know what kind of soprano. Yet. But you're a soprano." [laughs] So I had to retrain.

While I was singing, I was also an actor. I did classical theater, I did Shakespeare, and I did a lot of musical theater and experimental theater. Once I discovered acting, I said, "You know, acting is so much more rewarding and I'm frustrated with singing." So I dropped singing and did acting for many years. It wasn't until I moved to New York in the mid to late 90s that I took up voice again. And that was when I discovered I was a soprano.

After I moved here to Houston, I met my voice teacher, Cynthia Clayton. Cynthia sings with the Houston Grand Opera and she teaches as well. She's a professor of vocal performance at the University of Houston. She got my voice to open up more. It wasn't until I started studying with Cynthia that I enjoyed singing. Before then it was all terror. Something drove me to do it, but it was always terrifying, so I never had any confidence.

While studying with Cynthia, I released my first CD, *Billie and Dolly*.

So finding a teacher who understood your voice and how you should sing, did that coincide with you beginning to explore repertoire that includes both Billie Holiday and Dolly Parton? And did singing that material help you with the process of finding your voice?

That's a good question. I think it was all kind of happening at the same time.

I had been listening to jazz and bluegrass since I was in my early 20s. Both of the sounds had always been in my head. I think a lot of frustration I felt was because I didn't want to be pigeonholed into either. Each style seemed to have a specific vocal approach that I was not sure how to handle. So I didn't really pursue it.

I will tell you that the songs I selected for *Billie and Dolly* were all songs I always liked personally. From Dolly Parton's "Endless Stream of Tears" to Billie Holiday's "God Bless the Child" to "A Sleepin' Bee." "A Sleepin' Bee" is a song that my teacher in New York tortured me with! I loved it so much but I didn't have the chops to sing it. And when I finally got the chops to sing it, I said, "I want to do this song!" And it actually fit! It fit as a Frontier Jazz song. So my repertoire includes songs that I've been singing forever but had just been technically trying to master. Others are songs that I just emotionally connected with. The biggest challenge has always been technical.

Lee Hoiby's "Lady of the Harbor" is a song that I just felt like I wanted to *own* the first time I ever heard it. I didn't care about the technical part of it. It was just something I *wanted*. There are songs I just want to devour.

After a while, Cynthia Clayton got tenure while I was studying with her. She had to focus on her students, and as a result I wasn't able to study with her as regularly as I wanted to. So I looked around for another voice teacher and lucked upon a man here in Houston named John Barth, and he remains my voice teacher.

I will study until I draw my last breath. I believe in studying. John has taken my voice to a completely new level. I was studying with him when I released my CD *Notes From the Frontier*. And I feel that *that* voice is my voice.

People learn in different ways, especially when it comes to the voice. Because you cannot physically manipulate your vocal cords. It's not like a bicep that you can send a command to. You have to do a lot of other sympathetic action to get the cords to do things. People use all different kinds of techniques to get the cords to respond. Some people use visual images like "pretend you're smelling a rose. . . ." I'm not a visual person in that way. The technique I'm working on with John Barth is much more kinesthetic. My journey has been 99 percent technical. [laughs]

The repertoire you're currently singing, it's never an issue with your vocal teachers?
No. Not with Cynthia or John. Cynthia didn't pooh-pooh it. She thought it was great. She's a classical singer. But she did not say to me, "Oh, Jacqui, you should not be doing this classical song as a jazz tune. . . ." In fact, she and her husband, before Lee Hoiby died, they debuted some of Hoiby's work. And she said, "You know, I think Lee would have loved to hear his music done in a jazz style."

So nobody was saying I shouldn't try and mash these songs up. They were really just trying to get me to be a better singer. That's all they wanted. And if I was singing songs that made me happy, that was the entrée into the strengthening.

Jane Monheit told me the same thing about her teacher. There was never an issue of what she should or shouldn't sing. It was technical, and discovering what kind of singer you are and addressing that. It's interesting to learn that you had similarly open-minded teachers as well who put the student first.
The other thing that kind of kept me moving along was . . . I don't know if you've ever watched *Seinfeld*?

Sure.
There's an episode where Jerry Seinfeld goes to his mother complaining about

some stand-up gig that he's had. People were booing and this and that. And his mother, without blinking an eye goes, "Well, you know there's still that management-training program at Macy's!" [laughs] I am lucky that nobody in my life told me there's always that management-training program at Macy's. [laughs] People believed in me and always said, "Keep going! Keep going!" even though I never had any visible manifestation of my life as a singer.

That's so important, that encouragement. The songs on your two recordings, who does the arrangements?
On the second CD, I did the arrangements.

Wow. They're amazing.
Thank you! The first CD it was Henry Darraugh, who is the pianist and keyboardist on the recording. He also plays trombone; he's a wonderful guy. When I first put this group together, it started with Henry. He was the first person that I called up. A friend of my husband told us, "I know a guy who is a big band arranger. . . ." I wanted to mix jazz with bluegrass, but I needed an arranger. Henry did the arrangements on the first CD, mostly the horns. But working with him and working with my guys helped me start hearing what I was really feeling inside. We've all been working together for three years now.

When it came time to do the second CD, I had very specific sounds in my head. Now I don't arrange using notation. It's more like a choreographer. I know this guy can leap, this guy can turn, and these are the sounds I'm hearing. So I did all the arrangements on the second CD. But it was that foundation of that first CD and having Henry at least do the horns and hearing the guys work together that made me realize that yes, this does work. On the second CD, I put more of my stamp on it. Because I love bluegrass so much, I wanted more of an Americana feel. And I think I achieved that.

With "Summertime," which opens the second CD, I heard that cello entrance, I heard that banjo doing what it does, and I heard the piano arpeggios. I just don't know how to write all that stuff down. I just said, "Henry, here's what I'm hearing. I'm hearing really spacey arpeggios." So I have to do it verbally.

I don't have enough hours in the day; I can't go back to school and learn composition and arranging, you know? [laughs] A lot of stuff I'll just record it. I'll hear a motif and I'll just sing it, record it, and play it back.

Is there a bridge, some commonalities between jazz and bluegrass that you use in your singing?
Absolutely. It is so integral to who I am. I mean, Frontier Jazz is saying "you all think you're so different, but you have a voice together."

First of all, they're both uniquely American art forms. There is precedent for the two forms making out! [laughs] Making out musically! They've been on parallel tracks in my head for so long that I did not ever want to separate them. But I can tell you that people get very confused when I say I'm blending jazz and bluegrass together. One reviewer said (and I'm paraphrasing), "It's curious on paper, but it makes total sense once you hear it." And I think that's what's been part of the trajectory is getting people to understand that these two musical forms have a lot in common.

I have this project I'm still trying to get off the ground called Urban Banjo. The prototype of the banjo is an African instrument. Did you see [banjo player] Béla Fleck's film *Throw Down Your Heart?*

Yeah!

I was blown away when I heard Béla Fleck's *Concerto for Banjo.* He did it with the Nashville Symphony about a year ago. My banjo player plays a six-string banjo. So he can get a guitar voicing. That sound feels very old to me, like before I was born old. And people look at me and say, "Really? The *banjo?*"

I think Americana, that sound, is so specific, and that's what I'm trying to achieve through Frontier Jazz. That combined sound is what allows my voice to be what it is.

When you're talking about the banjo as a sound from before when you were born, you're talking about a sound before America came into existence. This is very old stuff. But it's all a part of our popular music. It's integral to jazz, rock and roll, and gospel music.

People just don't know what to make of it until they hear it. So my thing is "just listen to it. Listen." And it's hard for me to even get booking managers because they don't get it. And I'm never going to be a smooth jazz artist. Never. That's not what I'm about.

Cassandra Wilson said something along the lines of "jazz is not a style or a genre. It's a process." And that's how I approach it. It's about improvisation and exploration, and what comes out of it, that's what you would call jazz. It's the end product of a process.

I don't know what the Frontier Jazz Orchestra will sound like 10 years from now. I hope it evolves and allows my voice to keep growing. It is what it is right now, and there's nothing that makes me happier.

The second album is doing really well now, right?

Yes. It just finished its radio campaign. I was in CMJ's top 40 jazz chart for six weeks, which for an independently released CD is really good. And the reviews have been great. With the first CD, people were like, "well, this is interesting . . ." but I think they were waiting for a second product to see that this was a real entity, not some novelty act. I've gotten a lot of really good reviews. I can hear the respect in them now. And I'm working on the third CD.

You've released two recordings. Are they on a label or are they on your own label?

Both are on my own label.

Younger jazz musicians might be wondering how they can get their music on the radio. What's that process like? How do you do it? Do you have to hire a publicist?

Yes. You pay a publicist, someone who is well versed in radio and print campaigns. Henry recommended this lady Kari Gaffney from the Augusta, Georgia, area. She became a real fan of my work, so I hired her to be my publicist.

You hire a publicist because there aren't enough hours in the day. You have to call and harass and remind these radio stations because you're fighting major labels constantly. They are flooding the market and you don't have enough hours in the day to call and ask, "Did you open that envelope? Did you play her CD? How much rotation did it get this week?" Kari would call all of these stations with these questions. And then every week, I would get a radio report from her. I've done my market analysis, and I know where my audience is now because of the radio reports that she got to me.

Are these jazz radio stations that are playing your CD? Radio is so different from when I was a young and listening to FM radio.

No. A lot of "jazz" radio stations are actually smooth-jazz stations. Their listeners want their soprano sax and smooth-jazz thing, and so stations are not very risk-taking.

It's a lot of NPR affiliates. A lot of college radio stations. Here's my demographic: younger kids, like college-aged kids, because their palettes are so much wider now. They're not interested in boundaries. So it's college-aged kids and middle-aged white women. [laughs] It's the middle-aged white women who turn up at my gigs. I don't know why, but it's like "God bless you . . . because I need you!"

Who I need to convince are the booking managers and the festival organizers, and get them to understand that this is something that has integrity. The band and I have the chops to do this. I'm knockin' on a lotta doors to get people to believe and respect what I'm doing. Even getting somebody to open up the CD and listen to it is really hard.

But I believe in it so much, there's no questioning it any more. Fifteen years ago, even ten years ago, I couldn't have imagined feeling so confident and happy to be singing, that I'd be knocking 20 times on somebody's door saying, "You gotta listen! I *know* I'm good!" It takes a while to get to that point, to know that your instrument is reliable.

And that gets back to what I said about "languishing in oblivion. . . ." If I had had the musical chops at a younger age, I don't know if I would have sat down long enough to understand what kind of music really resonates with me. I don't know what would have happened. But I was obviously meant to be sitting in this meditative state [laughs] for 20 years or more! And asking myself, "What do you really love about music? What really resonates with you?"

Mindi Abair

Saxophonist, singer, and composer Mindi Abair is the first musician I interviewed for this book. In retrospect, that may seem strange, if only because Abair doesn't identify herself as a jazz musician. Then again, many of the other artists I interviewed for this book avoid using the word "jazz" to describe their musical output.

Abair's music is often lumped in the much derided, misunderstood, and in my opinion, underappreciated style of music commonly known as "smooth jazz." I say "misunderstood," because the roots of what might be better described as a groove-centric form of instrumental pop music come from a sea change in jazz that occurred in the late 1960s and early 1970s. During this period of tremendous social upheaval, jazz musicians began making music that wouldn't be out of place on soul and R&B radio stations and jukeboxes across the U.S. Musicians such as Ramsey Lewis, Les McCann, Donald Byrd, and Grover Washington Jr. enjoyed a degree of mainstream success playing a danceable style of jazz that embraced the backbeat, funk bass lines, gospel harmonies, and a sense of style that spoke to the politics of the time. Jazz purists, and especially music critics, hated it. Meanwhile, young listeners were intrigued by this new style of soulful jazz and were led to other strains of this music as a result.

Mindi Abair. Photo by Greg Allen.

Abair is certainly comfortable navigating the world of popular music. But her musical background is a little more complex than that of many pop stars. Her résumé includes playing saxophone with the quintessential boy band the Backstreet Boys and Boston's hard-rocking Aerosmith, but she cut her teeth as a player touring with jazz pianist and composer Bobby Lyle in a band that included former members of jazz-fusion pioneers Weather Report and the impossible-to-categorize rock, disco, soul, and R&B musical group Earth, Wind & Fire. She has recorded several hits as a so-called pop instrumental or smooth-jazz artist, but she names women like Tina Turner and idiosyncratic singer-songwriter Rickie Lee Jones as early inspirations. As a child, she grew up on the road with her father's band, the Entertainers. The track "The Alley" from Abair's 2010 album *Hi-Fi Stereo* features her father, Lance Abair, on a Hammond B-3, bringing it all back to home to the music that first set his daughter on a path to study jazz while planning to be a rock star.

At the time of this writing, Abair is the president of the Los Angeles Chapter of Music that, through programs including the Grammy Foundation and MusiCares, provides money and resources for music education and musicians' health needs. In an age of rampant piracy, a dearth of terrestrial radio airplay, and near-zero royalties from ubiquitous music-streaming services like Spotify, she is a strong advocate for the rights of composers and creators of music.

In this wide-ranging interview, which combines two separate conversations and is presented in this book in two parts, Abair talks about the importance of music education, her earliest experiences as a professional musician, and the "glass ceiling" that still exists in the music industry.

....

PART ONE

When did you first begin playing a musical instrument?
The first instrument I played was the piano. When I was little, I would just bang on my father's keyboards. And I think my parents just broke down when I was 5 years old and put me into piano lessons. When school band started in fourth grade, I was told to pick up any instrument and that we'd go on from there. I chose the alto saxophone. I was 8 years old. The saxophone was bigger than me at that point!

Many of the musicians I've interviewed had some kind of music program in their elementary school.
I now do a lot of work with young kids in schools through the Grammy Foundation and other outreach programs. We sometimes bring kids from the inner city to our sound checks and have lunch with the band so they can see how we

do things. I think it's great to have the kids interact with the musicians who are out there doing it. They can ask questions and be inspired by it. It goes a long way. No one is going to be able to fill the gap when a music program leaves a school, but we can all give it our best shot to try.

Your father Lance is a musician?
Yes. He plays Hammond B-3 on my track "The Alley" from my album *Hi-Fi Stereo*. He's also on my second CD.

Did your family support your early interest in music?
My father was a professional musician at the time. He was touring with a band called the Entertainers. He played saxophone and keyboards. No one thought anything about it really. My grandmother was an opera singer and a vocal and piano instructor. They loved that I was playing an instrument. Neither she nor my father wanted to teach me, because they both felt that a kid needs a music teacher, someone who is going to be firm with the student. They didn't want to be *that* person. They didn't want to be the person who might drive me away from music. They wouldn't teach me, but they got me teachers. I took piano lessons for many years, but there really weren't many saxophone teachers in our area. I grew up in St. Petersburg, Florida. Every once in a while, someone would show up at a local music store who would teach saxophone and disappear in a couple weeks.

What kind of music were you studying and playing as a kid?
On the piano, I was playing the normal repertoire. Bach inventions. Chopin. After a couple of years, I started to bring in music that I liked. Pop music, like Tina Turner or Toto. My piano teacher hated that. She thought it was all music of the devil. [laughs]

On the saxophone, I really only had had a handful of lessons by the time I entered college. But I would listen. I would do what they do in band, which was the usual course of study. But I would listen and play along with the radio. Which means I have an amazing knowledge of pop music. [laughs] I didn't own a bunch of jazz records, but I had top-40 radio. That was the music I really dove into.

It wasn't until later, in high school, that my father bought me a David Sanborn record. I heard that and thought, "Wow! This doesn't sound like what we're playing in school. He's like the pop music on the radio, but with a saxophone." So I started learning all of his records. That led me to the band the Yellowjackets. I loved the Yellowjackets. They led me to Miles Davis, but at the time, I got and listened to the newest Miles Davis record, *Amandla*, which featured Marcus Miller. That album was not necessarily "jazz" jazz. That sent me on the search for older Miles Davis recordings, which led me to Cannonball Adderley, John Coltrane, and all of these great jazz saxophone players. But that was not what I grew up listening to. I was playing along with saxophonists like Clarence Clemons or Maceo Parker or Junior Walker and songs by Janet Jackson, the Doobie Brothers, and Earth, Wind & Fire.

It took awhile for me to get to jazz. Most of my music now is not jazz. Probably the only reason they call me a "jazz" artist is because I play the saxophone. What I play is very pop, rock, and soul influenced.

What kind of music did your father's band play?
Blue-eyed soul!

Was playing music his job?
It was. I grew up my first four or five years on the road with his band. All they did was travel. My mother traveled with us as well. I was raised by her and the band. [laughs]

You attended Berklee College of Music. Was there a time while you were there, as you were learning your instrument and more about what you wanted to do as a professional musician, that you just thought, "I want to leave school. I just want to go out to L.A. and do it!" Did you experience that kind of impatience?
Oh, absolutely.

What made you decide to stay in school?
At a certain point, I was playing six or seven nights a week and going to school, and I thought I just don't need the piece of paper [the diploma]. No one is going to hire me because I've got a piece of paper saying I have a degree in music. They're going to hire me because I'm what they want. I'm the artist they want to hire. At the time, I thought, "Why not just leave and go to L.A.? It'll be the start of my career. I'll get started a little early, it'll be great!"

I called up one of my friends, the only person I knew who lived in L.A., and he was friends with Randy Jackson, who at that time of course wasn't on *American Idol*. He was an A&R guy at Columbia Records. My friend told me to call Randy and talk to him about my wanting to leave school early.

I called Randy, and he said, "Both L.A. and New York City are really big markets. Each city has an incredible amount of fine musicians, really excellent musicians who know who they are and they know what they want to say. They're experienced and they're going for it. So you're walking into a situation where you need to be as experienced as possible and ready as possible. It's going to do you no good to get out here, be in the right city, and the right club, and not be ready." I thought that was good advice. I took it. I stayed in school and came out to L.A. once I had the piece of paper in my hand. I figured I would spend my time at school becoming excellent at what I do, instead of going out to L.A.

when I wasn't ready or experienced enough to become the player my drive and ambition told me I could be. But I had to pay my dues first.

Advice like that from someone who was a veteran in the music industry must have carried some weight.
Yes. He wasn't some kid my age, 18 years old, telling me, "Yeah! We can just leave! That's the right thing to do, right?" And we both just agree with each other.

While you were at Berklee, were you studying both classical music and jazz?
I studied a lot of different things at Berklee. That was one of the reasons I went there, because they just had in their curriculum any kind of music that you'd want to get into.

I grew up listening to rock and roll. I grew up wanting to sing like Tina Turner. I wanted to be up there onstage like Bruce Springsteen, rocking around and jumping up on things. To just sit there, behind a music stand in a big band? That didn't make too much sense for me.

At Berklee, I played in rock and funk bands. One band I was in just played the music of Wayne Shorter. Another just did the music of Cannonball Adderley. So it was anything from jazz to rock and R&B and funk. I really wanted that. I embraced that. But I never wanted to be John Coltrane or Charlie Parker.

After Berklee, you went to L.A. to begin your career. Is it true that pianist Bobby Lyle heard you playing on the street in Santa Monica, took your card, and hired you to play on his *Power of Touch* album and then tour with him?
It's all true! I came to L.A. and quickly realized this is a very hard town to break into as a musician. Some of the best musicians in the world live here, and why would they give up their gig for someone new? I would try and sit in at different jam sessions and get my band booked into different places, and it was really rough.

When I first arrived, I got a job as a waitress, because I just needed to pay the rent. But I quickly realized, that was not what I came to L.A. to do. So, I quit the waitressing job, went out on the street, put my saxophone case out there and just played. I made my rent for a few months, which was great, and I got other gigs. People would come up and hire me for things. One of those people was Bobby Lyle. I recognized him right as he walked up. I'd seen his band before. He just stood and listened for quite a while. When I was done with one of the songs, he came up and he just said, "You know, you're really good. I should hire you." And I said, "Yeah! You *should* hire me!" I toured with Bobby on and off for five or six years.

In the early years, I didn't want him to tell that story. I was kind of ashamed that he found me on the street! But now I think of it as a badge of honor.

It's a really serendipitous thing. You have to be open to it when it happens.
It was an amazing thing for me; I was brand new to L.A. and I got hired to play in this band that was just the cream of the crop. Alphonso Johnson was on bass; he played with Weather Report for years. Al McKay was on guitar; he was the original guitarist with Earth, Wind & Fire. The band was phenomenal. And they all showed me the ropes, you know? If I did something that wasn't right, they'd tell me, "No, no. You should do it this way. It's more professional." They showed me how to be a professional in the music industry. How to be prepared, how to shape a solo, how to perform. The guys really brought me up a notch.

After that, things just snowballed. People started calling me for shows and tours. Bobby was a huge part of my coming up the ranks.

As your career started to develop, how did you manage to get some assistance with just managing your money at that stage and not getting ripped off? How did you find that help?
Just being around musicians and around the scene, I got a feel for what musicians should be paid for different jobs. I actually had money in my bank account for the first time. But I didn't have anyone else to handle accounting for quite a while. I didn't seek out a manager until much later when I was looking for a record deal. At a certain point, when I took off for long tours, like when I toured with the Backstreet Boys, and was gone for the most part of a year and a half, I got a business manager who paid my bills. My check went to a bank account the business manager controlled. At a certain point, if you're touring like that, you either have a husband or wife at home who's going to take care of that stuff, or you get a business manager, which is what I did.

Were there opportunities you said "no" to in the early stages of your career?
You know what? In the early days of my being in L.A., I said "yes" to basically anything. I played a lot of weddings; I played a lot of parties. There were people who would hire me to just stroll around and play saxophone. For me, these gigs were a chance to play, which is what we all want to do, a chance to pay the rent, which was great, and a chance to meet other musicians.

In Los Angeles, there are so many musicians doing so many things. It's not like you meet a couple of people and you've met everyone. You really need to go out there and meet people.

One time, I got asked to do a wedding with a band I'd never heard of. They needed a sax player and a singer, and I took the gig. I showed up and at the wedding I started recognizing the people there. They were all musicians. They were coming up and requesting songs that only musicians would request. I handed my card out to a couple of people and shook a couple of hands on my break. I got a call a couple weeks later. [Comedian] Adam Sandler was looking for a sax player and a singer for his upcoming tour. One of the guys at the wedding referred me after seeing me and hearing me.

I was just saying "yes" to everything. I wanted to meet people. I wanted to play.

I even played in the men's underwear department at Macy's!

That's brilliant.
Macy's asked me what department I wanted to play in. I was single, you know?

Yeah, where else are you going to play? Kitchenware?
No! That's not interesting to me. [laughs]

Going back to when you were young and on the road with your father, were there women musicians that inspired you and you looked up to?
I loved the way Tina Turner sang. I loved the fact that she was so sexy up onstage, but she rocked. It wasn't this overtly sexy thing; she just had this presence about her. I couldn't sing like her, but with a saxophone, I could scream and sing like her.

As a kid I really loved the rock band Heart early on. It was two girls, Nancy and Ann Wilson. I loved their songwriting and that there were two strong women out there just going for it. They were in a man's world, and they were rockin' it just as hard as any of the guys.

There weren't a lot of women in jazz when I was coming up the ranks. But I didn't get into jazz until later on. [Singer] Rickie Lee Jones always struck a chord with me. I always thought she voiced her background vocals like a horn player. She phrased like a horn player. I loved her songwriting and the way she approached music. I covered one of her songs, "It Must Be Love," on one of my records.

I actually met Joni Mitchell for the first time last night!

Wow! Really?
I was at a little Mexican restaurant that my first single was named after called "Lucy's." Lucy came over to our table and said, "Oh, by the way, my daughter is over there. Linda Ronstadt is at her table and so is Joni Mitchell." I looked over and said, "Are you kidding me? Will you introduce me?" I sing Joni's song "The River" on the Christmas tour I do with guitarist Peter White. So I met one of my heroes. She's just a great role model for a woman. She says what she wants to say and she says it well. She's smart. She's beautiful, just herself, just her spirit. It's not about being a beauty queen for her. It's about being smart and incredible with words and melody. I was a little geeked out, just sitting there, talking with her about different saxophonists we loved!

Her *Shadows and Light* band was an amazing group of jazz musicians, including Michael Brecker on saxophone.

That was a very important album to me as a sax player. I had the VHS of *Shadows and Light*, as well as the vinyl record, and the CD. Each one had different versions of the same songs and different sax solos. So I had to buy all of them! [laughs] I did not tell her that though!

Today, album sales are down, download sales are down, and yet people seem to be consuming more music in more ways than ever before. What is the mood like in the music industry now? Is it harder now to make a living as a popular musician? Or are things just changing for the better?

The whole world is changing. In the past decade, technology has changed the way that we live enormously. So it's not just the music business that is going through this change because of technology.

I have to say that what you said is totally correct. People are consuming music more than ever before. Music is more a part of our lives today than it ever was. It's just everywhere. And technology has given us that access. As a musician who has made a living playing music for most of my life, technology is changing the way all of us make a living. People aren't buying CDs anymore. They're downloading music. They're getting it from different sources. CDs are going to be dead and gone in a few years. Me, myself, I still love having the artwork and the liner notes. But I'm buying more music on iTunes than physical CDs because it's so easy! And we still make money from that.

What I find interesting is that if you're a great live band and people come and see you night after night, you've got a career. I think really that's what it's coming down to. Becoming a brand that is really you. You have to stick out. You have to be yourself. You have to have a reason for someone to come and buy your record. I think that blending in and sounding like other people is detrimental at this point. You really have to have a style and a sound that is your own, and you have to be a great live act. That's what people are spending their money to see.

And I love touring! So it's great to be out there on the road with my band.

I just wrote a book about stage performance, because in school they don't teach you how to perform on stage. They teach you how to play scales, arpeggios, and how to play over changes, and how to technically be a musician. But nobody really taught me that if you really want somebody to come back to your concert, if you want to draw people to come see you live and know who you are, you have to develop a live persona. I figured, I've done that my whole life, I should write down what I've learned. Write down all of the mistakes I, my friends, and other people have made and put them down in written form and get it out to people, because it's going to help musicians to make a living. The book is called *How to Play Madison Square Garden*.

I don't know if I would have written the book if this revolution had not occurred in the music business. It is such a different animal today, making a living as a musician, than it was just a couple years ago. We all morph and change. Many other revolutions have occurred in the music business and other businesses. You just morph and go with it.

Cheryl Bentyne

In 1978, when singer Cheryl Bentyne joined what was then the third incarnation of the vocal quartet the Manhattan Transfer (with members Janis Siegel, Alan Paul, and founding member, the late Tim Hauser), she found herself not only having to learn material from the group's previous albums, but several new arrangements for their next album, *Extensions*. Siegel presented Bentyne with an innovative arrangement of keyboardist Joe Zawinul's popular, jazz-fusion instrumental "Birdland," with lyrics by singer Jon Hendricks that paid tribute to New York's world-famous 52nd Street jazz club named after saxophonist Charlie "Bird" Parker. Bentyne's immediate reaction was, well, shock.

"I said, 'Sing this? Are you crazy? ... That would be unbelievable!'"

The arrangement, which would win the group its first Grammy Award for Best Jazz Fusion Performance, Vocal or Instrumental, was something new for Bentyne.

"I didn't really understand the bigger picture of what you could do with an instrumental piece," Bentyne continues, "that you could really restructure it, write lyrics to it, and make it a singable song."

Extensions (1979) and its follow-up, *Mecca for Moderns* (1981), were my introduction to the Manhattan Transfer. I was 11 when "Birdland" was a hit on FM radio, and remember my dad singing along with the group's doo-wop homage, "Boy From New York City." The group drew upon a dizzying range of musical styles to create a sound that was wholly contemporary, yet harkened back to the tight harmonies of 1930s and 1940s big band vocal groups. They were also very theatrical, and adopted a visual look initially inspired by 1970s glam rock and later, British new wave music. Over the years, the group has recorded and performed music from nearly every period of jazz, including compositions by Jelly Roll Morton, Django Reinhardt, Louis Armstrong, Count Basie, Ray Charles, Quincy Jones, Milton Nascimento, and Chick Corea.

Bentyne has enjoyed a lively and successful solo career while continuing to perform with the Manhattan Transfer. She has recorded several critically acclaimed albums, including *Let Me Off Uptown*, a swinging tribute to singer Anita O'Day, and *Let's Misbehave*, a beautiful collection of songs by Cole Porter that was released in the U.S. in 2012 following Bentyne's recovery from Hodgkin's lymphoma.

Given the breadth of her knowledge and experience with this music, it's not surprising to me that Bentyne is concerned that "the tradition" of jazz singing—a tradition that extends from "Cassandra Wilson ... to Ma Rainey"—is in danger of being lost.

"If a kid tells me he or she listens to Diana Krall," says Bentyne, "then I say,

Cheryl Bentyne. Photo by Sherry Rayn Barnett.

okay, who did Diana Krall listen to? Who did Billie Holiday listen to? ... When I was coming up, singers like Carmen McRae, Ella Fitzgerald, and Shirley Horn, they were alive and they were still vital. Now they're all gone.... If [young singers] aren't going back and listening to the women and men who have come before, who are no longer on the planet, then I feel for these kids."

When did you first begin playing a musical instrument?
I started playing piano when I was 6 or 7 years old. I had piano lessons for about eight years. I was always involved in these adjudications, which were like recitals except you were judged. You'd go once a year, play two or three songs, and then be judged on a state level. And for my age, I was playing much more mature music than other kids. That doesn't mean I was a better piano player, but I learned earlier. I started singing when I got to high school.

Were you drawn to the piano? Or was this something where your family

said, "Guess what? You have to take piano lessons," and you didn't have a say in the matter?

It was okay, but it wasn't something that I really felt in my heart to do. When friends would come over, my mother would say, "Cheryl! Play a song! Play a song!" and it started to aggravate me, because I didn't want to play piano in front of people. I was like the trained monkey in the house. I think that started really turning me off. I didn't want to perform on the piano even though I played okay.

But I'm really glad my mother drove me to piano lessons every week because it really gave me a musical foundation. I learned how to read music. I can still play a few bars of all the classic pieces. I have that foundation, which is really important.

What inspired you to sing when you got to high school?

When I got to high school I auditioned for the first musical they had, which was like a revue. You could come in with any song from any show or any film. And I was obsessed with the musical *Funny Girl*. I'd seen the movie and I thought, "Oh my goodness, this is me! I want to be a singing actress!" I'd never sung in front of people. I was kind of a "closet" singer. I would just sing in the patio of my house and mimic Barbra Streisand records in front of the mirror for hours at a time.

And the minute my parents came and saw me in this musical, my mother said, "I didn't know you could sing!" So she pushed me to go sing with my father, who was a Dixieland clarinet player. He had a Dixieland jazz band locally there at the Elks Lodge. He would play Friday and Saturday nights. So I started rehearsing with my dad, and I was like, "Ugh, this is old music." Louis Armstrong, all these old songs. But he gave me 25 dollars a week. And I thought, "I can make money singing? This is crazy!" So I started doing that. I had found my niche. My passion.

Did it become apparent then in high school that singing could be a career path for you?

Actually, I found singing to be easy, but I really wanted to be an actress. But I thought I'd make money in the meantime singing. And that continued after I was done with high school. I moved to Seattle. I'm from the Northwest, north of Seattle. I moved to the big city and auditioned for a band, the New Deal Rhythm band, which was wacky swing music. We'd dress up in goofy outfits, we'd do Cab Calloway, Ruby Keeler, and Carmen Miranda. I auditioned for them, and got the job. So for the next four years I got to make real money, rent an apartment in Seattle with a friend, and travel the Northwest and sing with the band.

So you didn't go to college. You went from high school straight to professional singing.

Yeah, right to my profession. I wouldn't say that too loud around young people who are going to a music college. Going to a music college would have been great, but I didn't have that luxury. I immediately just started to go to work. I consider myself lucky that I knew what I wanted to do at that age.

You know how you're fearless at 18, 19, or 20 and think, "I can do anything!" That was my attitude. That got me through it. In hindsight, it would have been nice to have a little bit more music theory so I could really write music. I kind of "punt" when I do a vocal chart. I don't do a lot of vocal-chart writing, although I can read music.

Musicians I've interviewed have said how important learning on the bandstand is. It sounds like your education was performing with other musicians in front of audiences. That was your university.

It was on-the-job training. And I believe that is the best way to do it. I coach singers and I do some master classes here, and my best advice is to find a little club and get a piano player and sing. When I moved to L.A., after I was out of the New Deal Rhythm Band, you could go to what they called audition nights or "hoot" nights where you'd go in with a couple pieces, you'd give the music to the piano player, and you'd get up and perform. And that is like throwing you into the fire. You gotta do it on the spot rather than rehearse, rehearse, rehearse or stand in line for two weeks for *American Idol*. It's none of that! You actually get up, you do it, and you fall down. And you get up again. Obviously it builds character, but it really forces you to learn your craft.

Did you have a vocal teacher around this time period?

Yes, I did. In Seattle there was a wonderful teacher that I found through my group. His name was George Peckham. He has passed on now. He was going strong on into his 90s. He was an amazing man.

I really believe that for even the best singers, it's good to have a set of outside ears to listen to you and get some good outside advice. Vocal exercises and warm-ups are really important because you have these delicate, little vocal cords and you can't just pound them every night. You have to warm them up. Just like you stretch before you do exercises. I'm looking for a new voice teacher as we speak.

I think it's important people understand musicians never stop learning.

Yes. The older you get, the voice changes. It settles, the break in the voice moves. I'm still working on stuff all the time. I have a gig coming up, a solo gig, where I'm doing all-new music. Well, when you do all-new songs, you also have to re-embrace your voice all over again and see where each song fits most comfortably, where the sweet spot is.

Fast forwarding a bit to the Manhattan Transfer, what were the first rehearsals with all four of you like? Can you take me through a rehearsal? Did one person take the lead and guide the rest? Were there exercises you would do as a quartet? Was it a free-for-all where everyone was throwing out ideas?

[laughs] Boy, the first few months were just a blur to me. Because I came in and learned all the back material that they were already singing, from their first three records, and then we immediately learned "Birdland" and all the music on *Extensions*, which was the first recording I performed on with the group.

Wow!

There weren't any warm-ups at that point. We'd sit and have coffee and talk for a while. It hasn't changed over the years, over 33 plus years. We still love to chat and eventually get to rehearsing.

In the group Janis Siegel is the taskmaster. She sits at the piano and plunks out parts. A lot of the time, since I'm the soprano and sing the melody, I have to sit and wait and wait and wait because Alan has to get his tenor part, and Janis her alto part, and Tim his bass part. So they have to do it a few bars at a time. Then we slowly start building it together, maybe eight bars, and then you go back and do 16 bars, and then you go back again. It's quite tedious, because we insist on learning it as a group. I know there are groups out there who individually go off and learn their parts, and then get together. We don't learn it that way. Sometimes I'll just sing with the bass part, soprano and bass, just to see where those intervals lie and get those parts really tight. It's very time-consuming.

At first we used to record around one microphone, if you can imagine that.

Sure!

And if one person got a part wrong, we'd have to record it again! It was crazy. Now we usually do two mics, sometimes four, but we'll stand kind of in a circle so we can actually sing with each other and look at each other.

What about the theatrical elements? In the earlier days of the Manhattan Transfer, did you have somebody come in and create costumes and choreography for your performances?

Absolutely. We had someone else come in. Actually, from the very, very beginnings of the Manhattan Transfer, they were *very* theatrical. Tim Hauser's sister Fayette was in a group called the Cockettes, out of San Francisco, and they were wild! Just crazy. And she would dress the group like glitter rock, you know? It was that glitter era. So they started out singing "Tuxedo Junction" but coming out with glitter on their lips. They were nuts! That was part of the uniqueness of The Manhattan Transfer. Here was this group sounding like an old 1930s big band ensemble but looking *insane*. It was an interesting combination of visual and vocal.

When I came in, [choreographer] Toni Basil did a lot of our early stuff. She was the brains behind all that. She even helped design our look, the futuristic space suits that were kind of like futuristic tuxedos. We were looking in some magazines one day and she said, "*This* is your designer!" and it was Jean Paul Gaultier. So way before Madonna got him, we were in Paris crawling through his closets looking for crazy shoes and stuff. It was wild. He designed our space suits and a couple other things. He built some clothes for us that literally fell apart when we got onstage! It was early in his stage-costume career, shall we say.

Basil would even help us create and build sets, teach us movement for the stage. When we got to our album *Vocalise* and started doing more bebop and vocalise jazz, we kind of put the dancing away and decided to just concentrate on the singing.

I'm guessing that once you joined the Manhattan Transfer you discovered and were exposed to music you hadn't been familiar with before?
Oh, yeah, absolutely, absolutely. One of the first things they did was play Weather Report's "Birdland" for me, the Joe Zawinul composition, which was kind of a hit at the time, and it was on the radio. And Janis said, "We want to sing this." And I said, "Sing this? Are you crazy? Oh my God. That would be unbelievable." So that was my introduction to the idea of singing an instrumental piece. I'd heard [the vocal trio] Lambert, Hendricks and Ross of course; I'd heard Jon Hendricks, but I didn't really understand the bigger picture of what you could do with an instrumental piece, that you could really restructure it, write lyrics to it, and make it a singable song.

Do lyrics change over time for a singer? Do they resonate differently later in life, and as a result, do you sing them differently?
You're telling a story, you're a storyteller. It's an acting job in a way. When I choose a song, I have to be able to relate to something when I'm singing it. Otherwise, there's no place to go emotionally. My job is to grab my audience and take them with me, wherever that may be. It may be a different place for them.

And it does change over the years. A love song might be about someone 10 years ago and about someone else today. Or losing someone might be about losing a love or a loved one who has passed on.

When you choose Cole Porter or George Gershwin, it's really important to try and find something new in the songs because these songs have been sung so much. I don't necessarily take melodies anywhere else, especially with those two composers, because they wrote perfectly. Porter wrote melodically, chordally, lyrically perfect songs. You can't stay away from them!

I've written about the healing properties of music and breathing. I came across your recording *Blissongs*[70] after I had read about your battle with Hodgkin's lymphoma. Did music and breathing play a role in your treatment?

To be honest, not a lot. It was an eight-month period where I was off the road. That was the hardest part because I wasn't with my group and singing. I was home. I did a lot of meditation during that time. It was a time for me to be quiet.

But I truly believe what you're saying, that music is healing. I remember when my father had a stroke, many, many years ago, I was standing by his bed, and all I could think of to do was sing. So I would just sing into his ear. I think that's an absolutely beautiful response to someone who is ill.

When I was sitting in the doctor's office during chemotherapy, I wouldn't sing. I would meditate and hum, but I wasn't listening to music. In hindsight, if I had put my headphones on and listened to my own *Blissongs*, it probably would have aided in my body healing more. But you know, I put it out there for others to use in meditation and yoga. And people are using it.

I am a believer in this music as healing. And I couldn't wait to get back and start singing again with the group. But during the time I was at home I wasn't singing. I was just still.

One of the musicians I've interviewed [flutist Jan Leder] goes into hospices and health care facilities and plays for the residents and patients.

Wonderful. I'd love to do that. They say that music can trigger life back into the brain. Oliver Sacks and many other therapists believe that. Who knows? Maybe that's the next chapter in my life. I think the power of music is vast and beyond our present discoveries of what it can do.

From your perspective, are you seeing more women in the music industry and in the world of jazz? Not just singers and instrumentalists, but as managers, publicists, engineers, or label heads?

Interesting question. My knee-jerk reaction would be there are *fewer* people in the *entire* music industry. It's funneled down to a very small number who are carrying on the tradition.

When I was coming up, singers like Carmen McRae, Ella Fitzgerald, and Shirley Horn, they were alive and they were still vital. Now they're all gone. When I teach singing or when I work with a master class, or after a concert if there are kids hanging around and I talk to them, the first thing I ask is, "Who are you listening to?" And if they aren't going back and listening to the women and men who have come before, who are no longer on the planet, then I feel for these kids.

If a kid tells me he or she listens to Diana Krall, then I say okay, who did Diana Krall listen to? Who did Billie Holiday listen to? Who did Cassandra Wilson listen to? Okay, she's got a lot of Miles Davis. Okay, who did Miles listen to? Louis Armstrong, where did that come from?

I have a huge map of where it started, and where it's come to, and I'm telling you, my list has come down to, for me, about three or four singers. And it's funneled down from dozens. I don't mean to make this sound doom and gloom, but I don't see the message being relayed in a huge way. I see a very small percentage of singers who have a very big responsibility. I'm not saying that the singers that are out there aren't great. But it's slim pickings.

Granted, the Internet has opened up a whole new world, and thank God for that. Hopefully, the young singers today will go back. That's what the Internet is really good for. You can log on and discover Cassandra Wilson and then go all the way back to Ma Rainey, you know?

I guess one ray of hope here is that anyone curious enough can do just a little bit of research using the Internet and YouTube and discover a whole lot. It's almost easier to study an instrumentalist or a singer than when I was younger. It's right at your fingertips.

Sherrie Maricle

Growing up in the 1970s in Endicott, New York, drummer Sherrie Maricle saw several big bands in concert, including those led by Count Basie, Frank Sinatra, Stan Kenton, Mel Lewis, Woody Herman, and [drummer] Buddy Rich. Hearing Rich was her first encounter with jazz drumming.

"I really fell in love with the drums when a teacher took me to see Buddy Rich and his Killer Force Orchestra," says Maricle. "When I saw that band, I got so excited ... I ran home and told my mother I was going to play the drums—that I loved big band and I wanted to do that. And that's all I ever wanted to do since I was 11 years old."

Starting in the 1940s, Buddy Rich's big band was managed by legendary conductor, drummer, and manager Stanley Kay. Kay served as the band's relief drummer as well, a scary position to be in, considering Rich's virtuosic ferocity on the drums and reputation for being a tough taskmaster.

In 1992, Kay contacted Maricle about forming an all-woman big band. She was intrigued, especially since he made it clear he had no interest in dressing the musicians "in leather skirts and fishnet stockings." Before meeting Kay, Maricle had little interest in all-women musical projects, mainly because of the way they were traditionally marketed.

"You can see in the film *The Girls in the Band*," says Maricle, "that even if women were playing great, their cleavage, lipstick, hair, dresses, makeup, and high heels were more important than the music."

Together, Kay and Maricle founded the all-women big band The DIVA Jazz Orchestra, with Maricle as bandleader and drummer. Kay managed The DIVA Jazz Orchestra until his death in June 2010. In addition to The DIVA Jazz Orchestra, Maricle also leads the quintet FIVE PLAY and the DIVA Jazz Trio. The three all-women bands have released a total of 20 recordings, including The DIVA Jazz Orchestra's *A Swingin' Life* (2014), recorded live at Dizzy's Club Coca Cola in New York City, with guest vocalists Nancy Wilson and Marlena Shaw.

In the following interview, Maricle describes her musical journey, from listening to big bands in grade school, to becoming one of the most highly respected drummers, bandleaders, and educators in jazz. Her many awards include the 2009 Mary Lou Williams-Kennedy Center Lifetime Achievement Award, the Kennedy Center Alliance Award for Outstanding Achievements in the Arts, a Doctoral Fellowship from New York University, the 2006 New York City Music Educator's Award for Outstanding Contributions to Music Education, and New York University's "Music Teacher of the Year" in 1997 and 2000. Maricle completed a Master of Arts in Jazz Performance and Doctorate of Philosophy in Jazz Performance and Composition at New York University.

Sherrie Maricle. Photo by Bill Westmoreland.

Stanley Kay famously said, "Music has no gender. If you can play, you can play." All-women music projects like The DIVA Jazz Orchestra and recent documentaries like the aforementioned *The Girls in the Band* have affirmed Kay's statement, and Maricle's work as a drummer, bandleader, and educator continues to help frame this music as something other than a masculine-oriented art form.

When did you first begin playing a musical instrument?
I was in fourth grade, and I wanted to play the trumpet, but I was told that girls didn't play the trumpet, so the band teacher insisted that I play a metal clarinet, which I started playing, but I didn't like at all. And I know I didn't like the music teacher! I was attempting to quit and he called my house and begged me to stay in band. So I did, but I also started playing the cello, and I had a great teacher; his name was Ivan Briden. So I started those two instruments, clarinet and cello, at about the same time.

When I was in sixth grade, the band director needed an extra person to play the bass drum for a piece featuring a lot of percussion, so I volunteered, and that ignited my endless love for percussion.

Did percussion speak to you in a different way than the clarinet or the cello?
I always loved watching marching bands and drummers in a parade. But I really fell in love with the drums when a teacher took me to see [jazz drummer] Buddy Rich and his Killer Force Orchestra. When I saw that band, I got so excited. I'd never really heard any jazz before. I ran home and told my mother I was going to play the drums—that I loved big band and I wanted to do *that*. And that's all I ever wanted to do since I was 11 years old.

That's wonderful you got to see Buddy Rich at such a young age.
I was born in Buffalo, but the town I grew up in was Endicott, New York. It's in the middle of New York State on the southern border of Pennsylvania. Every "road" band traveled through town. I got to see Count Basie a number of times. Frank Sinatra came to town, also Buddy Rich, Stan Kenton, Mel Lewis, and Woody Herman. Road bands were still going strong in the 70s, and I saw all of them many times. It was a really great place to grow up!

Were your parents fans of this music?
My mom loved and loves Irish music and country music, so I grew up every single morning listening to Johnny Cash or the Clancy Brothers. But my parents were definitely not jazz people. So I wasn't really exposed to it until I was in school and had teachers and like-minded friends who were interested in jazz. That's when I really started to investigate the music is a serious manner.

Was the next step to ask Mom and Dad to buy a drum kit for you?
I did. I started out with a practice pad and shortly thereafter pleaded and begged my mom for a snare drum. She ended up at a local music store but she didn't really know what a snare drum was. Unfortunately the music store owner sold her a half-broken, 12-inch tom-tom instead of a snare drum. I was so grateful to her that I didn't have the heart to tell her it was the wrong drum. So I kept it and practiced on that for a while. Eventually Mom got me my first drum set ... gold sparkle ... to which I added my "original" broken tom-tom.

I'm sure my mother thought, "Oh, my daughter's crazy! What's happening here? There are no girl drummers. Maybe she'll grow out of this phase." But I give her a lot of credit for allowing me to [play drums] and spending her money that she didn't really have on a drum kit. My mother was and is so generous!

In high school, did you have any opportunities to start playing jazz drums?
Yes. The elementary, junior high, and high school music programs were all great in Endicott, New York. The teachers and my peers were into all kinds of music. We had two orchestras, a full chorus, a concert band, a 300-person

marching band, and jazz ensemble. It was great. High school is where I really started to play jazz seriously.

My friends and I used to have listening parties and continually begged our teachers for more records, CDs, cassettes, and 8-tracks, whatever we were listening to in the 70s. I really got into [jazz] and tried to absorb everything I could, and absolutely loved it.

And I knew that was going to be my life. I knew it since I was 11 years old.

How did your parents handle this drive you had to make music your career?
My mother definitely pleaded with me to study computers or a career that "you could make money in." She didn't know any musicians personally.

As soon as I got into college, I started working a lot. There were dozens of gigs. Every hotel had a lounge band; there were loads of wedding bands . . . there was a local professional jazz group in town that I eventually started playing with called Music Unlimited. We had about 20 concerts every summer. I also played in a big band and dance group called Swing Street. I was also blessed to play many of the traveling road shows that stopped in the area, from the circus to Broadway to Englebert Humperdink. A lot of variety.

I remember my first gig very well. I played with a band called Bob Grover and the Tune Twisters at the Eagles Club [the Fraternal Order of Eagles], which is like an Elks Lodge, and I got 50 bucks for doing something I absolutely loved. I couldn't believe it. I was so excited after the gig I ran out—I didn't even take the money—and the leader had to come to my house to give me the money the next day! [laughs] I couldn't believe I could get paid for doing something I loved so much.

Around this time, I think my mother started to feel a little more comfortable, like, "maybe it is possible. . . ."

Were you in a music conservatory?
No, but I did start at Ithaca College, which had Gordon Stout, one of the world's great virtuoso marimba players, on their faculty. It's a great college and a great town.

But I was only 16 when I went there, and I was much too young socially, and it was too expensive. So after one semester at Ithaca, I transferred to the State University of New York at Binghamton, now known as Binghamton University.

You had the benefit of diving into the world of professional gigging at a relatively early age.
I worked all the time with all these wedding bands. Every time a show came into town I played with the show. I played Ringling Brothers Circus, playing percussion, I played everything and I played all the time. I developed really good sight-reading skills.

I'm a huge advocate of making yourself diverse enough to make a living. I feel really fortunate to have had these experiences from my teenage years through my early 20s. It truly prepared me to be a "professional" in a competitive market like New York City.

The academic environment for performing is much different than the real world. No matter how good the school is, to be a professional requires more skills than you can learn in school, largely from experiences that schools can't or don't replicate.

When you're doing a drum clinic, working with younger musicians, is this something you encourage? That they get out of the school environment and play gigs? And is doing so crucial to learning how to play jazz?
In all academic environments, all you do is practice. You rehearse every day, or at least once or twice a week with a school band for a semester and then you do a performance, but it's nothing like a real situation.

For example, when I play with the New York Pops, we rehearse for two to three hours and then we play at Carnegie Hall. It doesn't matter what kind of music you're playing, when you are in that kind of professional situation, you have to bring all of your experience at once. In school, there's not a realistic replication of what happens professionally. There aren't many nurturing, patient, understanding teachers [band leaders] in the real world.

And it's not just the ability to sight-read. It's all the things that come from being a performer, how to behave onstage, knowing you have to take a particular gig because you have this 50-dollar electric bill you can't afford to pay unless you get paid. [laughs]

But with jazz, I wildly encourage students to get out and play live with other musicians. But there are much fewer jam sessions than there used to be. In New York City, you used to be able to go almost anywhere, any night, and sit in. But now there aren't that many places where you can do that. I used to go to the Blue Note every single night. I lived right up the street and every night they had a jam session after the last set till 4 a.m. I also ran a session at the Village Gate for eight years. I got to play with so many different players, with different abilities, playing in different styles ... talk about school!

One of my fantasies is to create a network of clubs across the country in different cities, a connected scene, where students can go and play in real-life environments with professionals. There are so few places students can do this.

Let's talk about the beginnings of The DIVA Jazz Orchestra. Were there some fundamentals that were already in place for you when the opportunity to create this big band came to you?
Prior to DIVA, my then boyfriend, a great musician named John Mastroianni,

and I had a big band, and we were both composers. One of the components you must have for concert jazz group is your own music. It doesn't have to be original music, but it has to be at least original arrangements. I think that's one of the keys to success as opposed to just forming a band to play Buddy Rich charts or Count Basie charts. Why would anyone want to do that? There are real "ghost" bands doing that, but I think it's important to have your own creative vision and sound.

DIVA wasn't my idea. In fact, in my life up until that point, I'd never really been interested in all-women projects. You can see in the film *The Girls in the Band* [Judy Chaikin's historical documentary about women jazz instrumentalists] that even if women were playing great, their cleavage, lipstick, hair, dresses, makeup, and high heels were more important than the music.

In 1990, I met a man named Stanley Kay while I was drumming at the Shubert Theater for their 75th anniversary celebration. Stanley was conducting for Maurice Hines, a great dancer and amazing entertainer. I knew Stan by reputation from his association with Buddy Rich. So after that gig, I introduced myself as the drummer and he said, "Oh, you played great for us! Thank you." I was thrilled, because he was Buddy's assistant drummer and manager. That was a nice compliment!

So I stayed in touch with Stan and in 1992 he contacted me about starting DIVA. He called me up and asked, "Do you know any other women who play as well as you?" [laughs] And I said, "I do." And I took this very seriously because he was so serious. He wasn't going to put us in leather skirts and fishnet stockings. All he cared about was music. He had a lot of connections in the music industry already, and this [big band] was his concept. He wanted to start a brand-new big band, in the tradition of the "greats" but he decided to use women.

We had the first audition for The DIVA Jazz Orchestra in June of 1992, where 40 women came; we picked the first 15 and started from there.

One of the things that helped us, besides the fact that we could really play and had a library of great originals and arrangements, is that we had Stanley Kay. His reputation of excellence preceded him, so our recognition came quickly, and our acceptance and acknowledgement, because of our talent, immediately followed.

So my advice for anyone starting a big band, besides finding a great manager and advisor, is to seek out an older musician who is credible and has a good reputation and can introduce you to people. Seek out people who have done what you want to do and ask them for help. You have to ask for help, because you will never get what you don't ask for!

Anyone will tell you, any club owner, concert hall manager, or promoter will tell you, if you send unsolicited material, unless they know you, it will most likely go in the garbage. You have to have someone believe in you (besides you) and introduce you. That's the first step.

How does DIVA rehearse? After playing a chart, does everybody take time to go over notes and problems that need to be addressed? And how do you direct a band while playing the drums?

My style of leading DIVA is loosely modeled after the late Mel Lewis Jazz Orchestra. Mel was one of my teachers, and one of the most influential drummers in my life. He encouraged his band to contribute their opinions. He told me he would always say what he wanted to say in the course of a rehearsal, but all the musicians had a voice; it was very democratic.

On the stage [in performance], sometimes I'll give spontaneous directions like, "One more chorus!" If you'd seen Buddy Rich, you may have seen him yelling at his band, screaming directions like that; it adds excitement. Sometimes it drives my band crazy and they make fun of me for "yelling." [laughs] But, if I didn't yell they couldn't hear me!

We only rehearse when we get new music or play a show, like with Nancy Wilson or Diane Schuur. Everyone in the band is a phenomenal sight-reader and stylistic interpreter.

What's the difference for you as a drummer from playing in a trio, or FIVE PLAY, versus playing in a big band? What are some fundamental differences that you have to be aware of and address as a drummer?

All three of my bands are stylistically similar. There all have structured arrangements. The responsibility of a drummer in a big band is to make the form of the tune really clear, to set up those different sections of the song and also to support and enhance all the musical elements occurring within a chart. Actually, one of my clinics is called, "How to punch, kick, hit, and make it feel good." That's what the drummer's job is, to make the band feel very comfortable. It's the same for all three of my groups.

The other thing a drummer does is support the soloist. With smaller groups, there's more time to develop solos than there is with a big band. In my big band, people aren't going to play 15 choruses. We want to feature the sound of the total band. Everyone in my band always solos on every concert, unless time is an issue. It's tedious for me to see a big band and one person is doing all the blowing. And I am blessed with 15 incredible musicians who all deserve to be heard!

But in FIVE PLAY and especially in the trio, as the groups get smaller, the individual musicians' style and personality has more time to come out and develop in the context of the tune. In smaller groups, drummers are required to be a bit more intuitive and willing to leave space for the soloists, while also assisting in musical development, style, energy, and excitement. I don't usually go roaring into the first chorus of a piano solo in my trio because there might be 10 choruses!

Mel Lewis used to say: "There's no difference to me between playing in a small band or a big band. I play the same way." To me there are definitely some differences like volume, but the concept in either setting is to serve the music and serve the musicians. You don't want it to sound or feel like a drum solo with band accompaniment, even if the drummer is the leader. The drummer should lift and support the band from the center, like a heartbeat!

Do you have to play louder in a big band than in a trio?
Oh, sure. Dynamics are definitely relative to the size and style of the ensemble as well as acoustics of the performance space.

Playing large outdoor festivals or at the Hollywood Bowl for an hour is different than playing in a trio in a little jazz club with no microphones. I often tell my students, "You have to practice the way that you're going to play." You really do! Lead trumpet players can't practice in the staff and then [in performance] expect to play a double "G." You have to practice the way you want to play. So if you're in a big band and know you're going to be playing a roaring-fast tempo at double forte or a super slow ballad at piano, you have to practice that way. You have to practice the way you're going to play on the gig. You can't just think, "Oh, I'll play it right on the gig" because you won't!

Are there particular things you look for in an arrangement for the DIVA Jazz Orchestra? Are there musical elements that you just _have_ to have in an arrangement for that particular band?
We want our arrangements to be really, really fresh. It doesn't matter if it's a new arrangement of a standard, which a lot of our library is, or something original. It has to be really swinging. It can be re-harmonized, it can have dissonances in it, but for me, it's gotta swing and make the listener and player tap their foot. I want the arrangements to be fun and challenging for the players. But I want the audience to hear it and say, "I recognize that!" or "Oh, that makes me feel good!" I want our music to make people feel happy.

A lot of jazz can be very challenging to listen to. Sometimes it is challenging for _me_ to listen to. [laughs] So I don't want DIVA's music to be an overly intellectual experience where our audience walks away scratching their heads, wondering if it was or wasn't jazz.

Music that always makes me happy, like the Ray Brown Trio, Jeff Hamilton Trio, Woody Herman, Count Basie, Ella, Mel Lewis, Buddy Rich, Oscar Peterson, are role models of swing for my band. Stanley and I were in total agreement in this regard. Our music must be fun and challenging for us and hopefully make the audience smile.

Jan Leder

When flutist Jan Leder was an undergrad at SUNY Purchase, majoring in "a combination of jazz, jazz history, and American history," and studying improvisation with pianist Lennie Tristano, she decided to write a thesis about women in jazz. The topic quickly proved to be much more challenging to research than she had anticipated.

"I did the research and looked for anything on the topic," says Leder, "and ... there was nothing! The history of women in jazz had been completely ignored."

Realizing the contributions of female instrumentalists to jazz had yet to be documented, Leder scrutinized the discographies of hundreds of jazz recordings for the names of the women who played on the recording sessions. Six years after she graduated, Leder's research was published as *Women in Jazz: A Discography of Instrumentalists 1913-1968* (Greenwood Press, 1985), the first comprehensive history of women jazz musicians.

Like many of the musicians interviewed in this book, including trumpeter Ellen Seeling, pianist Connie Crothers (who Leder studied with for 10 years and has performed with as well), and drummer Sherrie Maricle, Leder is willing to speak up and speak out against gender discrimination that exists at jazz festivals and in the hiring practices of big bands, orchestras, and college music

Jan Leder. Photo by Stephen L. Tyler

conservatories. Three decades after the publication of her book, Leder feels little has changed when it comes to acknowledging the participation of women in the development of jazz music.

"When I published [the] discography," says Leder, "I was hoping I was doing something that would quickly become obsolete. I just did it because it had to be done. Well, hello, it's how many years later? I feel I'm in more of a ghetto than ever as a woman instrumentalist."

However, Leder's passion for music has allowed her to carve out a unique career in jazz as a flutist, composer, and lyricist. Leder has led and performed as a member of several highly respected jazz ensembles, including the NY Jazz Flutet, Art Lillard's Heavenly Band, Chip Shelton's World Flute Orchestra, and the 9th Street Stompers. She is an award-winning composer, and appears with her quartet performing her original "Gaspe" in the film *Sidewalk Stories* (dir. Charles Lane), which premiered at the 1989 Cannes Film Festival. Vocalist Diane Hubka recorded Leder's song "Thinking of You" for her CD *Haven't We Met?* (1998), and Leder herself has released two CDs of originals and standards, *Passage to Freedom* (1997) and *Nonchalant* (2000).

Leder also enjoys a career as a music-wellness practitioner, performing music specifically programmed for individual senior residents of healthcare facilities. She has lectured about her work with seniors and led workshops to help other musicians find work playing in healthcare facilities. In this interview, Leder vividly describes how live music benefits the health of infirm and comatose patients.

"There's a big difference between putting ear buds in a person's ears versus playing live," says Leder. "When music is played live, a personal connection is made, and that connection is profound."

When did you first begin playing a musical instrument?
I was 3 years old. I played piano.

Did you end up taking formal piano lessons when you got older?
Yes. My mother was the neighborhood piano teacher, so I kind of had the piano lessons built in. Except that when I was practicing, she would hear me practice, and that wasn't necessarily a good thing. [laughs] In junior high, I switched from piano to flute. I didn't know what instrument I wanted to play in band, and my mom said, "Try the flute. It's easy to carry and you can always change it if you don't like it." So I have to give her credit for that!

You made a transition from playing classical flute to jazz. When did jazz come into your life?

Jan Leder (second from left). Central Park, NYC, 1975.

I was studying classical music and taking flute lessons while listening to popular music. I loved the Beatles, Motown music, and R&B. I had very little exposure to jazz, but I found myself wanting something other than the classical
music experience.

So I spent a lot of my early days, my teen years, out in Central Park and
Washington Square Park playing with guitarists, drummers, and other musicians. When I played with these musicians, I wasn't reading music, I was improvising, which is, of course, what jazz musicians do, but I was improvising
in the context of rock and roll.

After a few years of that, a friend of the family told me about [pianist]
Lennie Tristano. I was attending Purchase College, State University of New
York, and would travel from Purchase in Westchester to his studio in Jamaica,
Queens. I received credit for every semester I studied with Lennie, which was
really unusual.

So Tristano wasn't a member of the school's faculty?
No, he was an independent entity.

I had applied to several college music departments, and every last one of
them rejected me. But I was applying for classical music programs, and my
heart was no longer in it, so I wasn't really surprised I wasn't getting accepted,
and it didn't really bother me. But I got into Purchase and ended up getting
credit for studying jazz with Lennie. And that was really a beautiful thing.

It was the late Michael Hammond, who then was the Dean of Music at Purchase, who sponsored my studying with Lennie and got me credit for it. My major ended up being a combination of jazz, jazz history, and American history. And I guess you saw the discography?

Yes!

That discography, *Women in Jazz: A Discography of Instrumentalists, 1913-1968*, was my undergraduate thesis.

What was a lesson with Lennie Tristano like?

It was amazing. I was 17 years old when I first began studying with him and very impressionable. I didn't know what to expect. I didn't know much about jazz, but I did know that when I was playing music with other musicians in the parks, I was improvising, and I knew jazz musicians did that! [laughs] I was pretty evolved as an improviser when I got to Lennie; I just didn't have any library of music in my head. I hadn't listened to much jazz and I didn't know its history.

At my first lesson he said, "Go get some records. Listen to Louis Armstrong, Billie Holiday, Lester Young, Roy Eldridge, and Charlie Christian." He just gave me a very basic diet of jazz. I would sing, not play, with the masters, learning their solos from recordings and singing them note for note. I spent two years just doing Billie and Prez [Lester Young], just listening and singing with them every week.

When you sing music, you really absorb it. But how did singing help you play the flute?

When you sing the music, you get the music in your head and your ears. You can't sing it if you don't hear it in your mind's ear. Maybe you can write it, and maybe you can play it on your instrument, but if you can't sing it, you don't really know it.

Remember, Lennie was blind, so we didn't use scores or notation paper. We used our ears, and I think that gave me such an advantage. The singing and scatting was a way to develop my ear, hear the intervals, and learn the language of jazz.

When I play and write music, I'm not thinking about chords and changes and technical things. I'm following my ear. It's important to know and understand music theory, but the most essential thing in improvising is the ability to connect to and play what you hear. Ear training was truly one-third of what we did in these lessons.

Would he accompany you on piano?

Yes. Usually, each lesson began with me freely improvising on my own. Then I would play scales and chords, scat with recordings, and then Lennie and I would play free as a duo. So for three years, in every lesson, I created music with Lennie Tristano. That enriched me in a way I can't even put into words. Playing with Lennie would elevate me to the place where he was at in the music, so we could be in the music together as just two creative people. When we played together, we weren't student and teacher, we were two musicians playing music together.

But even so, I don't think I actually appreciated what a legend he was at the time. I was very young, I didn't know the history of jazz, and he was a little off the beaten path, a little obscure, so to speak.

Maybe that benefitted you, because you didn't come to your lessons with any unnecessary baggage?
Yes. Lennie had his own way of looking at the world. He was an extremely intelligent man with strong opinions and very set in his ways. But he thought things out. His opinions were not flippant. He was a pretty serious cat, but he was also sweet and loving to me.

I believe he was quite different with his female students than [with] his male students. Lennie had a paternal way about him. He was protective. He was fatherly, even grandfatherly, and I know not everybody saw that side of him! [laughs] I know this from stories and one experience of my own when I arrived an hour early to a lesson. He was in a bad mood and just sent me away. [laughs] Back into the snow and ice! But most of the time, he was so sweet. He took his teaching very seriously.

I wanted to talk with you about your thesis. What compelled you to create a discography of jazz recordings that included or featured women instrumentalists?
I had to do something for one of the shorter four-week terms—I was basically making up my own program—and Michael Hammond suggested I write a paper on women in jazz. So for four weeks I did the research and looked for anything on the topic and . . . there was nothing! The only things I found related to women in jazz were very sexist magazine covers with a lot of T and A everywhere. The history of women in jazz had been completely ignored.

I wanted to know about the women instrumentalists who came before me. I wondered, is there a place for me in this music? I know about the singers, but what about instrumentalists? At the time, I couldn't even name a female drummer or trumpet player, and there was something wrong with that.

Michael Hammond sponsored this project as my senior thesis. I pored through discographies for over a year, picking out women on recording sessions. It was the only way to find them!

I did a lot of the work on the discography at Rutgers, on campus. [DJ, historian, and producer] Phil Schaap was on the radio then. I first met Phil at the

West End Café where I used to play and he used to host the jam session. He looked at my book, and found four musicians' names that were actually men. That could have been embarrassing! My thesis was published in 1985, six years after I graduated.

I was very happy that I ended up with 250 women in the discography. Half of those women are piano players. A very small percentage are drummers and a large percentage are flutists, cellists, violinists, and harpists, all the "female" instruments, right? The flute is typically thought of as a very feminine instrument, along with the violin and the harp, and there are about eight women harpists in my book.

I'm very proud of the fact that I contributed to a brand-new field of study which has since become ... I mean, honestly, when I published this discography, I was hoping I was doing something that would quickly become obsolete. I just did it because it had to be done. Well, hello, it's how many years later? I feel I'm in more of a ghetto than ever as a woman instrumentalist.

Look at the Jazz at Lincoln Center Orchestra or the Westchester Jazz Orchestra. It annoys me that these institutions seem to basically be boys clubs where women are not welcome.

You play music in healthcare facilities. Is this a big part of your musical career right now?

Yes. It is the bulk of my career and provides the bulk of my income. This month I have 33 gigs; two are in restaurants, and the rest are in healthcare facilities. As a matter of fact, I think playing in healthcare facilities has saved me. All I ever wanted was to make a living playing music and this is what has made it possible. Perhaps if I had doubled on sax I would have worked more in the public eye, but that was a decision I had to live with.

I need to make the distinction between music therapy and music wellness. I'm not a music therapist. Music therapists are licensed. In these facilities, music therapy is a rehabilitation program that involves measurement of change in response over time. It necessarily involves response, measurement of the response, and measurement of the response over time. What I do requires nothing of my listener. I'm hired as an entertainer because the facilities are required by law to provide entertainment for the residents. I don't think the hospitals or the hospice where I work are required by law to provide entertainment, but I believe the nursing homes are.

But what I do goes so far beyond entertainment. With my music wellness programs, there is what I'd call a theory to it, and I take it very seriously.

I don't just go in there and play music. I play specific music. I play music that I call personally significant music. That's a term I coined. I noticed that when I played certain songs for certain people, there's a different response than if I had just played a randomly chosen song. If I play a song for a nursing home resident that was a part of his or her adolescence or early adult experience, there is noticeably a more significant and positive response.

I was once asked to rouse a woman who three medical professionals could not rouse. I was playing in a home for a small group of people, and they asked me to play for a woman who was unconscious; I believe she was in a coma. She was African-American, quite old, and I decided to play her a spiritual. I played the song and nothing happened. They asked me to play another one and while I played, she woke up, sat up straight, clapped in time with me and smiled. The medical professionals were quite surprised!

Wow!

That was when I realized that this was not about my flute or me. This was about the song and this woman's brain. I tapped into a region of her brain that needs to be looked at. Dr. Oliver Sacks has looked at this, but what I want to tell him is that I believe what makes the difference between waking a person or not waking a person is playing personally significant music. The song I played for the woman I described to you was significant. It was a song she probably heard in church when she was a teenager, during those formative years when the libido kicks in and we form our identity.

You know how you feel when you hear a song from your teenage years? We all feel it! We associate really, really good times with certain music. And when that music revisits us later in life, it reminds us of our health and our wellness. Even if it was your wedding song and you're divorced, or if you lost the person the song reminds you of, it doesn't make you sad. It makes you happy for some reason. We associate the joy and not the loss with the songs.

There's a big difference between putting ear buds in a person's ears versus playing live. When music is played live, a personal connection is made, and that connection is profound.

It's rough being a jazz musician in this world, especially in an age where jazz isn't even listened to by most people. But when I play jazz, I move people. It's like a ministry of sorts for me.

Diane Schuur

While editing the transcript of this interview with singer and pianist Diane Schuur, I was intrigued to see that our conversation began and ended with references to rain. We begin by discussing a recording Schuur made when she was just 10 years old of the standard tune "September in the Rain," which appears on her album *Some Other Time*. On that album, "September" is programmed as a coda to a selection of songs Schuur heard growing up and recorded as a tribute to her late mother. Blind from birth, Schuur was blessed with perfect pitch and a full, beautiful voice that belied her years. You can hear what I'm describing on that track, recorded at a Tacoma, Washington, Holiday Inn in 1964.

Like many female jazz musicians of her generation, Schuur's talent allowed her to begin a musical career at a very young age. As you'll read in the interview, she began playing piano at the age of 3 and "was singing even earlier than that." She hit the road immediately after high school, and has enjoyed a hugely successful career as an internationally loved vocalist, pianist, and ambassador for the art of big band performance. She recorded two Grammy Award-winning albums in the late 1980s, *Timeless* and *Diane Schuur and the Count Basie Orchestra*, both of which brought the big band sound into the mainstream, and are classics of the genre. The popularity of those records is all the more amazing given the fact that after World War II, big bands became less active in the U.S. as jazz transformed into music for listening while sitting, as opposed to dancing, and rock and roll emerged as the new sound of America's youth.

Schuur, known as "Deedles" to her friends, has also recorded plenty of music outside of jazz repertoire, including classic country, blues (most notably with guitarist B.B. King), and popular songs. Her most recent recording at the time of this writing is a tribute to two mentors who were also good friends, saxophonist Stan Getz and singer Frank Sinatra. Everything Schuur sings is blessed with her inimitable and engaging style.

I must admit, for reasons I can't explain, I was a little intimidated at the prospect of talking to Schuur. But Schuur's immediate enthusiasm for this project calmed my nerves and reaffirmed my belief that a book collection of interviews with women across the spectrum of jazz would be welcomed not just by fans of this music, but by the musicians who play it as well. As Schuur told me at the end of our first conversation for this book, "A book about women in jazz? That's pretty fucking cool!"

Diane Schuur. Photo by Lani Garfield.

I was just listening to the recording you made at the age of 10, singing "September in the Rain" [from the album *Some Other Time*]. Did you have any kind of formal voice lessons before that recording?
No. I had voice training afterward. I went to the University of Puget Sound when I was 11 years old. Puget Sound is in the Pacific Northwest. That recording was pre-training for sure!

So as a child, you just started singing by ear to produce the voice we hear on that recording?
Right.

You had such a big voice. Is that just a God-given thing?
I think for the most part it is. A person can get coaching if they choose to. I did when I was 11 years old. I'm actually getting some coaching now because the voice does change as one gets older. I don't have an old voice by any means, but placement has to be a little bit different than when you're a little younger.

Were you also playing the piano at an early age?
Oh, yeah. I started playing the piano at the age of 3, and I was singing even earlier than that.

You also attended the Washington State School for the Blind. Did that school provide formal music instruction for piano or your voice?
You're right about the piano part of it. I actually started taking piano lessons when I was 7 at the Washington State School for the Blind. I went to that school from age 4 and a half to age 10 and a half, and then I went to public school.

Were you listening to a lot of jazz at age 10 or 11?
Yes. That was the main focus. Dinah Washington in particular, Duke Ellington, George Shearing, and Nat King Cole, although I did get exposed to rock and roll, country music, and classical music as well. My mom really loved jazz, and I was exposed to it constantly.

You didn't attend college, is that correct?
Just the musical training that I got when I was 11, which was Puget Sound. But no, I did not go to college after high school.

So you headed out after high school to become a professional singer.
Well, I was a professional musician from the age of 10. I was working up until I graduated from high school. I would come home from the school every weekend and work different places professionally. Once I graduated from high school I worked a lot in the Northwest. In the late 1970s, I started working in the Southwest; I moved to Tucson, Arizona, for a few years, then came back to the Northwest.

Was your family supportive of your career? Did they understand that you had this incredible talent and could make a living as a musician?
Oh, absolutely! They took me to the Holiday Inn, where I did that recording you mentioned of "September in the Rain" when I was 10. They took me to a lot of other places subsequent to that. I was, I guess, the star of the family, and helped to bring extra money into the household.

At some point, you must have started learning about the business of music, how to make sure you get paid what you're supposed to get paid for a gig or how to negotiate a contract.

Oh, yeah.

When did you have to start taking control of the business side of making music?
My father took care of the business up to a certain point, and then I went ahead and took control. I didn't have what you would call a formal manager with a contract until the beginning of 1985. That's when I met my first manager, Paul Cantor, who managed me for 17 and a half years. He was there for the height of my career with the Grammy awards and my appearances on *American Bandstand*, *Solid Gold*, and *The Tonight Show* with Johnny Carson 11 times and once with Jay Leno. He's [Paul Cantor] still alive today. He took the helm back then, and that's when a lot of things happened.

Before that time period, before you had a manager, was there a sense of camaraderie among you and the musicians you were performing with? A feeling that we're all musicians, we're all in the same boat, and we need to look out for each other?
There was camaraderie. I think I felt it most with the Count Basie Orchestra. Freddie Green, who was the guitarist with the orchestra, looked after me and kind of protected me in a way, and that was really cool.

Did you have any kind of mentorship early on in your career?
George Shearing was a mentor when I was growing up, and later on, Stan Getz. There's a man that I worked with named Overton Berry, who was a wonderful mentor. He's a pianist in the Seattle area.

Berry didn't instruct me on piano. He took me around to various places around the North and Southwest and started introducing me. In 1975, I did the Monterey Jazz Festival and then a gig with his group at an art gallery the day after. And then we just worked together pretty regularly until 1981 or '82. Berry was one of my biggest mentors, not only on the musical front but on a very spiritual front as well. Just a very wise individual and a great guy. I can't say enough about him.

Ray Charles once said: "When you're blind, you become a soul reader. Everything a person says is a soul note. It comes straight outta their soul, so you read a person immediately." Does this statement resonate with you?
Oh, absolutely! Absolutely it does. I couldn't agree more with what Brother Ray said, because it's the truth. I think that's what led me through all of the personal experiences that I went through, that ability to "soul read" people.

Not only musically and personally, but in business as well?
Yes, it's all interconnected. That's my own belief. Maybe other people don't share that, but it's absolutely my own belief.

We talked about you singing songs at the age of 10, as well as singing songs years later in the 1980s with the Count Basie Orchestra. Over time, do the meaning of song lyrics change for you?

I think they do. With life experience, with love experience . . . of course I still had the feeling and everything when I was 10 and singing "September in the Rain." I did another version of that song on the 1993 album *Love Songs*, a completely different version—a ballad! [laughs] But yes, over time, certain songs will resonate with me on a deeper level.

Do you teach or do clinics with singers?

I have at different times. Sometimes when I do college gigs I'm asked to do clinics with singers, and it's a lot of fun. I really get a lot of fulfillment out of doing them.

Do you talk specifically about lyrics with singers and instrumentalists?

No, not so much the lyrics, just more or less the approach to singing. Which is really interesting, because I'm older. I'm going to be 60 this year [2013] and I don't mind saying so. The relation between my age and my voice has changed. In the next couple of weeks, I'm actually going to have a session with a voice coach, because my voice has changed a little bit, and I have to work on placement now. Age has definitely changed that placement. My voice is different than it was in younger years. When I listen to albums like *Love Songs* or *The Count Basie Orchestra*, my voice is just different than it is now. So I'm going to be working on some of those elements.

As a singer, you are your instrument.

Absolutely.

Do you have some favorite big band arrangers or composers?

Billy May is great. Bob Florence, who arranged some of the Basie charts. Patrick Williams. Those are just three that I can think of off the top of my head.

What makes for a great arrangement for a singer and a big band?

They've got to be good at call and response. And they also, of course, have to be able to read and write music really well.

And an arrangement needs to leave room for the singer.

Well, let's hope so! You can't just be up there with egg on your face.

There has to be technique on both sides, both with the singer and the arranger, or the arrangement isn't going to be able to stand the test of time. Technique has to be involved along with intuition of what a singer would want. There needs to be subtlety, the build-up of a song, the crescendo of a song, and so on. It's all got to flow.

In performance, does the form of a chart change?

No. With a big band, it's got to be pretty structured, because there are so many instruments. It pretty much has to stay as written. It's a little bit more flexible in a small ensemble, like a trio.

Are there more women in the world of jazz these days? Not just as singers or instrumentalists, but as managers, publicists, or recording engineers?

I have a woman manager now for the first time, and that's kind of cool. She managed Diana Krall and Jane Monheit. I haven't met up with a female recording engineer yet. But there are women working at different venues doing sound production. I guess there probably are more women in jazz. There's more open mindedness about that sort of thing.

You've got Sherrie Maricle's DIVA Jazz Orchestra of course!

Absolutely! And I've been working with them for decades.

What's it like singing with The DIVA Jazz Orchestra?

Working with DIVA is fabulous because there's that woman energy. They're all just great players, all fabulous musicians. I just love working with them.

What is "woman" energy? Is there something different happening when it's all women playing the music?

Men are cool too. Don't get me wrong, okay? [laughs] It's just that ... how can I explain it? I guess musically, I get into the "soul reader" thing with these gals, on a professional kind of level. It's just really special, very magical.

What do you think of shows like *American Idol* and *The Voice* and the culture of competitive singing?

I don't like it. These shows demean people. I didn't grow up with that kind of competition, I wasn't subjected to it. I just don't take an interest in that kind of stuff. I'm just not into it. [laughs] But that's just my opinion. I don't want to dissuade anybody from watching whatever they want to watch.

If you approach music as if it were a sporting event, you're not going to be doing it for very long, because you're going to make mistakes.

Right. And that's what these shows really focus on. They just glom onto that. In front of millions of people that's got to be horrible, as far as the pressure is concerned. People need kindness and encouragement if they're going to pursue their dream, not cruelty and negativity about what they're *not* doing.

Have you been blessed with that kindness and encouragement in your career?

I would say so. I have been blessed with kindness and encouragement from a lot of different people.

How has the recording industry changed for you over the years?
The industry has certainly changed in the past 20 years. Because of the Internet and downloading, CDs are now more of a promotional tool than something you can pick up at the store.

My last album, the *Diane Schuur Live* CD, wasn't produced on a record label at all. We just recorded it live at one of our gigs and there you go. I went ahead and invested my own money in that recording, which is so different than having a record company spend a bunch of money and then the artist has to recoup that cost. I did that for years with GRP Records and so on.

When I talk to jazz educators, many express a concern that what they're doing is teaching young people to be great musicians, but that there are no jobs for those musicians once they graduate.
It's not as easy. They've got a point. I don't think it's ever really been easy in the jazz realm, unless you're a George Benson or Al Jarreau, who each had some crossover hits in the 80s. But I don't think in this day and age in jazz there could be a crossover hit. You know what I'm saying?

Sure. The Manhattan Transfer also had a couple of big crossover hits in the 80s. But despite there being so much music out there now, that kind of crossover doesn't seem to be happening.
Even in country music there's not the kind of crossover that there used to be in the 1960s and 70s. Which is one of the reasons why I decided to do a country CD, [*The Gathering*], which had a little bit of interest. I'm hoping at some point we can actually re-release it and see if anything can develop from that. But it's just a completely different time. It's totally different.

Record companies are just not supportive. It's just not the same thing. I hope I'm not being too much of a downer on this. I'm still looking for a label. I'm hoping that with the material I'm doing now that we can find a label and do a studio thing without having to spend a huge amount of money.

Some innovative young musicians have started their own labels.
I think it's great that young musicians are able to book themselves and all of that, but I need a manager and I need a booking agency to help me out. I can't do it all myself. That's just me.

I think that's the case with a lot of musicians. If you're not contained to one region in the U.S. and you want to book outside of that, you need a booking manager.
Absolutely. If it's going to be an international kind of an experience, without the right machinery behind the artist, touring is just not as effective. And I really speak from experience about this. To have a manager do booking may be

effective for a while, but it doesn't really last. I found I needed both management and a good booking agency to help me.

And I'll be blunt about this: careers go through cycles no matter who it is. Take for example Tony Bennett. He was going through kind of like a "cool" cycle, and then all of a sudden, there it is.[71] I myself am endeavoring to hit the reset button on some levels. I have been going through a kind of "cool" period in my career. I never stopped working, but we're just trying to rev things up.

They do love jazz in Europe and Japan. I just finished a performance in China. Since I'm a Grammy Award winner, I was asked to perform with several other Grammy winners, including Leo Sayer and Richard Marx, on a concert in Chengdu, Sichuan Province. And the audience, 40,000 people, just went crazy, even in the pouring rain. In fact, I was singing "Deedles Blues," and as soon as I sang the lyric, "*I met him on the corner / it was pouring rain,*" it started pouring rain! [laughs] It was pretty funny.

I look at the musical landscape now, and it seems that a lot of stuff is still shaking itself out.
It is. I'm glad to be a part of it.

Like Duke Ellington said: "I am an optimist!"[72]
Well, I am too! As long as I'm healthy and all of that kind of stuff, I'm gonna keep on doing it!

Pamela York

Canadian-born pianist Pamela York is one of Houston's most active jazz pianists, and performs regularly with her own groups as well as many of the city's leading musicians. York can be heard in venues such as Houston's Cezanne, as well as on festivals outside of Texas, performing standards, originals, and unique, groove-centric arrangements of hymns and spirituals. She was an early supporter of this project, and even agreed to be filmed playing piano for a video made to help promote the book in its early stages.

Like many of the musicians in this book, York initially started off studying to be a classical pianist, studying counterpoint, harmony, and music history while learning to play repertoire that included the music of several contemporary Canadian composers. However, in high school, she began to shift her focus to listening to and playing jazz.

"My band director ... was a bass player," says York. "He had taught [pianist] Diana Krall and [trumpet player] Ingrid Jensen. Both Diana and Ingrid had attended my high school, so there was already an expectation that if you were going to be in band, you needed to practice." [laughs]

And practice she did, pushing herself throughout her high school and college years to develop a feel for the blues, for swing, and extend her then angular, improvised motifs into longer, more lyrical phrases. Like Houston-born pianist and bandleader Helen Sung, who also began as a serious student of classical piano, York has tremendous respect and reverence for this music, and wanted to hear in her own playing what she heard in the playing of the pianists she so admired.

Says York, "I thought, if I'm going to do this, if I'm going to play jazz, I'm not going to fool around. I'm really going to study the masters of this music: Red Garland, Wynton Kelly, Oscar Peterson, Herbie Hancock, and Chick Corea. I focused on players who had a great rhythmic feel. . . . I really tried to dig into soulful piano playing."

York's debut album, *Blue York* (2001), is a trio set with bassist John Clayton and drummer Jeff Hamilton mixing standards, York's originals, and a reharmonized arrangement of the Christian hymn "What Wondrous Love Is This." She relocated to Houston in 2001, and released her second album *The Way of Time* in 2006, which includes her vocals on two tracks. In 2012, York released her critically acclaimed CD *Lay Down This World: Hymns And Spirituals*, a provocative set of arrangements of songs more typically heard and sung in church. Leading a trio of Houston musicians (Lynn Seaton on bass and Sebastian Whittaker on drums, with trombonist Andre Hayward guesting on two

Pamela York. Photo by Shannon Mucha.

tracks), the resulting music is not only a joy to listen to, but illuminates the transcendence musicians experience when they are playing music.

"I wasn't raised in any particular denomination or anything," says York. "But music stirred up something in me . . . I do feel that music satisfies me in a way that is hard to describe to people who aren't touched by music. In many different ways, it's more than just the notes."

When did you first begin playing a musical instrument?
I started lessons when I was 8. Before that, I had been just kind of playing around on a piano at my grandmother's house. One day, my parents surprised me. I came home and there was a piano in our house. They asked me, "Would you like to take lessons?" and I really wanted to.

Before that, I remember we had neighbors who had a piano. My brother and I would go over there—I was 4 and he was 2—and we would just sit at their piano. That's one of my earliest memories of the instrument.

Before you started taking lessons, did your parents perhaps hear something special when you were playing a piano?

I think maybe they did. When I was at my grandmother's house I would open up some of the music books she had and teach myself some things. My aunt, who plays a lot—she can read but she plays a lot by ear—told my parents, "Hey, if she figured that stuff out herself, maybe she should take lessons."

Where did you grow up?

I grew up on Nanaimo, British Columbia, which is on Vancouver Island.

What kind of music were you playing in these early lessons?

Once I knew the basic notes of the piano, my teachers gave me simple pieces by Bartok and Kabalevsky to play, so at an early age I was exposed to a lot of different kinds of music. Piano teachers in Canada often give you compositions by Canadian composers to learn, so that's nice. Sometimes you're required to perform repertoire by Canadian composers on your piano exam.

So you were playing repertoire by Canadian composers that was written specifically for students?

Yes. The composers wrote both complex and simple pieces.

Have you heard of the Royal Conservatory of Music in Toronto? Its musical curriculum is pretty much the national standard for Canada. When I was a kid, their examiners would come out to Nanaimo every six months or so, and I would take a piano exam. Once you were studying theory and counterpoint and harmony and history, you would take those exams too. It was and still is a very thorough system.

The examiners heard students in grades 1 through 10. You had to prepare for these exams just like you would prepare for a recital. Over the years, as you continued your private studies, you could take a performer's exam or a teacher's exam and eventually get an associate's degree from the Royal Conservatory.

So you had music education at a young age in your school.

Before college, my music education was formed through private lessons and playing in the high school jazz ensemble.

When did jazz come into your musical world?

In high school. My band director, Bryan Stovell, was a bass player. He had taught [pianist] Diana Krall and [trumpet player] Ingrid Jensen. Both Diana and Ingrid had attended my high school, so there was already an expectation that if you were going to be in band, you needed to practice. [laughs]

When I was 15, Diana came to our high school and showed me some ii-V-I chord progressions. I took lessons from her whenever she visited town to see her parents. She kind of got me started, told me who to listen to, taught me the importance of the blues, the importance of learning melodies, just basic stuff.

Were you listening to jazz before you met Diana?
A little bit. I had heard of [pianist] Oscar Peterson, who was a Canadian, and I knew about Bill Evans, but that was about it. Diana told me to listen to the Miles Davis Quintet and his pianists, Wynton Kelly and Red Garland. She also told me about lesser-known pianists who I'd never heard of, but were world class.

So you had a woman for a role model. I don't know if you thought about it in those terms?
I didn't!

So you didn't think a woman playing jazz was unusual?
At the time, I didn't really think about it. I was just really interested in playing music in school. My band director encouraged me. When Ingrid was in high school, I saw her up there playing the trumpet, but it didn't really occur to me that jazz was something . . . different.

Like a boys club?
Yeah. Exactly. I mean, I *was* kind of the only girl in the combo, and there were only a few women in the big band. But it wasn't like I thought that jazz was a man's world or anything like that.

Did you continue studying music in college?
Yes. Right after high school I got a full-tuition scholarship to what is now [called] Vancouver Island University. Back then it was a community college called Malaspina College and offered a two-year jazz associate's degree.

I went there for two years and played all kinds of gigs. I accompanied ballet dance classes—I never had a "regular" or "normal" job. I was able to save up money and attend my third year at the Berklee College of Music.

At Berklee, I was a performance major and studied jazz piano. I did take some arranging classes, but my one regret is that I did not fully pursue more arranging and composition skills. I was just really trying to be a jazz pianist. Lock myself in the practice room!

Saxophonist Mindi Abair, whom I've interviewed for this project, also attended Berklee.
She was there when I was. I think we had a class together.

She talked about playing in an ensemble that was dedicated to the music of Wayne Shorter, another that was all Joe Henderson. . . .

Yes! I played in the [Thelonious] Monk ensemble and the [John] Scofield ensemble, which was way out of my element, but it stretched me in many ways.

Did they have you play an electric piano?
They did. [laughs] I was really a fish out of water in that ensemble, but it was really good for me to learn some different tunes.

Were you ever anxious to get out of Berklee and just go and gig?
Because I had gone to the community college first, I was only at Berklee for five semesters, so that didn't seem like a long time for me. I can imagine that if I had attended for a full four years I would have been impatient to get out and go play. But it all went by pretty quickly for me.

And I did play out, though not as much as I could have. I did take some gigs, sometimes private parties, hotel gigs … I kept a good balance between school and playing out.

Did you know what you wanted to do once you had graduated college?
I was actually teaching toward the end. For about six months after graduating, I taught piano at a community school in Medford, which is a little ways out of Cambridge, and played some gigs. I was considering a master's degree, and applied to the New England Conservatory of Music. I got in, and got a pretty good scholarship, but at the time, the Canadian dollar was about 80 cents to the American dollar, and I just didn't want to be that deep into debt.

Another place I applied to was the University of Tennessee, Knoxville, because jazz educator Jerry Coker was there as well as pianist Donald Brown. Brown had played with Art Blakely and the Jazz Messengers. I had heard him in Boston—he used to teach at Berklee. I applied, got in, and about three weeks before the start of school, I got a call and found out I was the second choice for a graduate teaching assistant position. The first choice had taken a gig with one of the ghost bands, the Glenn Miller Orchestra or something like that. They said they wanted me to come, my tuition would be paid, and I would be studying with Donald.

I wasn't too thrilled about living in Knoxville, but I figured I could always move somewhere bigger afterwards. So I went there for two years.

Once you got to Knoxville, were there specific aspects of your playing that you wanted to focus on and develop further?
Having been classically trained, I wanted to be validated as a blues player and to have a really strong feel for swing. A lot of jazz players grow up playing in church or with some background in gospel, and that comes across in their playing, but I didn't grow up with that type of background. So I thought, if I'm going to do this, if I'm going to play jazz, I'm not going to fool around. I'm re-

ally going to study the masters of this music: Red Garland, Wynton Kelly, Oscar Peterson, Herbie Hancock, and Chick Corea. I focused on players who had a great rhythmic feel. I didn't want people to hear me play and think, "She's got a lot of technique but no feel." I really tried to dig into soulful piano playing.

How do you learn to swing? I guess you "get it" after a whole lot of practicing?
Yeah! And we all have our strengths and weaknesses, right? But that doesn't mean you can't "get it," whatever it is.

When I was at Berklee, I listened to a whole lot of Thelonious Monk. When I got to study with Donald Brown at Knoxville, I had a lot of quirky, angular stuff in my playing, that flavor of Monk, but I was lacking the longer lines and in how I was comping. Jerry Coker and Donald Brown really had me work on that, getting those longer lines and solidifying my ideas when I was improvising. A lot of people thought it was cool that I played a lot of short phrases. But I really had to work on not playing so many short ideas, and instead lengthen my phrases.

Musicians are always working on something. . . .
We're never "there," right?

What brought you to Texas?
I met my husband in Tennessee. We moved out to California so he could go to Westminster Theological Seminary, which is near San Diego. We were there for five years. His first job out of the seminary was in Texas, and we've been here ever since. He's a pastor at Providence Presbyterian Church in Kingwood.

Most people when they see me playing in a club think, "Your husband is a minister. Shouldn't you be in bed? You gotta get up early for Sunday morning service!"

The church isn't very far from jazz!
Right!

And you've recorded an entire album of hymns and spirituals titled *Lay Down This World.*
I didn't grow up in a religious home, but I got involved in a local church in high school, because the pastor's sons were in the band. In the summer, we'd play jazz for the morning services. At Berklee, I got involved with the Berklee Christian Fellowship, and had a lot of Christian friends. When I met my husband, I got into the whole world of hymns, which I hadn't grown up with.

I wasn't raised in any particular denomination or anything. But music stirred up something in me . . . you feel like, "Wow, there's something greater than me out there."

A lot of jazz musicians will tell you they're coming out of the church, that they heard their grandmother play the organ, they had it from a really early age. Not so with me. But I do feel that music satisfies me in a way that is hard to describe to people who aren't touched by music. In many different ways, it's more than just the notes.

I even find that when I practice and have had a satisfying practice session at the piano, I feel very fulfilled and actually am a better and nicer mother to my children. [laughs] It is that important to me to have that outlet. If I don't play, I'm more of a frustrated person.

In this day and age, between the Internet and so much piracy, why record an album?
To make a statement of where you are. I guess I'm a little old school. I still like to hear songs all the way through, in order, on a CD or whatever. That kind of satisfies me. But these days, the CD tends to be something like a souvenir that people can buy and take home after a live performance. I would say the crowd 40 years old and above still buys CDs. It used to be, even five or six years ago, many, many times, I'd make more money selling CDs compared to the artist's fee at a jazz festival.

What's it like being a jazz musician in Houston? I do wish there were more venues for just listening to music, not just a lot of restaurants with jazz in the background.
There's something about a venue that needs to be established over time. You can play a gig at Cezanne's and fill the room. But then, you play someplace else, and those same people don't show up. Other places have come and gone in Houston, and I think that's because they tried to do too much too soon. They tried to have music four or five nights a week right off the bat. You need to build a following.

It's great that there is live music in the local restaurants, but compared to a listening room like Cezanne's, it's not the same experience for the listener or the performer. I find that people who are used to quieter listening situations, they get frustrated and start shushing people.

Do you tour?
I used to go out of town a lot more than I do now. But I've got two kids now, and I've been so busy, I haven't pursued a lot of things. I'd like to return to some of the venues and festivals I've played before with the new recording.

I don't know if you've talked to many women for this book who are mothers, but having children is an added challenge to a career. It's pretty difficult. When I'm at a gig, I always say, this is the easiest part of my day. Or if I'm going through an airport and traveling by myself ... for a lot of musicians, that burns them out. But for me, I feel like I'm on vacation, because it's a lot of work at home.

I'm definitely on a slower track. [Bassist] John Clayton told me once: "You're going to have to have your own blueprint, because there's no blueprint for you to do this and *this*. You're just going to have to create your own career."

At music conservatories, they do push a certain blueprint. But music is so individualistic, and the path each musician travels is unique.
Music is not like other university programs, where you get your MBA and you do *this*. Or, you get your engineering degree and you go interview for a job. It's just not that clear.

At times, when I've been at home, up late with an infant, I think about my single girlfriends and they're doing this or that and things are moving quickly, and I just have to take a step back and remind myself, "It's okay. It'll be there."

Jacqui Naylor

In performance, some singers approach songs, especially jazz standards, as if the music and lyrics had been removed from a dusty, antique China cabinet, with "handle with care" stamped on each page. The very thought of incorporating any non-jazz musical elements into the performance of beloved songs such as "My Funny Valentine" or "Skylark" is sacrilege in some circles, although it may only be the most uptight of musicians and critics who find such hybrids disquieting.

When it comes to interpreting both classic and contemporary repertoire, singer Jacqui Naylor definitely ignores any warning of "handle with care." Which is not to say she is insensitive or irreverent; she holds the art of songwriting and song interpretation in the highest regard, but she's not afraid to challenge our preconceptions of the medium. How so? Check out Naylor's version of the aforementioned 1937 Richard Rodgers and Lorenz Hart composition, "My Funny Valentine," on her album *You Don't Know Jacq* (2008). The track begins with a lengthy and dramatic violin solo, with a distinct Romani (Gypsy) air. The arrangement then abruptly shifts to a steady, metal-like groove for drums, piano, bass and violin, calling to mind the music of . . . AC/DC? Yep.

Jacqui Naylor. Photo by Oliver Heinemann.

That's the groove and chords of the Australian band's shriekfest of a song, "Back in Black," with Hart's beloved body-shaming lyric on top. ("*Your looks are laughable / Un-photographable ...*") Naylor's singing on this track has a bold, yet cool, almost menacing quality.

"When I mash up two different songs," says Naylor, "I look for songs that work together organically, musically.... Mashing up songs gives me a way of reinventing songs in a way that hasn't been done before. I can sing a beautifully written song in a new way and hopefully bring different age groups and fans of different kinds of music together."

With her husband and co-arranger Art Khu, who also plays piano, organ, and guitar, Naylor has recorded a repertoire of songs that date back more than 80 years. On her critically acclaimed live recording *Dead Divas Society*, Naylor pays tribute to "departed, yet still spirited" singers who have influenced her as a vocalist and songwriter, including Ella Fitzgerald, Billie Holiday, and Peggy Lee, as well as Amy Winehouse and Freddie Mercury.

"I wanted to honor these singers and make the songs my own ..." says Naylor, "doing what we do as a band, mixing different genres and putting our own spin on things, and ultimately, give and record a great performance in a live setting."

Naylor and Khu's mixing or mashing up of genres reveals surprising connections between different decades of American songwriting. Their unique approach is also helping to redefine what it means to be a jazz singer in the 21st century. To that end, like any great artist, Naylor is not interested in imitating other singers, or treating jazz as if it were a museum piece.

"I don't feel like I'd be good at being anybody else," says Naylor. "I've never felt competitive with other singers. I spend time learning how to be the best 'me' that I can be."

....

When it comes to booking your tours, here in the U.S. or overseas, do you do the booking yourself? Or do you work with a tour manager?
When it comes to booking a show, if I'm not actually working with an agent, then it's usually on me. I don't mind that so much because my background is in marketing and advertising. I'm able to put on that other hat when I need to. I would prefer to just sing, but it doesn't always work out that way!

Early in my career, I was with William Morris for a time and worked with a couple of different agents. In my experience, agents are very good at the big things, but not necessarily with the small things. Some very big things happened as a result of working with these agents, which was great. But I still survive by performing in jazz clubs. In each city we play, there is usually just one club, maybe two, where the premier touring acts come through and play, and these clubs are usually not giant rooms. We play the Blue Note quite regularly, and that holds only around 250 people.

So, unless you're playing a whole week or more at a club, one night or two might not be enough for an agent to sink their teeth into. Agents can be good at getting me gigs at some festivals and performing arts centers, but my main clients or venues are places like the Blue Note, Yoshi's, Jazz Alley, and other, similar clubs I've worked with over the years.

Many of the musicians I've interviewed for this book take care of some if not all of the business-related aspects of their career. Is that something you just learn as a result of recording and releasing an album and then trying to find gigs? How do you learn how to do all of this?
I think a lot of people just learn by doing it, but I came at it in a different way. I came to music a little later in my life. I had a business degree and was already working as a marketing person for a clothing designer. Running a record label is no different than running a business. I take care of the musicians I employ and make sure when we're on the road that they are happy and cared for, just like one would take care of employees in any other business.

I just look at all of this like a business, and that helps me maintain a kind of balance. I've never done this because I wanted to be hugely famous or rich. I just want to make good music and share it with people. If something happens where I become hugely famous and rich, great. But the large label model never tempted me. Some labels approached me in the past, but the deals they offered were never good enough, especially in terms of the marketing. Unless they're going to throw a whole lot of marketing dollars at you, a major-label deal is nothing more than a poor loan.

My advice to a musician just starting out is to never stop honing your craft. Make this something you can enjoy and sustain so you can do it for a long time, so you don't injure yourself if you're a singer, and you're always becoming an even better singer, a better bandleader, and hopefully, a better human being. When it comes to the business, get help when you need it, but understand the pieces. Whether you're hiring someone as a consultant or agent or doing it yourself, understand the different aspects of the business of making music.

Did moving from your career in marketing to music require a leap of faith? Was it a scary decision to make?
It was scary, but I was lucky to have support and encouragement from my family. That was helpful.

At the time, I had been singing, but I hadn't made any records. I was gigging, but I was doing everything on the side. I went to New York to run a showroom we had there. I was there for about a year, and I enjoyed it, but I was working long hours and didn't have much time for my music. So when I came back to San Francisco, I made the decision that I was just going to do music. That I was going to make a record and really try and do this. And it worked out! [laughs]

I always loved to sing, but I wasn't raised to think that singing could be a career. I have to give credit to my main voice teacher here, Faith Winthrop. She taught a lot of great singers, and I had been going to her and studying on the side. She's the one who told me, "You know, I think you're a singer." I replied, "What? Do you mean like for a living?" And she said, "Yes!" This was maybe two or three years before I decided to leave my job and become a full-time musician. What she said, and my inclination to keep studying and keep getting better, gave me the confidence to make that leap.

I'm almost sorry I used the term "leap of faith" because I think it assigns art and music to a category of risk. But any change of career is a "leap of faith" if you're transitioning into something that speaks to your potential as a person.
I have a lot of determination in my being. That doesn't mean I don't have doubts, but I feel I have more determination than doubt. I have tools within me to overcome the obstacles I encounter. I'm not saying I'm looking for a career or a life without obstacles. What's more important is that I have what I need to overcome those obstacles.

There are certain things I want to accomplish as a human being in my life, and at this juncture, I'm glad I can use my voice to do some of those things, to express myself and give something to people. But if I couldn't sing tomorrow, I would still apply that same sense of determination and love and hope for life to whatever I did instead. And that influences not only the music I choose to sing and write and the way I perform, but what I am able to accomplish as a businessperson. Music and business may be separate in how I allot my day or week, but they're not separate in terms of me as a person. Does that make sense?

Yes, it does. The work I do outside of music, be it writing or editing, feeds what I do musically as well. Experiences I've had at work have helped me in situations where I'm composing, producing, or performing music.
Music is a conversation. It's like you and I talking today: we are having a conversation and bringing all of who we are to the conversation. We do the same thing when making music.

I've heard many jazz singers arrange and sing songs from the indie or alternative rock world in pretty unimaginative ways. But you sing songs from that world, such as R.E.M.'s "Losing My Religion" and "Once in a Lifetime" by the Talking Heads, and combine elements from completely different

songs into the arrangements. Did any of your vocal instructors encourage this experimentation? Exploring the repertoire outside of jazz?

No. [laughs] But I wouldn't say they discouraged me from doing it.

This kind of came later. A big piece of what I do when I perform these arrangements, say "Once in a Lifetime," with the bass line from the Joe Zawinul composition "Birdland," is something that was instilled in me by my teacher, and that is to sing the song as it was written. Even though I may be singing "My Funny Valentine" over AC/DC's "Back in Black," I'm singing the lyrics *and* the melody as it was written. And I think that's why the jazz community has not completely ousted me. [laughs] When I mash up two different songs, I look for songs that work together organically, musically.

Of course now whenever I hear "Back in Black," I hear "My Funny Valentine!"

Is there a conceptual bent here as well, when you combine two songs and bring an unexpected subtext to the music that wouldn't have occurred otherwise?

It's an added bonus. The more contrast between the two songs lyrically and musically, the better. Mashing up songs gives me a way of reinventing songs in a way that hasn't been done before. I can sing a beautifully written song in a new way and hopefully bring different age groups and fans of different kinds of music together.

How did you go about choosing songs and the singers you pay tribute to on your album *Dead Divas Society*?

The first thing that came to my mind was the album's title and the idea of recording an album as a tribute to my favorite singers, singers who have had the biggest impact on me. I honestly thought it was going to be an easier album to put together, but in fact, the opposite turned out to be true. And I'm grateful for that.

I had to look at each singer and ask myself, "What did I really learn from that singer? What is it about their singing that moves me?"

I searched for and listened to every song each singer sang and recorded and eventually created a list of about five songs for each that I considered recording for the album. But how do you pick your favorite Sarah Vaughan song? Talk about an artist with a huge repertoire!

For Vaughan, I chose something that is not as well known but that I loved. When I found the song "Gravy Waltz," I had never heard it. When I researched the song, I discovered Vaughan was the first person to sing and record it, that it won a Grammy award for "Best Jazz Composition" in 1963, and was written by the comedian Steve Allen and bassist Ray Brown. That was all very cool to me. When Vaughan recorded "Gravy Waltz," she was well established as an artist, but wasn't just singing well-known standards. She was looking for new, unusual songs to sing.

For Etta James I chose "Fool That I Am." It's not my favorite song from her, but what I love about that song is that *she* loved that song. She recorded that song on so many albums in so many different ways, and that was something I learned from her. She was one of these artists who sang a number of songs in different ways and wasn't afraid to rerecord them in different ways. She wasn't really attached to genre. She did rock and roll songs and then, later in her career, came out with these jazz albums and sort of reinvented herself. That really interests me.

Once I chose two or three songs for each singer, I took the songs to Art, and we added the element of us to each one of those choices. We worked on arranging the songs with our drummer, Josh Jones, and determined which of the songs spoke to us as a band. I wanted to tell *that* story. I wanted it to be "us" singing these songs.

We recorded the album live. I wanted the program to have a story and a through-line. We recorded it live in a studio with two different audiences of 75 people, which is unusual. There's nothing done to any of the tracks. The main thing I learned from all of these singers is a real skill, a craft, like, "You better be able to get up and sing the song without ProTools!"[73] [laughs] Go do your job!

I wanted to honor these singers and make the songs my own, our own, doing what we do as a band, mixing different genres and putting our own spin on things, and ultimately, give and record a great performance in a live setting. I feel like we did that.

Were you nervous about singing this material given the degree of influence and inspiration each singer has had on you as well as many other musicians and music fans?

The only singer where I had that kind of thought about was Billie Holiday. But what I realized was that there was a little bit of Billie Holiday in every other singer I was researching and listening to. When I listen to her, and I don't actually listen to her all that much, I realized that there are some phrasing things I do that are similar to Billie's. That's not intentional. I'm not trying to sound like her. It's because there's that element of her having listened to a lot of horn players and her influence on the singers we're talking about, like Sarah Vaughan, Ella Fitzgerald . . . she's in there.

Generally speaking, I didn't feel like I had anything to prove. I just wanted to do this. I feel I'm really good at being me. [laughs] I don't feel like I'd be good at being anybody else. I've never felt competitive with other singers. I spend time learning how to be the best "me" that I can be.

That's what I hear when I've heard you live and on your recordings. It's so important to find out who you are as a musician.

Going back to the business and marketing . . . for the most part, in jazz, the market doesn't really reward a singer or musician who sounds exactly like somebody else. We don't need another Sarah Vaughan because we already have Sarah Vaughan. I don't want to hear songs sung by other singers in exactly the same way as the original singers did them. I'd much rather hear somebody with the skill of Sarah Vaughan, but doing something totally different with that skill. That's what I'm always striving for.

Iris Ornig

The casual music listener may describe the role of the upright or electric bass as being relatively narrow: the bass player keeps time (the tempo of the music) while providing the root (or lowest) note of each passing chord. Keeping time and grounding the harmony are indeed both crucial components to making music, but historically, the bass has stretched its role and pushed both pop and jazz music into fresh new musical territory. For example, just try imagining the opening of the Beach Boys' hit single "Good Vibrations" without the contrapuntal melody played by pioneering bassist Carol Kaye. In an ensemble performance, be it jazz or the Beach Boys, once the bass leaves behind the root note of a chord, the musical texture shifts, like the turn of a kaleidoscope.

"The job of a bassist is multifunctional," says bassist, composer, and bandleader Iris Ornig. "The bass doesn't just keep the time. It keeps the har-

Iris Ornig. Photo by Pat Kepic.

mony together and even expands the harmony. . . . The bass sets the rhythm, as well as where the harmonies are going."

You can hear exactly what Ornig is talking about on her critically acclaimed album *No Restrictions*, where she, alongside pianist Helen Sung, and guitarist Kurt Rosenwinkel, collectively imply, state, and/or expound upon the ever-shifting harmonic content of the music. When you consider Ornig is also helping to maintain the groove and feel of each composition, it's apparent that "multifunctional" is really the only accurate way to describe her playing and the role of her chosen instrument.

Born and raised in a small town in Germany, Ornig was primarily a self-taught musician before she began studying jazz in St. Gallen, Switzerland, and later at London's prestigious Guildhall School of Music and Drama. Her initial exposure to jazz came by way of her family's radio, and would eventually compel her to relocate in 2003 from Europe to New York City. Since that move, Ornig has performed with some of the most highly respected musicians in contemporary jazz, including Gretchen Parlato, Ambrose Akinmusire, Joel Frahm, Mike Rodriguez, and Marcus Gilmore. Her current projects include "Iris Ornig Reimagines Michael Jackson," a collection of arrangements for her quintet of Jackson's best-loved songs. (Ornig has also re-imagined music by Bjork and cites Johnny Cash as a major source of inspiration.)

From Lucille Dixon Robertson, a gifted classical double bassist who, in lieu of being able to audition for white orchestras in the 1940s, played with Earl "Fatha" Hines, as well as the International Sweethearts of Rhythm, to contemporary players such as Kate Davis, Anne Mette Iversen, Tal Wilkenfeld, and Esperanza Spalding, women have been holding down the bass chair ever since jazz began, keeping the harmony together, while expanding it at the same time.

When did you first begin playing a musical instrument?
I remember in school I played the wooden flute. But the first instrument I really picked up by myself was the electric bass when I was 16 years old.

What compelled you to pick up the electric bass?
Certain circumstances. I had had an accident and couldn't do anything for a while and had to stay at home. A friend of mine from school said, "Hey, you're really not doing anything. How about you play bass in our band? We need a bass player!" I had no idea what a bass actually was, but I just thought playing in a band sounded really great. So I went to my mom, and convinced her to buy me a bass. Two weeks later, I was playing in the band, playing rock music.

You grew up in a pretty small town in Germany. Is that correct?
Yes. A small town by the Lake of Constance called Radolfzell. Its population is like 30,000 people. It's really small compared to New York City.

When did jazz music come into your musical life?
Earlier in my life, probably when I was 13 or 14 years old. I listened to a radio station where once a week they played jazz. They played Miles Davis, all the famous people, and I always looked forward to listening to it.

I was fascinated by what [the musicians I heard] were doing. I couldn't really understand what they were doing, but I just got really interested in the music. It never occurred to me to pick up an instrument myself. I come from a family with really no musical background. So I was just listening.

A year and a half later, after picking up the electric bass, the guitar player in the band I was playing in said, "We need a bass player for our music school's big band." I said, "Yeah, well, I'm playing electric bass, not upright!" And he said, "That doesn't matter." So, I went there, but I couldn't really read music. So I learned all the music that was written down by memorizing each note and played with the big band. And I loved it! I really loved it. Five years later I picked up the upright bass.

Were the musicians in that big band all students?
Yes. All students. All 16 to probably 28 or 29 years old.

In America, some schools are really good about providing music as part of a curriculum. Other schools have no music whatsoever. At the school in your town, was music something you could study if you wanted to?
No, not in our public school. The school with the big band was like a private music school. Every city in Germany has their own music school that is sponsored and represents their town.

I never took lessons. I did take a couple lessons with a teacher at the beginning to get a feel for what was going on with the bass. But I'm really self-taught.

I also studied economics after high school, because all my friends studied economics. I didn't know what I wanted to be, so I studied economics. But I realized, more and more, that actually my heart is with music. After two and a half years of studying economics, I switched to music. And then I had music lessons and education and everything.

You made a commitment to playing music.
Yes.

Was your family supportive of this decision?
Yes, definitely. They said, "If you want to do it, that's fine." My oldest sister

always said, "Oh, you should become a dentist, because then you can make money. With music you can't make money!" She was persistent for a while in trying to convince me to become a dentist. But she totally supported me.

A dentist? [laughs]
Yeah, I know. It's so bizarre just thinking about it. Of course, dentists make money, but why should I become a dentist?

Did you go to a music conservatory?
I went to a conservatory in Switzerland, which was very close to my hometown. I was there for three and a half years and got my degree.

And you were playing upright bass at this point, right?
I had just started playing upright bass toward the end of my time at the Switzerland conservatory. Before that, I played electric bass.

While in school, I attended a workshop of musicians all from London, and they told me I could complete a master's in one year at the Guildhall School of Music and Drama in London. They said I should apply to that program. I applied and I got in, and that's what I did right after I finished in Switzerland.

Going away to London for one year was an interesting experience, leaving my hometown, not knowing if I'd really like it. But I had a really good time.

What kind of music were you studying? Was it jazz?
In Switzerland, it was more open. I studied and played a kind of wide spectrum of popular music, Latin music, and jazz. In London, it was primarily jazz standards and the Great American Songbook.

Were you learning to read and notate music?
It's really funny. I'm a really good sight-reader. Probably because I really wanted that big band job and they had 30 charts or more. I had to memorize every note of each chart and learn everything by heart. Since that experience, I developed really good sight-reading skills. I taught myself how to read, and everyone has always said, "Oh, you're a really good sight-reader!" I guess that's because I forced myself. I remember the first few rehearsals where I just didn't even know where I was. I had no idea what was going on! [laughs] So, I guess that helped me a lot, that I spent time on just sight-reading.

Were you doing a lot of listening too? Were the big band director or other musicians giving you recordings and saying, "You should listen to this bass player"?
Basically, they would suggest a broad spectrum for listening, such as the music of John Coltrane, Miles Davis, Count Basie, and Duke Ellington. But I never had anyone suggest a specific album or player. That didn't happen. Everything I discovered was through playing with other musicians.

Of course, I'm a huge fan of [bassist and composer] Jaco Pastorius. I listened to him a lot. And then from him, got into Joni Mitchell and other music styles.

Listening to the band Weather Report, I discovered the music of Joe Zawinul and Wayne Shorter. I'm a big fan of Wayne Shorter. Through Weather Report I found Miroslav Vitouš, who is also a really great bass player.

Believe it or not, I'm also a huge fan of Johnny Cash, who is totally not jazz.

Is there something specific about Johnny Cash's music that influences the music you make with your quintet and what you do as a bass player?
I definitely like his feel and his darkness. That really touches me. And also his simplicity. I do believe you can hear that I'm really moved by him, but I can't tell you, "Here! This is exactly where you can hear it."

You made a decision to relocate from Europe to America.
That's correct. In 2000, I went to New York City to visit for almost four weeks. I had a friend who had a friend I could stay with. While in New York, I took lessons from different bassists, as well as some composition lessons. And I said, "I really want to live here!"

I made my decision in 2001 to come to New York City. But then, 9/11 happened. And I got scared, because it was a scary time. But in 2003 I said, "If I don't go now I will never go." And I just went. Everyone I knew was surprised, because I was well established as a musician and had a great job in a theater, and I just left. But I knew if I didn't go then, I would never go.

Why did you want to relocate to New York City?
All the history of jazz is there and all the great musicians are there. You can hear so much great music every night, and you get inspired. It's such a creative and energetic city, amazing and inspiring. Another reason was that I naively thought I'd get "discovered" there and tour a lot.

How does a musician survive in New York City? There's so much great music and so many sources of inspiration. But how do you pay the rent?
I remember after the first two years of living in New York, I had basically spent all of my savings. I kind of knew I'd have to use my savings, but I didn't know it'd be *all* of my savings.

Honestly, the first two years there were rough. You have to go around and try to get gigs and try to get known. And I do admit I had my points where I thought, "Why am I doing this? It's such a hassle." But, I kept doing it. And I've been in New York for almost 10 years.

Whenever I look back, I'm happy I didn't give up, that I just continued persistently doing what I wanted to do. I'm happy. I can make a living. I can't buy an apartment or go on vacation all the time, but I'm happy with what I accomplish.

I think some listeners have a narrow idea of what the bass does in a band like your quintet. What's the role of the upright bass in your band?
The job of a bassist is multifunctional. The bass doesn't just keep the time. It keeps the harmony together and even expands the harmony. Like when you hit a C chord, you can play a B and open up the sound. The bass sets the rhythm, as well as where the harmonies are going.

I think the role of the bass is underappreciated, but it's the most important instrument in a band. Just imagine an orchestra without the low instruments.

On your album *No Restrictions*, you have two chordal instruments in your quintet, piano [Helen Sung] and electric guitar [Kurt Rosenwinkel]. With two chordal instruments playing at the same time, you have the potential for a lot of notes clashing and getting in the way of the music. So how do you keep the music open and sounding good?
The important thing with both a piano player and a guitar player is that neither should have a big ego. It's important for everyone in a band to respect each other. Sometimes it's really difficult to find people who really want to play music and listen to each other. I had situations where I was playing with both a piano and a guitar player and both were playing so many notes and it was clashing and I thought, "Oh, my God. If one of you just stopped for eight bars it would be so wonderful." So you definitely have to find the right musicians, musicians who are willing to listen to each other and give room to each other. Both Helen and Kurt are amazing musicians. They listen to each other, respect each other, and give room to each other.

Are you seeing more women in your field playing jazz?
Women are still a huge minority. When I'm playing with others, I'm usually the only female musician. I try to mix it up with my own band, with two female musicians. It's just another experience and it's fun. It's not something where I think, "Oh, I really need to do this." It's just really fun and inspiring.

But women are still in the minority. It's the same in Europe. If you ask me to name a handful of female alto players, I'd probably stop after the fourth or fifth player.

Well, this book may change that!
Yes! It will!

Cheryl Pyle

Free improvisation is alive and well and living in New York City, and flutist, composer, and lyricist Cheryl Pyle, who arrived in the Big Apple from Berkeley, California, in 1980, is one of the keepers of the flame. She performs with pianists, guitarists, percussionists, and even painters in a variety of local venues dedicated to exploratory music, including ABC No Rio, ShapeShifter Lab, University of the Streets, and Downtown Music Gallery. Pyle seems to embrace as many stimulating improvisatory collaborations as humanly possible, so much so that it can be quite a challenge to try and keep up with her performance schedule and recorded output.

Pyle is a free spirit, albeit a free spirit with a BA in music from the University of California, where she was the principal flutist for its University Jazz Ensemble and played with such legendary musicians as Sonny Rollins, George Duke, Freddie Hubbard, Hubert Laws, and Joe Henderson. She would go on to serve as the musical director of the Berkeley Shakespeare Festival, perform throughout the San Francisco area as a member of the Loft Jazz Association, and from 1977 to 1980, serve on faculty at Berkeley as its flute teacher in the jazz department. Since relocating to New York, she has recorded and performed with jazz luminaries such as Joe Lovano, Andy LaVerne, Fred Hersch, Tom Harrell, and many more. Pyle is also a gifted lyricist, and has penned lyrics for several highly respected jazz singers, including Janis Siegel (of the Manhattan Transfer) and Sheila Jordan. And thanks to online platforms such as MySpace, Bandcamp, and Soundcloud, Pyle is able to collaborate and release music with kindred musical spirits from around the globe.

Despite high rents, hostile landlords, and New York's ceaseless mission to be a playground for trust fund kids, Pyle and the similarly creative artists she counts as her friends continue to infuse the city with the spirit that compelled her to relocate from California in the first place.

You're living in New York City now? That's your home base?
Yes. I moved here in 1980 after college, after my music studies at the University of California, Berkeley. I moved to New York City to play music and jazz, and that's what I'm still doing.

Where in the city do you live?
East Village, the Lower East Side area.

That area has changed quite a bit over the years.

Yes. When I came here, there was so much jazz in the Village. There were musicians everywhere, so many clubs. It was so inspiring in the early 80s. It's a lot different now. But it's a lot safer. [laughs]

When did you first begin playing a musical instrument?
I started late, when I was 19. I was going to pursue art studies in San Diego, where I was living and going to the junior college there. I really loved to paint so I thought I would major in art. I was playing a little flute, but I was just a beginner at that point. I took one music class with a music professor there, Robert Henninger, who had studied with Nadia Boulanger in Paris. He was so inspiring that I switched to a music major. That was it for me. I was practicing day and night, taking lots of music classes, working on lots of classical music, and trying to catch up and learn as much as I could.

Wow.
In the meantime I had a lot of friends who were really into jazz. One friend, a really good trumpet player named Fred Young, played Miles Davis for me. Miles' *Bitches Brew* had just come out, along with all the CTI recordings with [trumpeter] Freddie Hubbard as well as [flutist] Hubert Laws' *First Light*. Fred played those LPs for me and I just thought, "That's what I want to do!" It was an immediate, internal reaction.

I auditioned two years later for the music department at the University of California, Berkeley, which had a very traditional classical music department. I auditioned and got in to study music. At that time, the jazz department at UC Berkeley wasn't a part of its music department. My last year at college there, they had a really good professor named Ollie Wilson, who started teaching jazz studies there. But when I first started college, they only had "music activities" for jazz.

UC[B] did have a great big band. I joined it and started learning that format. I got to play all the flute parts. A lot of the saxophonists couldn't double flute well, so I got to play all those parts, which was great experience.

I was working part-time in San Francisco while going to college. There was a club, the Keystone Korner, which is a famous jazz club, just through the alleyway from my job in North Beach. I went there on every break five nights a week. I got to hear Rahsaan Roland Kirk, Art Blakey, Dexter Gordon, Horace Silver, Cecil Taylor, Ahmad Jamal—everybody was playing there! It was just so inspiring. I was meeting all of these musicians from New York, and they told me, "You should move to New York. That's where the jazz is!"

So, in 1980 I moved to New York, and I'm so glad I did. I immediately started meeting a lot of musicians and going to many clubs, including the Village Vanguard, Lush Life, Mikell's, and Seventh Avenue South. There was a club in the Village called Bradley's. The owner loved jazz piano, and he had a wonderful, amazing piano in this little bar. All the piano and bass duos were playing there and all the musicians would go there after their gigs at the Village Vanguard or Fat Tuesday's. There were also a lot of loft clubs, including the Jazz Forum, Jazz Mania—it was just a huge scene. Talking to musicians at Bradley's, musicians who were really my jazz idols, until four or five in the morning was just an amazing experience.

I did a demo tape and started getting some gigs. That first demo was with Fred Hersch [pianist], Ron McClure [bass], and Jordan Naess [drummer from Scandinavia]. I booked my first gig at the Jazz Forum in 1981, with Hersch, McClure, and Billy Hart [drummer]. And I was in jazz heaven at that point!

I met Roseanna Vitro around that time, and started writing some lyrics for Fred's tunes and other jazz composers. Roseanna sang some of those, as well as Sheila Jordan and other great jazz singers. I still play gigs, compose, and write lyrics to great jazz tunes.

When I first listened to your CD *Inside Dialogue* [2011], I didn't know the backstory, that it was recorded while you were recovering from skin cancer. When I listen to that recording, it sounds to me like a musical diary. There's something very healing in the music. It sounds like you were documenting your recovery. Is that accurate?
Yes. It was a survival CD. When I had skin cancer on my lip in 2010, I just wanted to prove to myself that I could still play flute. That was the goal, to just keep recording and playing flute. I still had stitches in my lip, and I tried adding some effects to my flute compositions. My lip was sore at the time, and I was working on getting my embouchure back. Since that time, I've just been trying to compose and record as much as I can. I had a little bit of a scare that I might not be able to play the flute again. But I'm happy to say that music and flute playing is still a daily endeavor.

When you play flute live with a rock or heavy metal band, are you playing amplified flute? Or do they want you to play more gently?
I just use a microphone. I don't really use any effects. I just want people to be able to hear the flute over the band! [laughs] I love the pure sound of the flute in most cases.

I grew up in the 60s hearing a lot of rock and roll. In high school, I loved Jimi Hendrix and Janis Joplin and all those bands. But when I heard *Bitches Brew* and Weather Report, where the music was a combination of rock and jazz, it was pretty incredible. Hubert Laws too. Chick Corea came out with a record around that time called *Light as a Feather*. There was a whole Brazilian influx at that time, lots of percussion, vocals, and flute. So I felt there were a lot of open possibilities.

I still combine elements and styles. I record with a heavy metal band in

Denmark. I really like going wherever the music takes me in the heart vein, you know? If the music has that "goose pimple" factor and makes you feel something inside, I'll go with it.

You mentioned the rock-influenced jazz albums that inspired you back in the 1970s. But there were also a lot of jazz albums out around that time that were heavily influenced by classical music. Were those records on your radar as well?

Oh, yes! All the jazz and classical flute players I love. I'm inspired by all of those musicians, jazz, classical, world music, whatever. It all gets mixed in and incorporated over the years in my flute playing.

With the technology we now have, digital recorders and the Internet, there's almost no excuse not to have your music out there in some tangible form. Would you encourage younger musicians to just get their music out there on the Internet?

Yes. The way to do creative music is to do it yourself. We all hear music in different ways, we all play solos a little bit differently, and we all construct compositions a little bit differently. To follow that, to follow your ears, and heart, and just get your music out there any way you can, is really important. Keep all those fragments for songs. Keep all of those ideas and work with them, develop them with other musicians. Jam as much as you can. The main thing is to keep playing music.

When I first moved to New York, we musicians would just get together to talk and play music, work on songs together, booking gigs, trying out new tunes, trying out new combinations of groups and different instruments. Over time, all of those experiences add up, and it makes the music better for everyone.

Is there less collaboration on the street, on the ground, in New York City today compared with the 1980s?

Well, I'm not sure. I can tell you a lot of people have moved because it's too expensive to live here. But I have several New York City gigs and online projects too. I used to walk around the Village area and run into many musicians. I ran into a drummer friend, Newman Taylor Baker, the other day, and was surprised to see a another musician in the East Village! [laughs]

After I recorded my first CD, I was playing about seven or eight clubs, and I could always pay the quartet.

Wow!

Yeah, wow. But all of those places are closed. Since 9/11, a lot of clubs have closed here.

Many of the jazz clubs are booking "name" people so they can bring people

Cheryl Pyle (right) with Roberta Piket (left). Photo by Eva Kapanadze.

in. I understand that. I just want to play as often as I can. So for me, whether it's a live gig somewhere or doing an Internet CD project, it doesn't matter to me. Playing music is the goal.

I've been playing a lot of free jazz recently. There's an East Village club, ABC No Rio, where that kind of old jazz New York thing is still happening. A lot of musicians go to there to hear the other musicians, and then we all jam afterwards.

Some musicians I've spoken to for this book, musicians who came to New York City around the time you did, have voiced a sense of missing a community, where when you go outside, you run into fellow musicians. They were living in the same neighborhood.
Yes, but I really think that now, the neighborhood is the world.

Your neighbor now is somebody in Norway or Denmark!
Exactly! When the scene started to change after 9/11, I was saying to friends, "Where have all the musicians gone?" I think I got my first computer in 2005, and I quickly discovered that everyone was online. I found many bands and musicians on MySpace and heard the new music they were posting. I found a lot of projects at that time through MySpace. Then we all migrated to Facebook.

We are so connected on Facebook and through other websites. I think more people should take advantage of social media. It's really a great way to make some wonderful music. I have recorded some amazing international projects this way, and feel very lucky to have found these great musicians many miles away.

Things are always changing and I'm just going with it. Wherever musicians are, that's where I'll be, near the music.

Roberta Piket

The heart has its reasons, which reason does not know ... We know truth, not only by the reason, but also by the heart. — Blaise Pascal from Pensées

I came across the above quote by the French physicist and philosopher Blaise Pascal while listening to pianist and composer Roberta Piket's performance of "Haunted Heart" on her critically acclaimed, solo piano album *Emanation* (2015). Composed by Howard Dietz and Arthur Schwartz and made famous in 1950 by singer Jo Stafford, "Haunted Heart" is typically interpreted by jazz musicians as a lush ballad, with a light and swinging rhythmic undercurrent. On *Emanation*, Piket takes a very different approach with the tune by using silence and space to convey what I hear as the interior experience of heartache and loss. It may be a cliché to describe Piket's approach to playing as a synthesis of reason and the heart, but the subject of how Piket and musicians in general, especially improvisers, engage with both logic and emotion comes up more than once in her interview.

"Most people are more left brain or more right brain," says Piket. "I think I'm pretty evenly split. I have the intuitive artistic side, but I'm also very analytical, and very verbal."

Echoing soprano saxophonist Jane Ira Bloom's statement, "I improvise like a composer and I compose like an improviser," Piket recalls a direction from her mentor, pianist Richie Beirach:

"Beirach used to say (to me), 'Your compositions should sound improvised, and your improvisations should sound composed.' Of course, the second part of that means when you're improvising, you want it to have a form ... you want to tell a story. But when you actually sit down to record and perform an improvisation, you have to let all that go, and just let those ideas flow through you."

Both as a bandleader and collaborator, Piket easily navigates the spectrum between the head and the heart and embraces with authority a myriad of styles and approaches in solo, trio, and larger ensemble settings. Her 2011 album, *Sides, Colors*, features her orchestrations for winds and strings, as well as Piket on organ and vocals. Other projects include the electric band, Alternating Current, an experimental trio with drummer Billy Mintz and saxophonist Louie Belogenis, and a neo-classical ensemble, the Nabokov Project, which sets poems by Vladimir Nabokov to music inspired by European classical music, with sections for free improvisation. Piket has also released two solo piano recordings, *Solo* (2012), and the aforementioned *Emanation*, and authored a series of jazz piano vocabulary workbooks.

As an educator, interviewee, and occasional blogger, Piket is happy to

Roberta Piket. Photo by Daniel Sheehan.

break down the processes involved in making great music, and share advice and guidance to young musicians and budding listeners as to how to further enjoy and appreciate creative music. If you've ever wondered, while listening to a musician play and improvise, what she or he is thinking or feeling, and what it takes to acquire the technical ability to play with such freedom, the following conversation will provide you with some answers.

Do you remember when you first began playing a musical instrument?
I come from a musical family. My father [Frederick Piket] was a very well-respected composer. He passed away when I was very young. When I was 8 years old, he died of cancer. He gave me my first lessons on the piano. I have early memories of him giving lessons every night after dinner when I was 6 or 7.

Were you drawn to the piano? Or did your father say, "I want you to learn the piano!"
You know, I don't remember. I think it was something I wanted to do. My father was the sort of, more laid back one; my mom was more the taskmaster. I think that if I hadn't been interested in it and excited about it, he wouldn't have made me do it. It was fun. He made it fun and entertaining. It wasn't like, you know, when you go to some teacher's house. It wasn't that formal. He was my father and it was fun to hang out with him.

Did formal lessons begin after a while?

Well, my lessons with my father were formal in that we had music books and I went through the pieces. I was learning to read music from an early age. Once my father passed away, I wasn't so interested in it. I kind of lost interest in the piano without him there.

I have an older brother, 10 years older than me, who is a musician. He and my mom were having a lot of difficulties. He was kind of already out of the house, and wasn't there to influence me. But I still kind of kept fooling around with music.

I remember in sixth grade I had a couple of friends, and we would sing together. We would sing harmony. And my sixth-grade teacher heard this and she was just shocked! It had never entered my mind that it was unusual to be able to make up a harmony on the spot and sing by ear. She was so shocked and impressed by this. She encouraged my musical interest by making me realize that it was something unusual, something special. Not just something anyone could do.

So from there I got a little more into music. In my early teens, I began playing piano again. My brother, when he was in his early 20s, got me into jazz. Once I began listening to jazz, that's when I really got excited about music.

When you say your brother got you listening to jazz, I can imagine a lot of different kinds of jazz that he might have had you listen to. What kind of jazz specifically were you excited by?

Initially, my brother had the radio on a lot. WRVR in Connecticut was on the air and played a lot of jazz. I was just kind of absorbing it all. To some degree, it all kind of sounded the same to me in the beginning. My brother started taking lessons with Walter Bishop, Jr. He played a Walter Bishop, Jr. record for me, *Speak Low*, on Muse Records. It's a record from the early 60s; my brother had picked it up at our synagogue. Our synagogue had a bazaar, where he found this record for 25 cents. And he was so mad it was selling so cheaply! So he bought like every copy.

When I heard that record, I just fell in love with the sound of the piano trio. I just knew I wanted to play jazz piano. That's the first memory I have of really being blown away by a specific recording.

At that age, were you starting to play piano with other musicians? Maybe in a rock or jazz combo? Or were you playing alone, and eventually decided, it's time to play with a bassist and a drummer?

It was maybe more of the latter. My brother played piano, he was and still is more of a rock guy. He never got as serious about jazz as I did. He plays piano, guitar, and sings. He still loves jazz and respects it, but he never became a serious jazz player. But he's very talented.

What happened was, I was kind of shy and introverted, and there weren't a lot of girls my age playing jazz [laughs] or any kind of music like that. I looked for people to play with, but it was always sort of a struggle.

I grew up in Bayside Queens, which is a very isolated, very middle class kind of neighborhood in Queens. I went to junior and high school in Manhattan. I went to Hunter College High School, which is a public school, sort of like Stuyvesant or Bronx Science, although it's a little more selective. It gets compared to those two schools in that it's a public school, tuition-free, but you have to take a test to get in. So I wasn't living in the neighborhood with a lot of friends. I had a few friends from the neighborhood, but most of my friends were from school, and they lived all over New York City, all over the five boroughs. And I never really developed musical relationships with kids in my high school. There weren't any girls my age playing jazz, as I said before. There were maybe two or three boys that were into jazz. But I was just too shy to approach them. I didn't really start playing with other musicians until I was 15 or 16.

One thing about my high school, it was great academically, but its music program was pretty much non-existent. No jazz band, no jazz ensemble. When I started at a music conservatory, the New England Conservatory (NEC), I think I was at a slight disadvantage because I didn't have those experiences, that training ground, that a lot of musicians have in high school. Just learning basic things, playing in a band, keeping time.... I was always good at playing changes. I was always good at harmony and improvising. But certain basics like having good time, things you develop from playing with other musicians, I was definitely lacking in those areas when I started at NEC.

But you had the facility to get into the conservatory. You were obviously playing well.

Honestly, I was really surprised when I got in! [laughs] I guess looking back ... it's not like now where you have these prodigies coming out of the woodwork. I mean, every day I hear about a new piano player who's 10 years old, 12 years old, who sounds like Chick Corea, you know? Or McCoy Tyner! I think back then, those kids existed, but there were way fewer of them. The jazz training, the jazz education has evolved so much from what it used to be, back in the early 80s when I was applying to college.

Maybe in some ways I was more developed than I was seeing. Like I said, I could play over changes, I did have that ability. But there were certain gaps. But I guess everybody at that age has those gaps. I guess I was good enough to get in. I didn't expect to get in! But I did.

I also got accepted into Tufts University, and Tufts and the New England Conservatory had a special five-year degree you could get but you had to be accepted independently by each school for the program. So that's what I did. I did that five-year program.

I see you got a bachelor's in Computer Science at the same time? Is that correct?
That's correct.

Why the dual degree?
Well, the computer thing was completely my mother's idea. See, my mom was smart. She never put it to me like, "You better do *this* or I'm not gonna pay for your college. . . . " It was nothing like that. But she was a very smart, Jewish mother. Very good at putting this idea in my head and making it sound as if it was my idea, which it really wasn't. Having been married to a musician (my father), she understood the hardships of being a musician, and she didn't want that life for me.

I guess because I came from this very strong academic background, and that I was always interested in the world around me, society, politics, social issues, it made sense to continue a liberal arts education, especially after a school like Hunter College High School. But as far as computer science goes, that was completely my mom's idea.

In a way it made sense. If you're going to do something as completely financially going off the cliff as a jazz musician, if you're going to study something else, why not study something more practical? But my heart wasn't really in it. I was always very good at it because I always had a very analytical brain. But it wasn't really where my heart was.

Not everybody can juggle and handle two degrees. Some people are kind of wired in a way that they're able to do that. But there isn't just one path that every musician must take in order to become a musician. There's a lot of variety to that experience. Some of the musicians I've interviewed for this book did not study music at all in college.
Yeah. That's exactly it. Herbie Hancock studied electrical engineering at Grinnell College. I've always been very split, left brain, right brain. Most people are more left brain or more right brain. I think I'm pretty evenly split. [laughs] I have the intuitive artistic side, but I'm also very analytical, and very verbal. So yeah, it kind of made sense.

I think it may be that being in that program slowed my musical development a little. But you know, anything that doesn't kill you makes you stronger. I'm glad I have that degree.

After graduating, I actually worked for a year for a computer company and I was just really unhappy. I felt like I wanted to be doing music full time, and I hadn't really given it the chance. I felt like I was young enough, that I should give it a shot. So I quit that job after a year. And it was a very good job. I was working for a company called DEC (Digital Equipment Corporation), which at the time was one of the most desirable companies to work for in that world. They paid well, and it was a prestigious company. They treated their employees really well. But I left and moved back to New York, and I just started doing music full time. Actually, I did that for about 15 years. Then I started doing a little bit of computer work. Nothing that I'd learned in college. Just fixing people's computer problems to make a little extra money. And it became a little financial fallback. But it's interesting how you come full circle sometimes. What I learned in school was programming, software design. And what I've been doing in the last seven years has had nothing to do with that! [laughs]

Let's go back to the conservatory. When you got there, did you begin discovering musicians who if they weren't role models, or even women, were just inspiring to you as a musician?

I had a lot of homework to do when it came to learning about the greats. A lot of people weren't on my radar. I was familiar with Thelonious Monk, Bill Evans, Bud Powell, and Charlie Parker, all the bebop heroes. I was also a little bit into fusion. I knew about Weather Report and Wayne Shorter. But when I got to NEC, I really started to broaden more, to investigate and transcribe. I was checking out Herbie Hancock, Wynton Kelly, transcribing a lot of Bill Evans solos. I had never done a lot of transcribing, so that was something new.

As far as female role models, of course there was Mary Lou Williams and Marian McPartland, who is a friend of mine to this day.[74] But there were very few women in the jazz department. Most of the time it was just me and one other person. Instrumentalists, I should say, there were always a few vocalists. But usually it was just two instrumentalists. And I know this has changed a lot in the past 20 years. It's changed enormously. But when I was in school, that's how it was.

Again, I was very shy, and very insecure about my playing. I didn't really reach out to people to play with them, because I felt timid and insecure about my abilities. Looking back, that was a disadvantage. As I progressed through the program, I became a little more outgoing and confident, and I ended up in some really good ensembles with some really good players. But I would say especially at the beginning I was very insecure.

After NEC, did you continue studying?

While I was in NEC, I studied with some really good people, including Fred Hersch, Jim McNeely, and Stanley Cowell. I also took a semester with the drummer Bob Moses, learning rhythmic concepts. Not playing drums, I would sit at the piano. And that was really great, really helpful.

After leaving Digital Equipment and relocating to New York City, a friend advised me to apply for a NEA study grant. At the time, the National Endowment for the Arts was still giving out grants for individual artists before Congress slashed all their funding. Somebody recommended I study with Richie Beirach. And honestly, I didn't know much about Beirach and his association with Dave Leibman. I was just looking for someone to study with. My friend said, "Look, don't worry about it. This is free money. Don't worry if this isn't the perfect teacher for you. Just go for the grant." [laughs] So I called Richie, and he asked me to send him a tape. I guess he kind of wanted to pre-approve me before he decided to take me on as a student and approve the grant. He accepted me. I didn't actually get the grant, but I started studying with him anyway. And a couple years later I did get a study grant to study with him. That's how I met Richie and began studying with him, for probably, five or six years, on and off.

Were you playing gigs in New York City at the time?
One of the first things I did when I moved back to New York City was buy a drum set. I would have sessions, and drummers would always have to bring their own drums. Good drummers don't want to carry their drums around to play a session, to play for free, you know? So that was one of the first things I did. I was having a lot of sessions, jam sessions. I always composed, and wrote. And I started booking some gigs. Looking back on it, I think maybe that's why I didn't get hired more. People had this idea I was a bandleader and that that was all I was interested in, which wasn't true. I always wanted to be, and still want to be a side person and have those kinds of musical experiences. But yeah, I started gigging with my trio pretty early on. I had a trio with Jeff Williams on drums for about 10 years.

My first record wasn't a trio record. It was mostly quintet with some trio arrangement. My first band was actually a quartet. Steve Kenyon played saxophone, Tom Hubbard played bass, and Jeff Williams was on drums. We did a little demo. I was using Jeff Williams a lot. But I used a lot of different bass players and different musicians I met. I think my main musical education just came from playing a lot of sessions with a lot of different musicians.

God knows I played a lot of gigs, restaurant gigs, and six weeks in the Catskills that felt like 10 years! I got a lot of seasoning that way, which I think a lot of young musicians now don't get. There are a handful that are lucky enough to get picked by more established musicians to be in their bands, and they get some of that seasoning. But a lot of young musicians now don't know any standards or tunes because there just aren't any gigs where you're doing that sort of thing. But part of it also is it's just not what they're interested in.

But I think it's good to know that repertoire, to know the standards, to have the bebop foundation no matter what music you decide you want to do. I play free music with a lot of players, but I think the best free players, not 100 percent across the board, but for most of us it's helpful to have that bebop foundation no matter what style of jazz you're playing, even freely improvised music.

Are there fewer opportunities for jam sessions now? Were there more jam sessions during the time period you're talking about than now?
As far as jam sessions in clubs, yeah, there were more of them. One of the only places for young musicians to go and jam is Small's; they have these late-night jam sessions every night after every show. I think that's great. But there used to be more sessions like that. Monday nights you were at the Squire, Tuesday nights you were at this place, Wednesday nights, the Village Gate had jam sessions, you know. There were more opportunities like that, I think that's true.

But then again, there are a lot more schools, there are a lot more educational opportunities for young musicians now. If they want to find it, they'll find it.

You make your own opportunities. If you can't jam in a club, you can do it in your house!
Right. Exactly. And sometimes that's better! I used to always say I'd rather play in the house than go out somewhere and be told what to play for like, 20 bucks. At a certain point in your life, it just becomes insulting.

You talked about bebop as a foundation. That leads into a question I had about two tracks on your first solo piano album. "Variations on Monk's Dream" followed by the Thelonious Monk composition "Monk's Dream." And I love the variations. Can you talk about what's going on, what you're doing on "Variations on Monk's Dream"? How is it connected to the Monk composition?
To put it in the most essential terms, I just took the motivic material from "Monk's Dream" and developed an improvisation on the material. It's something that I got into when I was studying with Beirach. He has a strong classical background. It's just a way of approaching music. It's sort of a classical influence there, the idea of improvising based on a motif or several motifs rather than just playing over chord changes.

I was looking at the CD cover the other day and thought, "Man, I called this 'Variations,' but it's really just one variation. I should have just called it 'Variation' singular!" [laughs]

"Variations on Monk's Dream" sounds through-composed to me; the music never repeats and changes constantly.
Yeah. It was completely improvised, and every time I play it, I play it differently. But I worked on it. Because I think the first thing to do is really internalize the motives, so you can play and express them organically. You can't be thinking about it like, "Okay, now I'm going to play this motive. Now I'm going

to play this motive...." If you do that, it's going to sound really unmusical and stilted and awful.

An interesting thing Beirach used to say to me was, "Your compositions should sound improvised, and your improvisations should sound composed." Of course, the second part of that means when you're improvising, you want it to have a form, to be something that develops in a way that it sounds coherent. To use an old-fashioned term, you want to tell a story. But when you actually sit down to record and perform an improvisation, you have to let all that go, and just let those ideas flow through you. And that's what I tried to do.

With "Monk's Dream," I go into the more traditional treatment of the tune, with chord changes, a 32-bar form, a solo over changes. It's a contrast, but I think it's a nice contrast to the variations.

Since this was my first solo CD, one of my goals was to show my range and to present a variety of music. I've done eight other recordings, but this is my first solo piano record. So I wanted to show variety and keep it interesting. When you're doing a solo piano record, you don't have different instrumental timbres and textures, so you have to find other ways to keep it interesting.

As far as playing the tune "Monk's Dream" itself, I actually play the first A section of the head normally, and then after that, the melody and harmony goes up in minor thirds. Normally the bridge is in C, but I play it up a half-step, in D flat.

So these are just ways of playing with and exploring the tune, but I'm still playing that 32-bar form.

Where should a young pianist begin if she or he decides they want to play jazz? Listening to and studying your solo piano CD seems like a good place to start.

I know some teenagers who play insanely well and they have such a foundation already. They have all the fundamentals, they're swinging, and they play great. And then, I hear from friends of mine who do more teaching than I do, especially at some of these music schools, some of the colleges in Manhattan, if you can pay your way and you don't need any break on the tuition, they'll take you. No matter what you sound like or how much you care about music. Because they want the money. I know this for a fact. They'll tell the teachers, "just keep passing them." Even though a student might not be practicing and they're not really serious. But there are a lot of talented and hard-working kids out there.

As far as getting into the music, I would say the first thing is listening. That's one thing I've noticed about a lot of students that I've had is that they want to play jazz, but they don't listen to enough jazz. And I think these days, there's no excuse for that. There are so many amazing resources online. You can go to YouTube and you can hear everything! It's crazy. You can search for any musician on YouTube and hear them playing. We never had anything like that.

About six or seven years ago, I did a "suggested listening" discography.[75] And I put it on my website; it's on one of the pages. But it almost feels outdated now. Not because the records aren't great and aren't worth listening to, but because all you have to do to hear any of those musicians on any of those recordings is go to YouTube and just type in their names. But it almost seems kind of old-fashioned to buy a bunch of records! [laughs]

But listening is something a lot of young musicians don't do. And unless you're listening, it's all theoretical. How can you explain to someone what "swing" is if they don't hear that? You can tell them, you can analyze it for them, but they need to hear that and absorb it, you know? Which is difficult, because it's not in the culture now like it once was 60 years ago.

Jean Cook

Well, I don't know what jazz is. And what most people think of as jazz, I don't think that's what it is at all. As a matter of fact, I don't think the word has any meaning at all ... —pianist Cecil Taylor[76]

There is an improvisational vernacular that exists somewhere between the intersections of rock and roll, contemporary composition, and free jazz. Or maybe, at this point in time in the timeline of this music (not using the "J" word here just yet . . .), it's actually a tradition, rather than a vernacular. Then again, perhaps what I'm attempting to describe is less about vernacular or tradition, and more a way of thinking about music.

The reason violinist Jean Cook finds herself playing in so many diverse musical settings, be it alongside post-punk indie-rocker Jon Langford, in collaboration with bassist William Parker, or as a member of the new music collective Anti-Social Music, has a lot to do with the way she thinks about what to play and why.

"I play in a lot of different contexts," says Cook, ". . . when I play with William Parker's double quartet . . . nobody knows what's going to happen. We just start playing . . . what we're exploring is just the idea of, we're here and what happens when we're here? How do you respond to the things that are here? And what does that mean?"

Jean Cook. Photo by Morgan Klein.

While Cook is classically trained, and the sonorities she explores on her instrument in performance wouldn't be out of place in contemporary classical music, in order to play the music she now plays, she has pushed herself to develop a feel and technique beyond that which is required to play in the string section of an orchestra.

"One of the things that I had to unlearn was the idea of being accurate," says Cook. "I'm trained in a way that I have the ability to make many, many different kinds of sounds out of my instrument.... I had to learn not to be so exact about that sort of stuff and just focus on the feeling and what the ensemble is trying to say."

Like the pioneering pianist Cecil Taylor, Cook uses both concrete and poetic language to explain her approach to playing and improvising music. She describes her classical training as "the letters I have that spell the words ... the words I have that form the sentences."

Her description of Taylor's music is similarly succinct: "I hear space. I hear clarity. I hear the willingness to embrace the side of music that isn't so neat and pretty or leading you in such a specific direction with its melody. When music is really open, I can connect with it. It's just a little bit more profound."

....

When did you first begin playing a musical instrument?
I started playing the violin when I was 3 years old. Both of my parents are musicians. My mother is a cellist and my father is an oboe player. My sister is a cellist as well. My mom wanted me to play the cello, but I wanted to play the violin. My family has a photograph of me when I was 14 months old, back when I could barely walk, and I'm holding two pencils, one underneath my chin and the other one I'm holding like a violin bow. Apparently, when they took that photo, they were all singing to me and I was playing along with my imaginary violin.

Everything I know about my earliest years on the violin is through the lens of proud parents. [laughs] I don't know how much of it is true, but I did want to play the violin at a very early age. I was very clear about that. When I got big enough to hold a violin, they gave me one.

Were your parents your first music teachers?
They were very supportive. But they didn't know how serious I would be about the violin, so they put me in Suzuki. I kept at it, and my parents decided I needed a private teacher. They got a friend of theirs, who usually taught much, much older students, to agree to take me on. From then on, I began studying more seriously.

By the time I was 10 years old, I was playing in orchestras and entering and winning competitions. I started performing as a soloist with orchestras as well. That's when I started to think that music might be something I could do as a career.

When I was 16, I went to the Aspen Music Festival where I was surrounded by super serious students of classical music. There were the kids who practiced three hours a day, the kids who practiced five hours a day, and the kids who practiced *eight* hours a day. I was the kid who practiced three and half hours a day. At that point, being among people who were so driven, and in an environment that is very political, I realized there are other things that I wanted to do. I loved playing music and I loved playing music with other people. But everyone around me was so stressed about winning competitions, getting recitals, learning repertoire, and beating everybody else in this very competitive environment, I just felt that there were other things I could do in this world. I decided the path I wanted to pursue was not necessarily that of a classical soloist.

I thought I could help musicians as an organizer and administrator, so they could just play music and not worry about the business side. So I started helping out my parents. My mother and father put on a concert series at the Kennedy Center in Washington D.C. They brought soloists over from Korea who were not well known in the U.S. and gave them their Kennedy Center debut. I helped to produce the series.

I went to college in New York City and got a degree in sociology. While I was in New York, I did an internship with the Orpheus Orchestra and worked at Columbia University's radio station, WKCR. After college, I went into presenting. I worked with a group that put on concerts at the Kennedy Center. The concerts included dance, straight-ahead jazz, world music, and performance art. In 2000, I moved from Washington D.C. back to New York and co-founded the non-profit new music ensemble Anti-Social Music (ASM). ASM presents music that embraces classical, jazz, and many other genres and influences, including rock and punk rock music, and to date has premiered over 120 pieces. I also began playing violin and touring with rock bands.

Going back to your experience at the Aspen Music Festival, it sounds like your family was very supportive of the decisions you were making at the young age of 16.
You're right. They didn't put a lot of pressure on me and were supportive. There are parents who don't know how to support a child who is very driven to play music, but my parents did. They'd both been to the conservatory and had lots of friends who were professional musicians, but they also recognized that there are other things in life as well. They came over to the U.S. in 1968 and

they wanted to be able to give me a life where I have agency, where I'm able to make choices and determine what path is going to make me happy.

I'm not saying my parents weren't surprised at my choices. When I first started playing with rock bands, they had no idea what that was all about. They understand music and understand why music is important to people, but they haven't come to hear me play with rock bands.

How did you first begin exploring improvising on the violin?
When I was younger, my father introduced me to jazz. He played me recordings by Ella Fitzgerald, Sarah Vaughan, and Billie Holiday. But I didn't study chord progressions. I didn't study music theory. I have a good ear, but I didn't have that kind of context. I didn't listen to jazz records and play along with them.

I learned to improvise playing rock music. When I started doing sessions with different bands, the musicians would ask me to play something, and I'd have to make something up. They would tell me if what I played was or wasn't what they wanted and through that process I learned how to create something spontaneously that people wanted to hear in a specific context.

I've actually learned most of what I know about improvising over changes on the bandstand.[77] With most of these bands, there's no rehearsal. We just get onstage and they'll start a song I've never heard before, yell my name when it's time to solo, and I have to figure out what to play.

When I'm free improvising, there's a lot of melody in what I play, but sometimes, it's just texture, and that actually comes from my interest in the textural aspect of my instrument.

When I worked at WKCR, Phil Schaap introduced me to [pianist] Cecil Taylor's music. When I heard Taylor's music, I thought, "I get this!" I got that stuff in a way I didn't "get" other types of jazz I was being exposed to. While I appreciated that music, I didn't personally identify with it in terms of what I was doing. I'm a huge Charlie Parker fan, but I never wanted to play like Parker. With Cecil Taylor, the music sounded like the contemporary composers I listened to in high school, notated music from the European tradition.

In just about any interview you read with Cecil Taylor, he talks about his predecessors. He's a huge Billie Holiday fan, for instance. But when you hear his music, do you hear how it might connect back to Charlie Parker or Billie Holiday? Do you hear the music in those terms?
I don't come to it with that perspective. I kind of look at every musical thing I encounter in a little bit of a vacuum. That's just the way I hear it. That doesn't mean I'm not subconsciously connecting it to other things, but when I hear Taylor's music, I hear space. I hear clarity. I hear the willingness to embrace

the side of music that isn't so neat and pretty or leading you in such a specific direction with its melody. When music is really open, I can connect with it. It's just a little bit more profound.

Would you say your classical training has provided a foundation for the music you play now?

I don't think I can really separate myself from my training, because it started so long ago, and the lessons aren't really in my head, they're in my fingers. I can't really imagine what it would be like if I didn't have the training, because those are the letters I have that spell the words. Those are the words I have that form the sentences. That's just what I have to work with.

It's not like you threw away everything you learned in the classical world and started from scratch.

The thing about being a classical violin player is that when you play in an orchestra, you play in a section. There isn't really an emphasis on you specifically, not like it is for an oboist, for instance. When you're the only person in an orchestra playing a particular line, you really have to nail it, because if you don't, everyone's going to hear it. But violinists in their section are different. If you don't quite nail a part, the section is still going to sound pretty good. I'm not saying violinists in symphonies can't nail things. But in the environment violinists get put in, there isn't so much of an emphasis on rhythm and time the way there is for other classical instruments.

I was trained as a melodic instrumentalist. I don't think about chords. Or rather, I didn't, but I think about them more now. When I first began improvising with bands, people would shout [chord] changes at me and I wouldn't know what they meant! [laughs] I also had to get a grasp on what time is about and how to express myself within the context of time in a way that also informs how the time is evolving in a group performance.

One of the things that I had to *unlearn* was the idea of being accurate. I'm trained in a way that I have the ability to make many, many different kinds of sounds out of my instrument. I have the ability to, in a very subtle and nuanced way, get in between very, very specific kinds of sounds. I had to learn not to be so exact about that sort of stuff and just focus on the feeling and what the ensemble is trying to say.

What's ahead for you musically?

There are certain kinds of music that I've always been interested in that I want to explore more. I played in a drone band once. The participating musicians played and recorded simultaneously in three different cities. We stared playing on August 8, 2008, at 8 p.m. and played for 64 minutes. We had no notes, no instructions. We couldn't hear each other either. I mixed all of the separate recorded performances later and created this drone record. The idea of just sitting down and not knowing what you're going to play for 64 minutes, but it's basically going to be just one note, [laughs] is something I'm really interested in. It forces you to think about what *is* interesting about playing that one note. In performance, you find yourself meditating on a single note.

I did a workshop with Cecil Taylor 10 or 15 years ago. Taking a look at music that he had notated and then hearing him explain, "Well, this is really just about the idea of the note 'B.'" [laughs] I was reminded of that when I did the drone recording. You're playing and you're playing and after a while, you're playing all kinds of things. There are multitudes of experiences contained in a single note. It's kind of profound.

I play in a lot of different contexts, but feel the most comfortable when I am surrounded by people who are looking for the same thing as I am. Like when I play with William Parker's double quartet. When we get together to play, nobody knows what's going to happen. We just start playing, and I feel like what we're exploring is just the idea of, we're here and what happens when we're here? How do you respond to the things that are here? And what does that mean?

I love the idea of looking deeply into something like a single note and that in the process of looking deeper, you can explore all kinds of emotions and all kinds of powerful experiences. That's something I'm really interested in.

Samantha Boshnack

To describe Seattle-based trumpeter, composer, and bandleader Samantha Boshnack as "industrious" would be an understatement. As a musician who is always stretching, she refuses to scale down the size of her musical ambitions or be intimidated by the challenge of turning those ambitions into reality. Boshnack's projects as a bandleader include the Sam Boshnack Quintet, whose repertoire includes music inspired by 19th century feminist and journalist Nellie Bly and music for Karin Stevens Dance Company, and the 14-piece B'shnorkestra, an "alternative chamber orchestra" with a repertoire that draws on improvised music traditions from around the world, including Balkan folk music and Balinese gamelan. She is also a member of Reptet, a four-horn plus rhythm section sextet, who perform original compositions influenced by jazz, punk, avant-garde, and eastern European folk music.

While her skills as a composer and trumpet player are formidable, so is her gift for fundraising, marketing, and audience outreach. The B'shnorkestra's 2013 recording, *Go to Orange*, was funded in part through a campaign on the popular online crowdfunding platform Kickstarter. She is also the recipient of several grants, including an award from New Music USA, 4Culture, and the Seattle Office of Arts and Culture.

"Sometimes, when it comes to finding funding," says Boshnack, "the bigger the ensemble the easier it is to get funding. Because the only way you can do it is with outside sources."

So is this jazz? Once again, we find that word may or may not be helpful when it comes to describing music that is, in the words of composer John Zorn, "a bit of a freak," and is equally informed by many other styles of music besides jazz.

"The only reason I might use the word 'jazz' to describe my music is because of the improvisation," says Boshnack, "although a lot of other styles of music include improvisation. . . . I think in this day and age when we are all involved in so many kinds of music, playing all sorts of stuff all the time, you end up coming up with music that incorporates a lot of different things and can't be categorized."

Although Boshnack says she rarely writes music "that swings in the real jazz sense of the word," there is plenty of precedent in jazz for her globally-inspired compositional vision, including Carla Bley's recording *Escalator Over the Hill* (1971), the recorded legacy of Sun Ra and his Arkestra, and Duke Ellington's album *Afro-Eurasian Eclipse* (1971),[78] to name just a few. That said, Boshnack's music is not beholden to any particular tradition, other than a tra-

Samantha Boshnack. Photo by Daniel Sheehan.

dition of artistic exploration and celebration. Like any great musician, she is always pushing herself to venture outside of her comfort zone, and then share what she discovers to a listening audience.

When did you first begin playing a musical instrument?
I started playing the trumpet at age 10 and then piano at age 13. I originally wanted to play clarinet or flute in the school band, but I think my dad wanted me to play more of a "jazz" instrument. I picked up the trumpet and fell in love instantly with the instrument. I lived kind of in the country in upstate New York. I had a really good band teacher, but it was a very small school.

What kind of music did the school band play?
Normal elementary-school band stuff. But I did play classical stuff on my own and began taking lessons as well.

So you started getting serious about this instrument.

Yes. The minute I picked it up I remember I played, like, four hours a day. I was really excited about it. There was a jazz band at my school, but it met once every other week, and it wasn't really real jazz. I listened to jazz at home a lot.

You said your dad wanted you to play a jazz instrument. Is he a musician?
He played guitar when he was young. He listens to a *lot* of music. He knows a lot about it and writes a music column. I remember listening to a lot of Charlie Parker, Miles Davis, and Kenny Burrell because my dad would give me recordings.

After high school, did you attend a music conservatory?
I went to Bard College. They have a music conservatory now, but at that time they didn't. I studied with Erica Lindsay. She's a really great saxophone player and she was my mentor. I didn't know I was going to study music; I thought I might go to law school or something. [laughs] But then I kind of got sucked into the music program because they didn't have a lot of trumpet players. I ended up spending all of my time in the music building. Erica got me composing. I hadn't really done any of that. She also really worked with me on my sound. I don't know if I ever really improvised before I went to college.

So once you got to Bard, you found the right person who heard something in what you were doing and was able to develop that.
Well, I actually did apply to a bunch of music schools and auditioned but I didn't get into any of them. My senior year, I got more interested in writing the application essays than practicing for auditions! But all of the conservatories I visited just didn't feel like a very good fit for me. Bard seemed a little more open.

While at Bard, did you get to hear music in and around New York City?
Oh, yeah. And some musicians would come upstate to play. I remember hearing a show that Erica played with [slide trumpeter] Steven Bernstein and [trombonist] Roswell Budd. I actually went out and bought a slide trumpet after that. [laughs] I was also listening to a lot of recordings.

How did you end up in Seattle?
My college professors during my senior year were kind of encouraging me not to go to New York but to go somewhere else. I think this was because I kind of had a late start with everything and I needed to work on my craft more. I thought I would go to Chicago, because I was kind of interested in that scene. But my boyfriend at the time had a friend out here [in Seattle], and we took a trip to Seattle. I met a group of musicians called the Monktail Creative Music Concern, which was kind of like a free collective. They were playing a gig at this place they'd never played before and I just happened to find them. I sat in

and it just felt like a fated thing. I just really liked these musicians. I actually still play with a lot of the musicians I met that night.

My goal after getting out of school was to go somewhere where I could write music and get it played and maybe be able to help pay the bills by teaching lessons. Talking to people, it seemed like Seattle was a place where you could probably do that. It's more expensive than some cities, but less expensive than others. So I just kind of leapt into it and just fell in love with Seattle. [laughs] [Keyboardist] Wayne Horovitz is a huge part of the scene here, and I play in two of his bands. There's a lot going on. It feels good.

Here's a quote from the composer and saxophonist John Zorn: "The term 'jazz,' per se, is meaningless to me in a certain way. Musicians don't think in terms of boxes. I know what jazz music is. I studied it. I love it. But when I sit down and make music, a lot of things come together. And sometimes it falls a little bit toward the classical side, sometimes it falls a little bit towards the jazz, sometimes it falls toward rock . . . but no matter which way it falls, it's always a little bit of a freak. It's something unique, it's something different, it's something out of my heart. It's not connected with those traditions." Can you relate to that quote?
Yeah, definitely. The only reason I might use the word "jazz" to describe my music is because of the improvisation, although a lot of other styles of music include improvisation. But I rarely write anything that swings in the real jazz sense of the word and I rarely play straight-ahead jazz. I'm more likely to play a salsa gig than play that. I think in this day and age when we are all involved in so many kinds of music, playing all sorts of stuff all the time, you end up coming up with music that incorporates a lot of different things and can't be categorized.

Did improvisation initially begin for you in a traditional way, improvising through jazz standards, or were you improvising in different kinds of settings and ensembles?
I kind of jumped into it doing both at the same time, doing more free or modal improvising and doing some standard stuff. I think I was even playing in a rock-soul band and learning how to improvise with them as well.

So one way of playing wasn't a foundation you built on as an improviser?
The more modern stuff, that's what spoke to me more. I felt better improvising on that than I did on the real straight-ahead jazz. I had listened to so much straight-ahead jazz and I knew in some ways I could never . . . it's hard to feel you can do anything to that music that hasn't been done better already. It's hard to feel like you can add your own voice to bebop, you know? Just because it's already been done so well.

Would you agree that composition and improvisation are two sides of the same coin? Your compositions incorporate improvisation, right?

Yeah. And I'm composing through improvisation most of the time. The nice thing about composition is you can work on it and make it better than what the original idea was.

Or you can bring it to these larger ensembles you're involved with, like B'shnorkestra. How do you manage to keep such a large ensemble together?

I wrote a lot of grants and managed to get a few and that allowed me to debut the ensemble. I wrote eight pieces all at once for that debut and our first recording. The grants gave me a little chunk of change to rehearse the band and do that debut concert. At that time I didn't have a conductor. I played trumpet.

The thing about Seattle is you have all of these musicians who are so good and so nice, and the musicians were really down with the project. These players don't always get to do stuff like this. There was something special about the people assembled for the project. It just felt like a band, even from the very beginning.

I'm not rehearsing the band all throughout the year. It's more like, when we have shows is when we get together. It's been nice having a conductor [Joshua Kohl]. With a band this big it's so hard to hear everything and really rehearse it the way it should be rehearsed. Before the B'shnorkestra project, I didn't have a lot of experience with strings. There are different ways to talk to string players than to horn players or drummers. I'm learning more and more about the strings all the time.

Going forward, I'll just keep trying to find more opportunities and write more music. With every show I just try to do something new and push it ahead. It's a learning process.

You never thought, "Oh, this is impossible. It's too much money, too much work, it's too complicated. . . ." You just went ahead and did it.

Sometimes, when it comes to finding funding, the bigger the ensemble the easier it is to get funding. Because the only way you can do it is with outside sources. I had no idea when I was getting ready to do it how it would change me. But it definitely changed me a lot. When I was onstage during our debut performance I thought, "I just love this!" [laughs] Writing for B'shnorkestra is my way of writing for orchestra because I don't know how to break into that world.

Is there an audience for this kind of music in Seattle?

Yeah. I'm building it. It felt like people got excited about the band when it debuted. The nice thing about the project is the sound is even more far away from a jazz sound than Reptet just because of the strings. The string players would probably never call themselves jazz improvisers, but they're improvising. But then there are players in that band that are really jazz players. So I think the band brings together a lot of different audiences.

From your perspective, are there a lot of women involved in creative music? Or is it mostly men and a smaller number of women?
Well, there are a lot of really great female musicians in Seattle. At Bard there really weren't. I had my teacher, but other than her, it was all guys. When I came out here the women really supported me. I think everyone really helps each other. B'shnorkestra has a fair amount of women, and I started my own quintet and that features two other female musicians.

But yeah, you're usually a minority. You definitely still play gigs where people are like, "I haven't heard a woman play the trumpet like that." I remember in the beginning it being kind of hard and doubting myself. Guys will downplay *your* success and say, "Oh, it's because you're a girl!" But then after awhile it's just like, whatever. As a musician, male or female, you always find ways to doubt yourself!

Connie Crothers

The music of pianist Connie Crothers can be described as a bridge between interpreting standard tunes, including soloing over the harmonic progression that supports a tune's melody, and spontaneous improvisation, where music is created in the moment, without any advance preparation.

"For many years the jazz world was sort of divided into groups," says Crothers. "There's been a huge chasm between the standard-tunes players and the free improvisers for decades, and this really worked against me because I have always done both from the beginning."

Born in 1941, Crothers began studying and playing classical piano repertoire at the age of 9, and quickly began composing and performing her own music as well. While studying music composition at the University of California at Berkeley, she found herself becoming disillusioned by how musical expression was discouraged in favor of "procedure and structure" and "compositional rigor." She also began listening to jazz. After hearing a recording of pianist Lennie Tristano's "C Minor Complex," one of the earliest recorded examples of spontaneously improvised music by a jazz musician, Crothers was inspired to begin exploring improvisation. Initially, this proved to be a formidable challenge.

"I sat down at my piano," says Crothers, "and said to myself, 'Now... improvise!'... All I could do was stare at the keys. I could not improvise even with all my many years of training.... I realized that improvising had been left out of my training. And it was a shock to me!"

Crothers soon made the fateful decision to relocate from California to New York City to study with Tristano. She would go on to perform, collaborate, and record with some of the finest musicians and composers in jazz, experiences she describes in detail in this interview. Throughout her career, Crothers' music has remained uncompromising, yet completely engaging; she sees no need to "dumb down" what she does in order to appeal to some as-yet untapped market of consumers.

"People can handle great art," says Crothers. "In fact, they want it. They're being starved."

Like many of the musicians I interviewed who were born before the women's rights movement, Crothers' music-related projects are informed by her political activism. In 1982, she founded the artist-owned, collectively run label New Artist Records, and chose *Swish*, an album of duets with drummer Max Roach, for its first release. Given the economic challenge of survival as an independent artist in the U.S., she encourages musicians to take as much control over their creative work as they possibly can.

Connie Crothers. Photo by Peter Gannushkin.

Crothers' belief in the future of this music is inspiring. And while she does emphasize the importance of "roots" and "lineage," she also adamantly believes jazz is evolving as an art form, and that we are, in fact, "heading into something incredible."

....

Your music illuminates the connection between so-called "straight-ahead" and "free" jazz.
For many years the jazz world was sort of divided into groups. For instance, there was a kind of division between the free improvisers and the jazz musicians who played tunes, as well as other divisions based on other consider-

ations. But now we're moving into a new era. I feel that it is already underway; certainly it is in New York City. I call it a jazz renaissance. But it's happening underground. It's not on the surface. It's underground.

But the thing that I think has to happen in order for this to come to fruition is that all the groups need to open up and find out about each other, because there are so many valuable musicians in each group. And if they find out about each other, the art form will just blossom! I look forward to that. I hope to be a part of that. In fact, in a way, I already am because I have several friends, associates, and know fellow musicians in more than one of these groups, much to my great joy.

You said this renaissance is taking place underground. So it's taking place outside of academia, outside of the colleges and universities?
Yes! Way outside! Way outside. But it's taking place outside of the mainstream venues as well. So some of the leading proponents of this jazz renaissance are still unknown.

I bring this up because among the musicians I've interviewed for this project, no two have taken an identical path toward becoming a musician. There doesn't seem to be a set path for achieving your potential as a musician.
That's true.

When did you first begin playing a musical instrument? How old were you?
I was 9. My instrument was the piano. My grandmother, who was like my mother, bought an old upright—everybody did that in those years, you know? My grandmother had a friend who taught piano lessons. So I studied with her friend who was studying with a teacher, Edward Hoy, who was the most highly reputed teacher in the San Francisco Bay area. My grandmother's friend got me a scholarship to study with him.

I was studying only classical music. From the time I was 9, I was writing my own compositions. This teacher presented me a lot in recitals and concerts and had me present my pieces on my programs. So from the time I was 12 to 15 I was performing quite a lot. Big works! [laughs] I used to play three sets of big works by Beethoven, Bach, and Chopin, as well as some of the more modern composers like Ravel and Debussy. And my own pieces were included on these programs.

Even as a child, I realized that I did not want to spend my life performing other people's music. As much as I loved these pieces, I realized that that would never fulfill me and that I was going to have to create my own music.

However, when I was 12 years old, I gave up composing. And the reason why I gave it up is because I realized that the idiom that I was familiar with was not current. I didn't feel it had contemporary value. And so I just let it go. And I didn't get back to composing until I was in my late teens.

What made you decide your music, the music you were composing, didn't have a contemporary value?
I knew it wasn't a contemporary idiom. I was mostly hearing the sound of the kind of music that was composed in the 18th and 19th centuries in Europe.

When did you being improvising?
When I was in my late teens, I went back into music, with the serious idea in mind to become a composer. I went to the University of California at Berkeley, and while I was there, still an undergraduate, I audited graduate courses and studied with a Berkeley composer. I was extremely serious.

But I also knew pretty quickly that this wasn't for me. During those years certainly, composing was very much about procedure. And I didn't think that that's what music was for. For me, the reason we have music is to express feeling. And that wasn't going on in the Berkeley environment at the time. Instead, it was about procedure and structure. The favorite phrase, instead of feeling or beauty, was "compositional rigor!" So it was just not for me.

So I thought, "Well, I don't know anything about jazz, but it's the other great art music of our time, so I'll find out about it!" I listened to the radio, I

Connie Crothers. Photo by Scott Friedlander.

bought a few records, but I didn't really get a handle on it. I studied with an arranger, a local radio personality named Cous Cousineau, who was really a terrific guy. But that didn't get it for me either.

And then I heard a track called "Requiem" by [the pianist] Lennie Tristano. It's about four minutes long, and during the length of that track, I had an amazing experience where I saw my future. It was unnerving, because I had a very wonderful, happy life in California that I did not want to leave. I knew nothing about New York City; I knew nothing about improvising or about jazz, but I knew that that's what was going to happen. It was almost as if it had already happened. It was a very incredible experience.

I started to try and find out about improvisation. During a lesson with Cous we were listening to Lennie Tristano's "C Minor Complex," and I said, "Now I know that's not improvised . . ." because I had a way of knowing. I was a jazz composer and a piano player, and knew enough to know that the musical complexity and pianistic demands I was hearing were way past what anybody could do if they were improvising. I just knew that that track had to have been composed. Of course, Cous set me straight right away. He said, "Every note on that piece is improvised." When he said that to me, it made a believer out of me. I knew that's what I wanted to do.

When I realized that I wanted to improvise, I sat down at my piano, and said to myself, "Now . . . improvise!" And I sat there for about a half hour. All I could do was stare at the keys. I could not improvise even with all of my many years of training and the ability I had developed—I could really play, you know? I even knew by then that those classical composers were improvisers, like Bach for example. I realized that improvising had been left out of my training. And it was a shock to me!

The thing that I credit myself for is that while I was sitting there, wanting to improvise, I didn't bullshit! I didn't just fake it. I knew I couldn't do it, and I didn't fake it. So it was a moment of truth for me. And when I came to New York City, I didn't really know if I could improvise. But it worked out. It's amazing what such a huge premonition—well, it wasn't even a premonition. When I heard Tristano's "Requiem," I was catapulted into my future. Like it had already happened. It all worked out and proved to be true.

How did you connect with Lennie Tristano when you got to New York City?
[Saxophonist] Lee Konitz came into the area and advertised at UC Berkeley and I took formal lessons with him, which showed me I could not procrastinate for any reason. Lee Konitz was very gracious, and he taught me some important things. But I knew that I couldn't settle. I had to go to New York City.

So Lee Konitz called Lennie and recommended me. So as soon as I got to New York City, I started studying with him.

In addition to performing and recording you also teach. What are some practical instructions you offer your students who want to begin improvising?

Number one: sing with records.

Is that something Lennie had you do?

Yes. "Sing with records," is what Lennie told me. He told me that when he was first starting to teach, he knew a lot of theory and could present that very well. But he said to me, in those earlier years, what wasn't happening with his students was spontaneous improvisation, the kind of spontaneous improvisation he knew about. But he discovered that having his students sing with records opened that up. Lennie told me he felt that was the greatest discovery of his teaching life.

Now when I present this to my students, I recommend they start out with the musicians in the first decades of this music. We all need our roots. It goes back before John Coltrane; it even goes back before Charlie Parker. People have to find out where we came from. We need our lineage.

Beyond that, during those first few decades of this music, there was a different energy and all of the musicians were in this energy. And I think some of it is because they never stopped playing. That improvisation energy was more open than it is today. Now there have been outstanding innovators since then of course, but I like to say, if you really want to find out about spontaneous improvisation, do a lot of singing with people like Louis Armstrong, Roy Eldridge, Lester Young, Billie Holiday, Charlie Christian, and other musicians from those years. Then move on to Charlie Parker, Bud Powell—I have a whole roster of musicians I like to suggest. Or I will say to people, if a solo reaches for you, sing with that one, because it has a personal meaning.

Beyond that, I don't teach in the academic way about improvisation. My approach is not based on putting melodic material into chord changes. I feel that's false. That's not improvisation, that's a substitute. And people commonly understand that as improvisation, but in fact, it's not. What I try to get to instead with people is have them play the strict melody of a tune with no ornamentation whatsoever. Not like on the sheet music, but like how they would sing it, just very simply. And then, instead of trying to think chords, just hear the melody, and let the melodic line get released, with the melody being your source. I like to say the melody has everything in it. It has the harmonic sound, so you're getting the harmony from your ear, rather than thinking "C7."

Besides that, the melody of the tune has the form. If you internalize the melody of the tune, you don't have to count beats and bars, you don't have to be cognizant of your sections. The melody gives the whole thing to you. And when you release your improvisation after that point, you can bring in anything. If you start thinking chords before you release your improvisation, it's like trying to fly with a weight on you. It doesn't happen. You're going to be stuck thinking chords for the rest of your playing life. I have helped people get out of that.

Chord changes with bits of melody and chord scales can get you complicated music, but it's limited. There's a limit to it. But if you contact spontaneous improvisation, that's boundless. There's no boundary on it. It stretches out infinitely!

Simple and complex are identical. The opposite of simple is complicated. And anything complicated cannot be complex. So I get musicians into being able to contact whatever they work on from the simplest expression, and the simplest expression of a tune is the melody.

My own musical work, and the way I work with the people who study with me, is not predetermined in any way. It's open. So when I say spontaneous improvisation, it's open to everything. I don't believe in mistakes. I encourage people to improvise freely and when they're playing from a melody on a tune, to accept what they might think of as "wrong" notes.

With more advanced people, I open it up for them to improvise with harmony while remaining deeply within the tune. I don't believe in honoring the harmony. I think that's a mistake with the chord-changes approach to teaching; you go around and listen all around town and no matter what the content is, if musicians are playing a standard tune, you hear the same harmony. You may hear variations of it. But mostly, what you'll hear honors the harmony too much. It's no wonder people want to throw out standards. I'd be sick of them also if that's what I was doing.

There's been a huge chasm between the standard-tunes players and the free improvisers for decades, and this really worked against me because I have always done both from the beginning. So I kind of caught it from both sides, you know? Not so much now, but certainly when I was coming up. Free improvisers thought that if you played tunes, it's not pure improvisation. And the tunes players thought if you do any free improvisation, well that was just bullshit. I may be oversimplifying! But in my opinion, that's the next step for this music. To take that huge world that separates those two modes of improvisation and just throw it away, get rid of it! Because in my opinion those two modes of improvisation can merge and the next evolution of this music can express that.

I feel like I'm coming from a long lineage. As I like to point out to people, I think the first instance of free improvisation on record is Louis Armstrong's intro to "West End Blues." That's the 1920s. Roy Eldridge told me he improvised free with Chu Berry and Clyde Hart, and I heard him do it in a concert once, atonal music by the way. Lennie Tristano, who was the first person to go into the recording studio with this in mind, had free-improvising sessions with his band three times a week for two years before they took it into a club. They did this in Birdland. They played some tunes, and they also did some free improvisation. So the separation of those two modes of expression is a mistake! And when we wake up to that and let them converge as they naturally do, that's our next level. I can't even imagine the music that's going to result from that except, of course, I've tapped into that. [laughs] I know what that feels like.

The kind of playing you are describing requires a high level of musicianship.
Oh, yes. People have to give their lives to developing their understanding of music. Absolutely.

A lot of people don't understand the amount of work that has to go into what you're describing here. It's not that one mode of expression is easier than another.
Free improvisation is more challenging in a way. Because if you have that understanding of music, you're never going to be able to fake it. You can't. You have to tap into that deep well of understanding every time you express your music. That's your mode. You can't be in another mode. With no parameters to guide you, it's on you to create music that's beautiful and has an inner logic. I find this extremely intriguing and really exciting—thrilling in fact!

I just want to describe something to you if I may. At the 2011 Vision Festival, I played a set with my quartet, with Richard Tabnik on alto saxophone, Roger Mancuso on drums, and Ken Filiano on bass. We agreed ahead of time we would choose some tunes and play the heads of those tunes during the set, but that at any time any one of the four of us could drop the tune and go into free improvisation. We didn't say we would play free improvisation at selected times, like, play a head,[79] play a chorus or two of the tune, and then play free. Any one of us could play free even if the rest of us were still in the head. And this really worked! It worked even better than I thought it would.

Do you remember what tunes you chose for that performance?
The heads I wrote expressed one thing, but we associated each head with a tune that we liked. For example, we started with a head I wrote called "Helen's Tune," and midway through we played a head I call "Carol's Dream."

And they reminded you of other standard tunes?
Yeah. Like a lot of times, when we play "Carol's Dream," we actually play the tune "You Stepped Out of a Dream." But "Carol's Dream" is way, way away from "You Stepped Out of a Dream." It's just that we [the quartet] have that association. But "Carol's Dream" is another piece, actually.

It's hard to describe this. It's not like I've just written like a melodic statement over some changes. Quite the contrary. It's more like an association. So during that stretch, some of us were playing "You Stepped Out of a Dream" and some of us were not. It shifted and changed from moment to moment in an uncoordinated way. And it worked! [laughs]

From my perspective, it seems that this evolution in the music is happening at a time where more women are a part of this music and are being acknowledged for the roles they've played in its development.
When I first came to New York City in 1962, this was before the women's movement, when I went to a club, it was like walking a gauntlet. It was just understood that if there was a woman on the premises, the men were gonna hit on her. Now, this is called sexual harassment. In those years it was considered to be that's just how it is, you know? Like, what's there to think about? No one gave it any thought. I heard from a good source that Lester Young's sister Emma Young quit music for that reason when she got married. A lot of women in those days were kicked off of bandstands and out of the recording dates because of the prevailing notion, which was very strong then, that men were better, that women were not as good as men. If you thought that way, it was considered hip. This sexual harassment was very intense.

But the exceptions were the guys that I met who were studying with Lennie who were in my generation. They were not like that at all. I met Roger Mancuso, who is in my band today, and he related to me as a musician right away. And so did [saxophonist] Lenny Popkin, the tenor player. Over time, we moved into an era where sexual harassment could still go on of course, but it was not as acceptable.

What I noticed for decades was that it was almost like an unwritten rule that there should never be more than one woman on the bandstand. Time after time if there were any women at all on the bandstand, it would be just one. This was even true if it was a singer's group. The singer, if she were a woman, would be the only woman on stage. Or, if there was a woman instrumentalist, there would only be just one. But this is changing and it's changing especially among the younger women. There are bands where there are a few women or maybe the band is mostly women. This is a major change.

I had a band for a long time that featured Carol Tristano. She's a great drummer. It was a band I co-led with Lenny Popkin. For the most part, we played with Cameron Brown. So there were two women in the band. Carol, like me, is not big in stature. And she's very sweet. She's not tall and big. She used to sit down at the kit and she had this sweet expression. And you could feel it, you know? The audience would just think, "Oh, well. We're not gonna get much from this drummer. She's a little chick." But then she would take her first solo, and the whole place would go crazy. Audiences are more receptive than people give them credit for. The audiences had no problem with her as soon as they heard her cut loose with a solo.

In this music there have been hundreds, even thousands of great women musicians. One example that immediately comes to my mind is Vi Redd, who I think is one of the most important alto saxophone players in this music. I could go down a long list.

Louis Armstrong's Hot Five was originally Lil [Lillian] Hardin's band. She was a bandleader. Not only was she a bandleader, she was a promoter. She did promotion for Louis. She got him away from Fletcher Henderson, and the rest is history, right? Bear in mind that when she was in the Hot Five she was still in her 20s. She was an extremely accomplished musician and jumped over hurdles to accomplish what she did. But after she broke up with Louis that was it for her. But what she did should be regarded as a cornerstone of this music.

Mary Osborne is one of the most important musicians in jazz. She's the missing link between Charlie Christian and the guitar players who came afterwards. The missing link the historians have been seeking is her. She was Charlie Christian's only protégé. She's major. Billie knew about her, and hired her for that TV special. So there were two women in that band. [laughs]

People don't realize how avant-garde Billie Holiday was back in the day.
That's right.

You talked about going back to the earlier decades of this music and listening to people like Charlie Parker, Billie Holiday, Frank Sinatra, and listening to their solos not so much as time capsules of a style, but for their immediacy. And if you sing with those solos, you tap into that immediacy with them. You're there in that moment with them.
That's it.

And the solo you're singing becomes something else altogether. It transcends these labels we're stuck with.
You got it. That says it very well.

Like you, I'm excited by the potential for change we're talking about.
We're moving! We're moving. Jazz is not dead! In fact, we're heading into something incredible. I get surprised all the time by individual performances.

Say a young person comes to you and says, "I want to play music." He or she wants to play it as well as they can; they're not interested in something that's commercial or playing anything other than who they are —
That's the only kind of student I get!

Do you talk to your students about the economic realities of being an artist in this country?

Everyone has this problem. It's not new. It's not a new problem. Jazz in the first few decades was supported by the gangsters. They were like the Medici. But when they stopped supporting jazz, there really wasn't any money. If you got a good gig in a festival or went on a European tour you could get some money. But there has never been any money for jazz musicians, not in this country.

There is a saying, a tourist in New York City stops a New Yorker and asks, "How do you get to Carnegie Hall?" and the New Yorker replies, "Practice, practice, practice!" People know what this joke means, and it is a musician's life, especially a jazz musician. When you're a jazz musician, you have to create the music at the very split second you are performing it. That's an amazing challenge. To be able to do that with any depth you've got to spend tremendous quantities of time not just in the beginning, but all of your life. And none of the time that you spend is paid, none of it.

So most every jazz musician I have ever known had other ways of bringing in income. Even an amazing successful musician like [drummer] Max Roach worked at the University of Massachusetts. Lennie Tristano was a teacher of course. I don't think Roy Eldridge had another job, but he told me there were some lean times and at one point in his life he considered becoming a radio technician.

All musicians have this problem. It's in the core of life for all artists, the enormous amount of time that you must bring to your art to be any good at it is not paid. At the very same time that your professional counterparts are coming up in their profession and getting paid, you're not. It's not just that the gigs are few and far between and the times are lean. It's that most of the work you will do in your lifetime will not be reimbursed. So you have to see the enormity of that and come up with any kind of strategy you can. I have to say many of the people who study with me, just as I was when I was young, are extremely poor.

It's a juggling act with finances and this time commitment you're talking about. And it's hard to prepare someone for it if they haven't experienced it. They have dreams of "making it" as a performer! Every musician starts out with that.

When I was at the music conservatory, the big thing musicians I knew dreamed about was recording records and touring. And at that time in the music industry, you had records coming out by great jazz musicians, like Mike Stern or John Scofield, that were kind of popular. And you thought, "Well, I could do that!" Now the landscape has changed. Even recording doesn't seem to be a great option for generating income.

Well, here is one of the things that was operating in those years, and I'm not commenting on any specific individuals when I say this. In order for you to stay out there as a performer and make your money, you needed to accept some compromise. It may not be that you're going to have to play rock. But you're going to have to compromise with the business people. They're going to want to have some input in what you record and what you present on their stage. It's the difference between the market and pure art. They have this idea that people can't handle great music. "Great art? They can't handle it!" I've heard people say this in the business. But they're wrong, because in the years when the gangsters put their money behind the people they liked, that's when the musicians went to ultimate fame and this music was the dominant music. So Louis Armstrong was, after Caruso maybe, the first international superstar. And Roy Eldridge, when he was playing at his greatest, when he was a featured star with Gene Krupa, was a pop star. So now all of these many years down the road with the money people having the say, jazz is at the bottom. Their idea is a proven failure. People can handle great art. In fact, they want it. They're being starved.

Today we have independent labels like New Artists Records and festivals like the Vision Festival that are run by artists who say, "We have got to get this music out there somehow!"
Get away from those money people and do it yourself!

Malika Zarra

Singer and composer Malika Zarra came to music at the relatively late age of 19. The reason for her decision to begin studying the art of singing is intriguing, and speaks to the pan-cultural spirit of her music.

"I felt very strongly that art could be a tool that could have an impact between people coming from different cultures and backgrounds," says Zarra. "I could have done other things. But I felt that music and singing would be easier for me, because I was surrounded by music at home."

Zarra was born in Morocco, in a small village called Ouled Teima. Singing and dancing, as well as listening to both traditional and Western music on the radio, was a part of daily life at home. After her family emigrated from Morocco to Paris, Zarra, who says she was "very, very shy" as a child, had to reconcile the differences between her native and Parisian culture. Many of her songs, especially those on her album *Berber Taxi* (2011), speak to the experience of being a stranger in a new, unfamiliar land, and how friendship, family, and one's native culture can help with navigating an unfamiliar, sometimes not-so-friendly world.

Since improvisation is an integral part of Arabic and African music, Zarra was initially drawn to jazz. However, singing jazz presented its own unique cultural challenges.

"I used to sing a lot of jazz standards and liked it, but . . . I would forget the lyrics," says Zarra. "There are references in jazz songs that I don't have, because they're not a part of my cultural background. So I started writing my own lyrics in my own language."

In 1996, Zarra traveled from Paris to New York City, where she met several talented and supportive musicians, including saxophonist and educator Arnie Lawrence, who helped her explore different cultural influences in her singing and composing.

Like Ayelet Rose Gottlieb and Sofia Rei, her fellow singer/composer/lyricists in the four-voice a capella group Mycale, Zarra has managed to absorb several cultural influences while remaining grounded in the roots of her native land. The result is a truly global music that's a little more profound and enriching than the "world music" one may hear piped in a day spa and or yoga studio.

"If you're not able to see where things are coming from and where you are coming from," says Zarra, "the experience becomes diluted."

Malika Zarra. Photo by Becca Meek.

When did you first begin singing or playing a musical instrument?
I started quite late, actually. I was 19 years old when I started playing the clarinet in a marching band.

But growing up in Morocco, there was always music in your house?
Yes, definitely. Usually, in most African homes, music is very important, and we weren't an exception. My mother used to listen to a lot of traditional music as well as the radio. We listened to Western music on the radio as well.

Your family chose to emigrate from Morocco to France. . . .
Yes.

Why did they decide to do that?
Economic reasons. This is the only reason why.

The place where you grew up in Paris is described as a "suburb." In America, a suburb is generally an upscale, usually white community, located outside of a city. But that's not the kind of environment you grew up in, correct?
Yeah. It was like what you in America call "the projects." Most of the projects in France and Europe in general, they are in the suburbs.

Did you have any sort of musical education before the age of 19?
Not really. I mean ... there was a little bit of music in the schools, but in France

it wasn't that important at that time. We had maybe one hour per week that was drawing and painting and the next week would be music.

At some point, maybe when I was 13 or 14 years old, I had a music teacher who became a big influence for me. She gave me a resonating feeling about what art could be and what art could bring to the people's lives.

Did you listen to a lot of music as a teenager?
I didn't have the resources to buy recordings. But I would go to the library in my neighborhood to listen to records.

When did you start singing?
I guess six months or a year after I started playing clarinet. I was 20 years old.

What happened that inspired you to start singing?
It's kind of weird, but this is how I started . . . at that point, I felt very, very strongly that art could be a tool that could have a lot of impact between people coming from different cultures and backgrounds. For me, [making art] was kind of a challenge. I felt I would be better at promoting art, because I was very, very shy. *Very* shy. I felt that maybe I should, just for myself, learn an art activity so I could overcome my shyness. I could have done other things. But I felt that music and singing would be easier for me, because I was surrounded by music at home.

I went to study at the conservatory and I didn't like it. I didn't like classical music. I felt it was a little bit too far for me. I really didn't know which kind of music I wanted to do because I really had no music education.

Little by little, I came to jazz because my clarinet teacher was a jazz musician. So through him, he showed me a lot of records. And then the improvisation thing was something very close to me because in Arabic and African music, improvisation is a very important item. So I thought that it would be good for me to start with [jazz]. I really liked the rock energy, but I felt it was too, too far for me because I was very shy. But I always liked that rock energy.

So, finally, jazz won! [laughs] At least at that time. That's how I started. I studied at private schools and took private lessons.

During this time, you were studying both the voice and clarinet?
Yes.

Was the decision to sing and sing lyrics, other people's words and eventually your own, part of your desire to bring people from different cultures and backgrounds together?
For me, at that time, I thought that *any* art could have that kind of impact. I guess I chose singing because I just felt that I didn't need to buy any other instruments! And it's something closer to me, since my mother sang a lot.

Do you remember the first time you sang in front of an audience?
This is weird. I never thought about that. [laughs] I don't remember when I sang the first time. But I have a vague idea that I was, like, very, very scared. [laughs] Yeah, that's it. Let's not talk any more about that!

But that's an experience many musicians share. The first time you sing or play in front of people, it can be scary, but it can also be very empowering.
Yes.

Once you get through it, you say to yourself, "I enjoy this. I'm going to figure out how to do this!"
Actually, it took me a long time to really feel my own joy with myself. I think for a long time, what made me happy was to see the reaction of the audience. That, for me, was the biggest part of my happiness for a while.

When did you begin writing your own songs?
I think around 1995, 1996. I used to sing a lot of jazz standards and liked it, but at the same time I felt that . . . I always would forget the lyrics. There are references in jazz songs that I don't have, because they're not a part of my cultural background. So I started writing my own lyrics in my own language, my mother language, for the jazz standards I was singing.

I went to New York in 1996, and met some amazing musicians. One of them was [saxophonist] Arnie Lawrence, who really helped me explore my different cultural influences. After that, I started writing my own songs.

You made a decision to relocate from France to New York City. That's a big life decision. Can you talk a little bit about that?
Well, first of all, I have to be honest with you. The first time I came to the U.S. was in 1996. [Before that], while I loved a lot of things in the American culture, one of them being the music, I was never attracted to go to the U.S.

In 1996, I really felt I needed to go and check out the mecca of jazz, and I really fell in love with New York City and the people that I met, the kindness, the simplicity of the relationship with people. I really wanted to come back after that and stay for two years to learn from the city and the culture. But I wasn't able to come back to stay until 2004. I got rejected when I wanted to come back and study. Arnie Lawrence tried to get me into The New School, but I didn't have the money for that. So he asked me to come to the U.S. anyway to see what instead we could do. But, when I tried to return to the U.S., I got rejected. It was a horrible experience.

In 1996, that was the year when the plane crashed,[80] [saxophonist] Wayne Shorter's wife was on that plane. I remember really well, when I got my ticket, the agent, the tourist agent, told me, "You know, be careful, because right now the U.S. is rejecting a lot of people from entering the country. Especially people like you, born in a Muslim country. And you went to New York not too long ago." In Paris, at the airports, American [security] employees would ask you, "How much money do you have? Where are you going?"

When I got to New York, even though I had a French passport, the agent I saw, I think it was at Newark Airport, really gave me a hard time because I was born in Morocco and had recently traveled to Morocco. I was telling her I had traveled to Morocco just to see my family. I was detained for six hours. It was the most horrible thing I've experienced in my life.

I found out years later when I returned to the U.S. and had my visa, that the reason why they rejected me was because of a drawing I had from a friend, a musician, a trumpet player, who I'd met on my first visit to New York. To survive, he was a dog walker, and he drew this picture of himself surrounded by dogs and gave it to me as a souvenir. I kept that drawing in my calendar along with all the business cards everyone was giving me. And I completely forgot about this. So when I returned to the U.S. in 2004, I asked them why I had not been allowed to enter the U.S. just a few years previously. I finally got a letter from the immigration service that explained I had been rejected because they had found a drawing in my belongings that was proof that I wanted to work in the U.S. illegally as a dog walker! [laughs]

Oh, no!
This really ruined my life for years because of that drawing.

People were making a connection that wasn't based at all on reality.
Exactly. You have no control over this.

I'd like to talk about a few specific tracks from your album "Berber Taxi." First, can you explain the meaning of the title of the song "Berber Taxi?"
"Berber Taxi" is not an original composition of mine. It's a traditional Moroccan song. I couldn't find the name of the composer of this song, so that's my own title, my own creation. My mother taught me this song. It is a song she sang as a teenager. They used to sing it because she grew up in the mountains. As you know, there's a lot of Berber or, as we call them, Amazigh people in Morocco. They are the native people of Morocco and a lot of other countries in Africa. When the Arabs invaded these countries, they had to retreat and hide in the mountains. So a lot of them lived in isolated places. And in this song, it's like the young people, they don't see a lot of new people, and the only way to see new people that they would fall in love with would be through a taxi driver. They are waiting for a taxi driver to bring them to their love.

Are you singing in Berber on that song?
Yes.

Did your mother speak Berber around the house?
Not really. Because my father is from another region, a southern region of Morocco, with an Arab background, and he wasn't really comfortable with that language. So we ended up speaking the Moroccan dialect.

The rhythmic changes throughout the song give me the image of a person who is new to a city, maybe an immigrant, surrounded by lots of activity, lots of transitions happening very quickly.
That's interesting. I never thought about that. I like it! [laughs]

The next song I'd like to talk about, "Houaria," reminds me a bit of Wayne Shorter's writing, or maybe a composition by the band Weather Report. Is this one of your own compositions?
Yes.

What does the title translate to?
It is exactly where I was born. It is the tribe of my father.

Was it inspired by jazz music in any way?
I can't avoid it. This [jazz] is also my culture. I went to school for that. So yes, I use jazz harmonies, and then there are rhythms, and call and response from traditional Moroccan music.

The third track I wanted to ask you about may speak to your experiences living in France after emigrating there from Morocco: "Mon Printemps." What's the story behind this song?
This one, it's a composition that I co-wrote with Irene Jacob. She's an actress and singer in France. She's the sister of my guitar player, Francis Jacob. What I'm talking about in that song is how friendship can inspire you so much and how the breath of spring can come into your life, just like the love of your friends, and have a lot of impact. "Mon Printemps" means "My Spring."

Would you say there is a larger international presence now in jazz music? Or just in music in general? Are you seeing more musicians who come from different cultures and ethnic backgrounds coming together to create new hybrids of music?
Everything, music and all of the other arts, is becoming a melting pot. And there's a good side of it and a bad side of this. The good side of it is a large number of people now have the opportunity to discover something from other than where they come from. At the same time, I think what's difficult today is to be able to define and understand where this and this item comes from. If you're not able to see where things are coming from and where you are coming from, the experience becomes diluted.

The challenge in a world that is more international is always to be able to identify where things are coming from and not be superficial. This is very important, and it's not easy to do. Even if you are mixing things, how much time you spend to really dig in and be sincere about this, to see and to know where you are getting this or this information, that is very, very important.

Unfortunately, our society wants things to be very fast and easy. Everything is created to be consumed easily, like food. Changing the subject! That's why I enjoy spending time in Morocco. Because it's a place where you don't have all this processed food and you still know what you are eating. And the result of this food is your health!

I think for each human being, it's important to have the patience to try and look for what is true and where things are coming from.

Nioka Workman

In a 2003 interview for *All About Jazz*,[81] Philadelphia-born bassist Reggie Workman credits Philadelphia's musical culture and a nurturing home environment for inspiring him to study music.

"Now that I look back on the situation," says Workman. "I realize how much the culture has to do with the evolution of a people. . . . A lot of our institutions . . . the school systems and so forth, didn't encourage too much cultural evolution, but that was a natural thing in our community. I think my parents recognized that and it developed from there."

The impact that the home environment and the culture of a community can have on a young person is a recurring theme in my interview with Reggie Workman's daughter, cellist, composer, and improviser Nioka Workman. Workman grew up in Brooklyn, and initially studied both music and dance at the New Muse Community Center (where her father was the music director), Henry Street Settlement, and Third Street Music School Settlement. Not surprisingly, her family supported her in all of her aspirations.

"They definitely are all about supporting whatever it is you decide to do, as long as you're happy," says Workman. "But music, that's who we are. . . . my uncle [Arthur Harper] played with [trombonist] J.J. Johnson. I have cousins who played with Chuck Berry. . . . I have all kinds of music in my family. It's just part of my life."

For decades, the cello has provided an especially unique voice in the world of jazz and improvised music. Cellists such as Fred Katz, Tom Cora, Hank Roberts, Diedre Murray, and Abdul Wadud have expanded the role of the instrument by embracing musical idioms from around the globe, as well as extended techniques,[82] amplification, and electronics, to produce an expansive, sometimes startling vernacular of sounds. Workman explores all of these sonic territories as a solo performer, in the electric cello and guitar duo Iron Blossoms with electric guitarist Hui Cox, and as the member of her six-piece acoustic chamber ensemble, Firey String Sistas! Workman's technique is rooted in her study of classical and jazz repertoire as well as the music of the "masters of soul, funk, and R&B." This, together with her passion for and understanding of a wide variety of other creative mediums, including dance, performance art, and theater, has allowed her to develop a deeply personal and compelling style on both acoustic and electric cello.

In 2011, Workman formed the Firey String Company [FSCO], an organization dedicated to presenting educational workshops and concert programming and creating "nurturing environments for creative and improvising string players to perform, share, learn new skills, produce new work and net-

Nioka Workman. Photo by Clifton Anderson.

work." FSCO is especially committed to empowering female musicians, and in her interview, Workman points out that women have always participated in the development of jazz.

"There have always been a lot of women playing improvisatory music, which is what I prefer to call it," says Workman, "and now, a lot more are being recognized for what they do ..."

When did you first begin playing a musical instrument?

Officially, I started taking lessons at the age of 10. But my father had a lot of instruments around his studio space. And my folks, they wanted us to try different things before they locked us into taking traditional lessons. So, we did dance, we did karate, art, and all kinds of things. We tried the piano, violin, I tried the bass — oh my God, and the bass was too *huge*. But I didn't know they had smaller versions [laughs] or else I think I would have tried that out!

So I kind of went through an exploration period for a while before I landed.

Was it required in the household that the children play a musical instrument?

Not at all, not at all.

You were living with your family in New York?

Yes. Brooklyn is where I was raised. But I was born in the Village. We were there for a while, then we were in Queens for a minute, and then settled in Brooklyn when I was in elementary school. I'd say age 10 is when I started playing cello. In junior high, my dad was the director at the New Muse Community Center, and that's where I started taking official lessons. You had all kinds of things going on there.

What kind of music were you playing then?

A lot of my teachers were going back and forth with my father. He wanted me to start with jazz. Actually, you could say that he was the first teacher because he gave me a few tunes to learn. "Embraceable You," [trombonist] J.J. Johnson songs, whatever music he had around he gave me and encouraged me to play by ear.

So he wanted me to learn and play jazz first. But in any traditional lessons I had, the teachers said, "She needs more opportunities. . . ." So they started me with the Suzuki Method.[83] When I went to Henry Street Settlement for a while, that was *strictly* Suzuki. [laughs]

Would you go home and in addition to practicing whatever it was you needed to practice, play the music your dad was encouraging you to play?

Oh, yes! I always wanted to play music with my father. That was my goal in life, you know?

How about improvising? Was that a part of your musical world as well?

Well, with my dad, I was mostly playing by ear. I don't think that improvising is what we did. We just played music, you know? I mean, all of it is improvisation, but traditionally, that came in later after the classical training.

Were you on track as a younger musician to be a classical musician before making a decision to play jazz? Or was it much more organic than that?

I did everything organically at first, and at age 10, I was put on a classical track. So yes, at the New Muse Community Center I had theory and cello and lessons and all that. Then I went to Henry Street Settlement, and then I went to Third Street Music School Settlement, all of these different schools.

But I wanted to improvise and do new music and jazz. So, after I got out of school, I just started branching out.

Using the word "jazz" sometimes is a little misleading.

Mm-hmm.

And when I listen to your music, I hear a lot of different things.
I did a gig last night with [singer] Antoinette Montague. What a wonderful artist.

She sang a mix of all kinds of things. Blues was the main music that she felt the audience really responded to. But she sang "Here's to Life" and all these beautiful songs by Nina Simone. To be able to go from a kind of an art song to kind of a Broadway-type song to an R&B song ... I think you just have to stay open and study and learn different things. To use just one word, "jazz ..." I don't know. What does that word mean?

It sounds like your family supported your decision to make a career for yourself as a musician.
[laughs] Well, yeah! They definitely are all about supporting whatever it is you decide to do, as long as you're happy. But music, that's who we are. I mean, my uncle played with J.J. Johnson. I have cousins who played with Chuck Berry.... I have all kinds of music in my family. It's just part of my life.

So you didn't have anybody discouraging you, saying, "This is going to be really tough for you financially, you're gonna have to think of something to fall back on!"
[laughs] Oh, boy. I hear you. If you love the process, where just being a part of the music is an honor, to just be alive and continue to grow and learn and share with people ... it's a choice. You just make a choice.

Some people choose to know when their vacations are, know when their retirement is, know when you're gonna get paid. [laughs] You do have to pay bills, and some things you just have to do. And yes, I'm trained in the Suzuki Method. I can do that kind of thing, and I've done a myriad of jobs to support what I'm doing. And I've heard that "advice" over and over again. But I know where my heart is and I know where my focus is.

When were you first exposed to dance? Does that go back to your childhood as well?
Oh, yeah. Back at New Muse, I was told, "Nioka, you can't do it all. You can either do dance, or you can do music!" [laughs] "Why can't I do both?" "Because your grades aren't doing so well! You have to cut one of them!"

I believe I would have been a dancer if not a musician. So if I can stay around it, if I can be around it in collaboration, that's wonderful. [Dancer, choreographer] Marlies Yearby has inspired me so much, because she is just so free and spontaneous and creative. And Maria Mitchell, who is really a historian, she studies so much, and puts all of her information into her choreography. Those two people really have inspired me to just stay connected, really stay connected to dance.

Can you talk a little bit about the relationship or the similarities that music has to movement? Is dance music? Is music dance?

We just went through a whole summer with [the] Joffrey Ballet. I usually go in there by myself and kind of work with the class. Oh, *so* much to talk about. Because it's not songs that I do [with dancers], it's mostly sounds and shapes and rhythms. A lot of their training is in ballet, so it's up, up, up. Everything is above the ground, up in the sky. They train to think "up." So when they hear the rhythms that sound kind of African and really deep and low in the bass register, they're like, "Oh my God. I didn't know what to do! I don't know where to put my body. It's so heavy. What is this?"

Unless they come from another country! A lot of the people from India or from Latin countries or African, even some Asian countries, they're okay with relating to that. Like, "Okay, yeah! Give me more!" So it's interesting what the [musical] connections are to the body, and where in the body they feel it.

I'm getting ready to do a piece with someone in Minneapolis dealing with cancer, and the first thing I went to with her was chakras and how some people use meditation and sound to heal, to open meridians, to open blockages, and heal themselves. So we're going to explore that a little bit.

I feel like I'm a little behind, because I know people like Sun Ra years ago have worked with that area of study.

Where music has a physical healing power?

Yes, yes, physical and mental healing powers. It's so amazing how the healers use just one note, but then, how does that work when there are several notes in different combinations? How does *that* affect people?

Do you wonder sometimes what dancers are hearing when they're onstage and performing? Dancers often hear things that musicians don't.

Yes. What's interesting about Marlies' work is if you're not in tune with her, then you're in the way. If the sounds are not in tune, if you're not following her, then you're in the way, because their *breathing* has sounds. So when they fall on the floor, you hear, "Hoo!" or "Whew!" Those sounds help them to remember the movement. When dancers practice, they often work without sound.

When did you start composing?

I would say in the 1990s when I was around The New School. I liked the idea of taking my eraser and erasing. [laughs] Putting something down and then saying, "Oh, I don't like that, let's try *this*!" So the freedom of it was pretty cool! I liked that.

I've been trying to study the masters, like Duke Ellington, Charlie Parker, and try to take their music apart and say, "Okay, where did he come up with this idea? What was first, the lick or the chords?" I'm always doing my homework.

Did you have some formal instruction when it came to composition?
A little. The impetus is just out of curiosity and fun. I had a little training at Queens College and at The New School with Jimmy Owens, Cecil Bridgewater, and John Blake. These were mentors who would look at things, give advice, play through things, and say, "Go back in the shed!" [laughs]

Did theater and performance art also come into your life at a young age?
I think just hanging out with Dad and traveling—we were in Japan when I was like 8 for a year—and just seeing what was on television, or the kabuki theaters. It was always around. I think [singer] Abbey Lincoln was a performance artist, in a way.

There is an educational component to what your group, the Firey String Sistas, does. Do you go into the schools with that group and work with the students?
Yes. We play, and we have a Q and A. I thought it would be great if we could create something so different that we'd get the kids just riveted while educating them.

I think a lot of schools are just hungry for that.
Right! I was in the public school system for a few years, and I just feel so sorry for the kids. Because most of them are just bored. They become problems, because most of them are bored, you know? It's just the way that education is presented to them.

There's a video on YouTube of you playing a composition called "Simone" on the electric cello.
It's a composition by Frank Foster. Frank Foster was a fantastic artist. Unfortunately, he passed a few years ago. He was a saxophonist, flute player, and bandleader for many, many years. His last band was called the Loud Minority. [laughs]

That's a great name!
He was just an amazing person and artist. [Trumpeter] Cecil Bridgewater is a mentor of mine, and he gave me that piece to play. I started studying it, taking it apart, working it out.... I've arranged it for strings.

When did you start on electric cello?
I think in the 1980s with a trio. The flute player played an electronic wind instrument [EWI] and the pianist, an electric keyboard. So, they were like, "Hey, why don't you get an electric cello?" It was a great idea!

In the video of you performing "Simone," are we hearing a live sound feed?
I'm triggering loops with a foot pedal. I prerecorded all the loops, and then

I play against them. And that's what I do a lot with the dancers. It's kind of another development that I'm working on with them.

You've also worked with composer Anthony Davis. Can you tell me a little bit about that experience?
First of all, he is an amazing person, just a sweet person. My first experience with him was [in New York City] at The Kitchen when I was a part of the Kitchen House Blend. That was a 10-piece ensemble that met, I think, every two months or so. . . . Some amazing musicians in there. Anthony was commissioned to write for the ensemble, and playing that piece was an amazing experience for me. I wanted to study with him, but I didn't get the opportunity to do so.

I saw him again in another situation. . . . We played his piece "Hemispheres" with dancers, and it was just incredible. I just had to pick his brain and ask him, "Okay, how do you do this? How does it work?" And the way he showed me was just so simple. Just starting with the motifs and just expanding on it. That's all! [laughs] Inspiring, very inspiring. And his operas are incredible. I haven't had the opportunity to play one, but I've heard them.

Improvising and composing seem to be two sides of the same coin. Does being able to improvise help you as a composer? Or vice versa?
I think they have to go together. I think I've chosen to go even further into just the sound, the motion of sound, and how it moves and then, how is it built? How do you build a sound, and how does that work? I'm not close to just one form of improvisation.

Do you think there are more women musicians playing jazz (or whatever you want to call this music) than before?
That's an interesting question. It's like you say, the word "jazz"—where did that word come from? What does it mean? Everybody has a different definition of it. Some people say, "Jazz? Well, I don't hear *that* as being jazz." It's so interesting. It's almost like "rock and roll" when doo-wop singers sang it. It was called "rhythm and blues." Or "blues."

People are defining what that music is. For some people, jazz is just bebop and people want to preserve it as such. Just like for some people, classical music is Bach, Beethoven, Mozart, and that's what it is.

There have always been a lot of women playing improvisatory music, which is what I prefer to call it, and now, a lot more are being recognized for what they do—which is fantastic.

Patrizia Scascitelli

New Orleans in the 1800s was by far the most ethnically diverse city in the South. It was one of the main ports for Irish and German immigrants, and the first city in the U.S. with large settlements of Greeks, Croatians, Filipinos, and Italians. Just before the turn of the 20th century, thousands of Sicilians arrived in New Orleans from Catholic Mediterranean countries. Their influence is still very much a part of the city's culture, from the foods at Central Grocery on Decatur Street, to St. Joseph's Day in March, when altars commemorating the saint appear on the porches of Italian Americans' homes so people can leave offerings. Going back to the earliest days of the music that came to be called jazz, Italian immigrant musicians played in Dixieland or "jass" bands, the Original Dixieland Jass Band (erroneously described as "the creators of jazz") being a famous example.

In 1971, Italian-born pianist and composer Patrizia Scascitelli had just completed her diploma in classical piano performance at St. Cecilia Conservatory in Rome. That same year, the conservatory announced it would offer the country's first jazz degree program, taught by pianist and well-known film composer Giorgio Gaslini. In Italy, the announcement was big news, and Scascitelli, a prodigiously talented classical pianist who was enamored with jazz, jumped at the chance to study it formally.

Patrizia Scascitelli. Photo by Patty Bianca.

"The course was a big success," says Scascitelli. "We had so many people in the classes, including outsiders and many self-taught musicians."

It may be hard to imagine now, when magazines like *DownBeat* and *Jazz-Times* are filled with advertisements for undergraduate, graduate, and post-graduate jazz degree programs, that up until 1950, music educators in the U.S. were, for the most part, horrified by the idea of creating a curriculum around jazz. In 1945, [trumpeter] Miles Davis famously left the Juilliard School in order to learn bebop by playing in nightclubs. It wasn't until the 1960s that a significant number of schools in the U.S. began offering jazz classes for college credit.

In Italy, things were moving a bit slower.

"After this first course . . . the director of the conservatory decided to get rid of the jazz course," says Scascitelli. "It was all over the newspapers. They couldn't handle it. For them, jazz was bringing confusion that could change the traditional way to see music. I was lucky to get my degree!"

After completing that jazz program at St. Cecilia, Scascitelli went on to build a successful career in Italy as the country's first female jazz pianist, as well as in the U.S. as a pianist, composer, and bandleader. Her interview here provides yet another fascinating perspective on how much jazz has evolved over the years, as it traveled from its home, the port of New Orleans, to major cities across the country like New York City and Chicago, then overseas to Europe, where new generations of musicians continued to study an art form originated by African Americans, and now played by ethnic groups around the globe.

When did you first begin playing a musical instrument?
I began playing piano at the age of 8. I was born and raised in Rome and went to a private, Catholic elementary school. I started piano lessons there with a teacher that was also the church's organist. She was blind, and after a few months it became difficult to continue. One day, she told my mother that my progress was very fast and she could not keep up with me. She suggested to my mother that she go and search for a good teacher for me.

Were you already serious about playing the piano at the age of 8?
Yes. I didn't have a piano, so I made one out of cardboard, with painted keys. I got a piano at home when I was 9. Then I started taking serious piano lessons.

What kind of music were you studying at such a young age?
When I was 9, after leaving my first teacher, I studied with Tito Aprea, who was a very well-known piano teacher and had a big name in Italy.

He didn't teach kids, but he felt I was an exceptional musical child. He had me study all of the classics like Bach—everything you work on to prepare to get into a conservatory. So within six months I did all of that and went to take the entrance exam. I had just turned 10 years old.

At that time, St. Cecilia Conservatory was very strict, and it was very difficult to get in. At the audition, I was competing with at least 200 other students for only about 20 openings. They all were much older than me. I was the little one!

But I passed with almost the "top vote," which was a 10, because the teachers' committee said, "We can't give her a 10. She's just a kid!" So they gave me 9.5 points. [laughs] It was like getting a scholarship. Once you got into the conservatory, your lessons were free.

From then on, you were on track to become a professional musician?
Yes, definitely. I was really into music.

Were both your mother and your father supportive of you becoming a musician?
My father was not interested in music. It was my mother who was really supportive, and continued to be so during my musical career. She was a good singer and still is at the age of 90! She was not a professional, but during her youth she had performed in numerous college shows. Most importantly, she always loved music.

At her age she's still going strong and tells me, "Oh, you have to keep playing! Keep going on with your music."

When did jazz come into your musical life? How did you get exposed to jazz?
I was playing a lot of classical music while at the conservatory. I started to become curious about jazz because a senior student I knew played a bit of jazz and had a couple of jazz records that I listened to a lot. One was of Louis Armstrong. No one at home listened to jazz, although my mother loved opera and popular songs.

In Italy during the 1960s, there were many popular songs on TV shows that were played with jazz arrangements. Famous singers would sing popular American songs that had these jazz arrangements with the lyrics translated into Italian. So jazz was not something completely new to me. When I was 14 or 15 years old, I started listening to Ray Charles and lots of R&B music and I became a really big fan. I also listened to a lot of pop and rock groups. Later on, I started listening to modern jazz, including Ornette Coleman.

Once I finished my classical studies and received my diploma, I saw that there was a jazz course at the conservatory. It was a great historical event be-

Dopo un paio d'anni di lavoro sotterraneo, inteso sempre a valutare il lavoro di combo. Patrizia Scascitelli, una delle rare figure femminili che operano nel jazz, e arrivata al suo primo album e/al successo.

JAZZFEMMINA

Patrizia Scascitelli in *Ciao 2001* magazine, 1975.

cause it was the first time it was being offered at such an important music institute and a good opportunity for me to learn jazz. They offered a three-year course [degree program] with a phenomenal teacher, Giorgio Gaslini. In addition to being a well-known jazz pianist and modern composer, he was a successful film composer who collaborated with the filmmaker Michelangelo Antonioni.

In 1971, none of the other Italian conservatories had jazz in the curriculum, but in Rome at the St. Cecilia Conservatory, jazz was introduced in such a big way. I took this course and got my degree in jazz. For me, it turned out to be a culture clash, but very interesting and fascinating because I went from playing all classical music to Gaslini. [laughs] It was incredible.

The course was a big success. We had so many people in the classes, including outsiders and many self-taught musicians. After this first course though, the director of the conservatory decided to get rid of the jazz course. It was all over the newspapers. They couldn't handle it. For them, jazz was bringing confusion that could change the traditional way to see music. I was lucky to get my degree! [laughs]

This opportunity to learn jazz in a conservatory only lasted for a short time and then it was shut down?
Yes. It lasted three years. That's all.

Are there jazz programs now in Italy?
Oh, yeah! What I described happened back in 1973. Despite the closure of this first jazz course, some private schools began their own jazz programs. In the mid 80s, jazz was offered in several Italian conservatories and now is in all of them.

In America, for a long time, jazz was not taught in music conservatories. You had to learn the music in clubs and on the street.
Yes, I know. It was the same in Italy.

Why did you decide to relocate from Italy to New York? That's a pretty big life decision.
I know! Before I moved here, I had visited New York City three times. The first time was on a trip organized for students of the conservatory to see the New-port Jazz Festival. That was my first time here and was great! I saw [pianist] Thelonious Monk; I saw [saxophonist] Rahsaan Roland Kirk; I saw many great jazz masters. It was spectacular.

At the same time, this made things more complicated for me. I had a crisis. I didn't know what kind of music I was going to play professionally.

But the music had made the choice for me when in 1975 I returned to New York a second time and met [trumpeter] Don Cherry. I performed with him in Italy later on. I was the first Italian female jazz pianist and all the maga-zines and newspapers wrote articles about it. I had a recording out too, *Ballata*, which was based on the Italian folk music but played in a jazz way.

The third time I visited New York was in 1976 when I was invited to play two concerts with my band at Hunter College and Columbia University. The big change occurred at the end of the 1980s. My plan was to come back to New York City for maybe four years to learn and absorb jazz and then return to Italy. But then, I got so involved with everything, playing and teaching in this city that I love, and I didn't go back! [laughs] I had a green card, and in 2001, I became a U.S. citizen.

You mentioned hearing Thelonious Monk. Who were some other pianists that were inspiring you around the time you were traveling back and forth between Italy and New York? And were there musicians in Italy who were also inspiring you?

In addition to Monk, many other pianists, including Bud Powell, Oscar Peterson, and Bill Evans—the masters—inspired me. I was also inspired by other instrumentalists like John Coltrane for his sound and spiritual message.

In Italy it was difficult to find a teacher in the 1970s. It was such a struggle to learn jazz. Many players were playing swing and were not interested in teaching.

I think this was because they thought that jazz was not possible to teach. The other reason was the differences between the two generations, one who wanted to continue with traditional jazz, the other being more interested in John Coltrane and free jazz. In Giorgio Gaslini's course, there was not enough time available for him to teach theory. His teaching was based on listening and commentary about the records. There were also opportunities to play with various ensembles and to improvise on given themes.

I decided to learn jazz theory on my own. I learned from the four volumes by John Mehegan that I got on my first visit to New York. I remember buying them when I walked into a music store in Times Square, I think it was Colony Music, and I said to the seller, "I would like to learn jazz." Luckily he gave me one of the best methods. But it was so difficult because I had trouble translating it from English to Italian.

I ended up spending many days at home translating and playing and learning how to practice. Finally, I could organize modern (chord) voicings, and I began to listen to a lot of Chick Corea's music.

When you play with musicians, do you also learn things?
Yes! When I find musicians that make me discover new things, I go on to play for hours without getting tired. I have met and played with many musicians between Italy and New York, musicians of jazz and other music genres, and I've learned by playing with them.

After I moved to New York in 1982, a pianist friend told me about [pianist, educator] Barry Harris' jazz classes. It was a great thing, because I didn't have money for private lessons and his classes were at a price that everyone could afford. And so every Monday, from one in the afternoon to one in the morning, I attended the classes and learned so many things from this great teacher. I can say that he gave me the jazz basics of bebop and more. Most of all he gave me a lot of confidence.

Were his classes free?
There was a donation. Sometimes you could pay only a dollar. It was incredible. You could pay just one dollar and stay all day. I met a lot of good musicians there. But because I was on my own, I had to work to make money. I don't come from a rich family, so from day one, I had to work. But it was good,

because I never had to work a job that was not related to music. I was in a jazz-rock band a week after coming into the States.

Very soon I started to play and write arrangements for singers and teach privately at various schools. Because I can play classical music, I also play church gigs. But what I did more of was a lot of work with singers.

You have such a unique voice as a player and composer. I think your background is very apparent in your music.
Yes. But sometimes I wonder if I am doing too many different things. I am involved with many projects that require playing in different styles from jazz to Broadway to classical. Sometimes I feel that it takes time away from playing jazz.

Is that going to be good for me? Will it enrich me with new experiences? Or is it going to be distracting and take away from my focus? In the end, this is what I am, and I am glad to have all of these opportunities to play.

Also, I think that to play and listen to only jazz can be restrictive. You really have to listen to all kinds of music to have a large view, do you know what I mean? Personally, I cannot just listen to one type of music.

Of course I realize how important it is to have the skill to improvise, because nowadays one often needs to be prepared to change what' s written in the music charts. On many occasions, I see classical musicians not being able to do that, having trouble because they are so strictly attached to the music that is written on the chart. If I didn't have the jazz training, I could not do many jobs.

Sometimes I wonder why there are so many jazz schools when there are not enough jobs and venues for jazz musicians.

These schools are teaching students to become teachers.
And to be able to work in the different situations I described earlier. I think that the teaching in the future will have to move towards a global vision of the music with an emphasis on improvised music.

More and more classical musicians are learning how to improvise, either in school or on their own. But improvising used to be a part of the classical tradition.
Yes! Of course! But then in the early 1900s that all changed. Maybe things are changing?

When I work as an accompanist and do these jobs, I have to improvise. You can't always learn this stuff in just two or three rehearsals. We know how to do tricks! [laughs] Sometimes I see charts that are so bad and they have to be changed. Even some of the Broadway stuff, I change it, and people say, "Oh, that sounds really good!" [laughs]

What are your upcoming plans? What do you want to do in the future as a pianist, composer, and bandleader?

Here in New York I have a six-piece band with great musicians, and mostly we play my compositions that I recorded on my CD *Open Window*.

I love making music with the sextet because every time we perform, something new happens. It does not matter if we play in a jazz club or a theater, as long we can keep the music happening and make progress. Although it is a problem to find good venues where we can perform. The music business is really crazy these days.

I do perform once a month at the 55 Bar in the West Village [New York City] with other bands, and sometimes I'm there with my sextet. When I am in Rome, I play with a great quartet. I'm looking forward to going back in the studio to do a new recording.

Also, I have been playing concerts for the Italian Cultural Institute as an ambassador of music representing the Italian culture. Two of my projects are presented through them. One is called "The Musicality of the Italian Language," where I explain how the Italian language has created musical terms and styles. The other project is called "Music and the Story of Italian Immigrants." I start with the old music of the first immigrants, including early jazz in New Orleans. With regard to this, when I did the research, I found many interesting things, such as the first ever jazz recording was made by Italians [The Original Dixieland Jass Band] in 1917. Back then, Sicilians were in New Orleans playing jazz with African Americans.

There have been contributions to jazz from immigrants from all over Europe.

Yes. Knowing this makes me realize that we Italians have a long tradition of playing jazz. As long as I keep making a contribution to music and the people are happy, I'm satisfied and happy too.

Jane Monheit

The Great American Songbook refers to a wide and varied repertoire of songs composed from the 1920s to the 1960s for Broadway and movie musicals or as popular songs of their time. These songs, known as "standards" by jazz musicians, are distinguished by their engaging melodies, sophisticated harmonies, and literate lyrics. Like the European classical lieder and art songs of the 18th and 19th centuries, the melodic and harmonic content of songs from the Great American Songbook serves to support and compliment the lyrics, as well as reveal new layers of meaning. Composers such as George Gershwin, Jerome Kern, and Richard Rogers partnered with gifted lyricists, including Ira Gershwin, Otto Harbach, and Oscar Hammerstein II, to create a "songbook" that was embraced and interpreted by both popular artists like Bing Crosby, Al Jolson, and Judy Garland, to name just a few, and jazz vocalists.

Like many singers of her generation, Jane Monheit grew up hearing songs from the Great American Songbook on both musical theater and jazz recordings.

"Both of those genres include the same repertoire of songs," says Monheit. "I would hear the original cast record of a show, and then I'd hear Ella Fitzgerald and Louis Armstrong doing the same songs on a jazz record. I was hearing all of these amazing songs interpreted both ways every day of my life."

Throughout her career, Monheit has recorded many of those songs, including "Over the Rainbow," "Cheek to Cheek," "In the Still of the Night," "Look for the Silver Lining," and "Moon River." However, more recently, she has begun to explore what she describes as "volume two" of "great popular songs" from around the globe, a newer repertoire that includes songs by Brazilian composers Ivan Lins and Antonio Carlos Jobim, well-known rock and folk songs by the Beatles [John Lennon and Paul McCartney], Randy Newman, and Joni Mitchell, and pretty much any other song composed after 1970 where the "forms, melodies, and harmonies" lend themselves to re-interpretation by a great jazz singer.

The lyrics of a song are a crucial component for Monheit; the importance of interpreting lyrics is a subject many of the singers I interviewed bring up when they speak about their musical and artistic growth.

"In my teaching in the last year," says Monheit, "I've been dealing mostly with lyrical interpretation. I'm 35; I'm a mother, and as a result of these changes, I have become a better lyrical interpreter."

A powerful example of Monheit's gift for lyrical re-interpretation is her medley of two classic songs by the Beatles, "Golden Slumbers" and "The Long and Winding Road," on her recent album *The Heart of the Matter*, where she

Jane Monheit. Photo by Matthew Holler.

conveys an emotional vulnerability that a weary and bitter Lennon and Mc-Cartney took great pains to hide in the acrimonious last days of their professional relationship.

In her interview, Monheit also speaks about the changes that the recording industry has undergone since her debut album, *Never Never Land* (2000), and the larger changes that have occurred in the U.S. as a result of the women's rights movement. Many of her observations inspired the section titled "Think Visual" in the introduction to this book. I also quote her at the top of the section about the women's liberation movement.

"We're all just people," says Monheit, "and it should not matter what our gender is when it comes to what instrument we choose or how we are regarded in the music industry."

When did you first begin playing a musical instrument?
Outside of the voice? I started singing first, but I think everyone does that. Little kids sing and dance. They do both naturally, they do them from the time they're tiny. Little kids sing and dance without thinking about it, but it gets socialized out of them, at least it does for boys in America.

I started studying instruments formally around the age of 8. I studied clarinet and piano.

Did you make the decision to study these instruments or did your parents?
I think I just wanted piano lessons at a certain point. I was playing on my own as it was. My parents never pushed me to do anything. Every musical decision I made was mine alone, although I did grow up in a very musical family. It wasn't a big thing for me to say that I wanted piano lessons. (My grandmother was a piano teacher.) It was more like, "Oh, of course she wants lessons. Of course she's singing. Because that's what we do in this family!" As far as studying woodwinds, that was just part of my school's music program.

Your school had a music program in place?
Yes! This was Long Island in the 1980s and 90s, when I was in grade school. I graduated high school in 1995. At the time, there were still very strong music departments in New York State, and I was very lucky to have amazing teachers. There was a jazz band, a choir, a regular band, and an orchestra just in my tiny elementary school alone. At my high school, there was a wind ensemble, a big symphony orchestra, multiple jazz bands, combos, brass ensembles, woodwind ensembles, madrigal groups, three different choirs, jazz choir, show choir, and festival choir. We had everything you could possibly imagine.

Around this time, when did you become aware of and start digging into jazz?
It was just there from the moment I was born. There was never a time when jazz wasn't there. And that goes for a lot of other genres of music as well. I had jazz in my life every day because my mother is very close to her parents. They lived about 20 minutes away, so they had a big hand in raising me, and they are hardcore jazz listeners. My father is a bluegrass musician, so I had that in my life every day, as well as Broadway and musical theater.

So one genre of music didn't speak to you over another? You were just taking it all in.
Absolutely. Although growing up, I especially loved jazz and musical theater. Both of those genres include the same repertoire of songs, songs of the Great American Songbook. I would hear the original cast record of a show, and then I'd hear Ella Fitzgerald and Louis Armstrong doing the same songs on a jazz

record. I was hearing all of these amazing songs interpreted both ways every day of my life.

When did you realize that you wanted to make music your career?
I always knew music would be my career. You can ask anyone who ever knew me, from the time I was a tiny kid, every teacher I ever had, knew I was going to be a singer. And not just my music teachers but every friend I ever had will tell you, "Oh, yeah, Jane was always going to be professional singer!"

And I never doubted myself because the people around me didn't doubt me, which was amazing. I was a very lucky kid in that regard. Not only was I born with a totally unnatural amount of confidence [laughs], but the people around me had confidence in me as well. And that is a very powerful thing for a child.

So there was never anything like, "Jane, music is fine. But you should really study to become a dentist, just to have something to fall back on."
Nope.

You're a musician that embraces different kinds of music. Early on in your career, did you define yourself by saying *this* is the kind of the singer I want to be, be it a jazz, cabaret, or musical theater singer? Or did you decide that "I'm going to be a combination of different things"?
You know, I never thought about it much. And in my opinion, those kinds of labels, "cabaret" or "jazz," are for the consumers. It makes it easy for them to find us. It's marketing. It's business. But those labels don't really describe most of us with any accuracy. Many singers are more than one thing. I mean, we're human beings. We love all sorts of things. I don't think any artist truly feels comfortable with labels.

Look at a singer like Jamie Cullum, who will take a standard and then put this incredibly modern groove to it. There are people doing all kinds of interesting things like that now. To me, the whole fuss over whether or not I'm a jazz or cabaret singer just seems ridiculous. The question should be, am I singing a song in a way that makes *you* the listener feel something? If yes, then I'm doing my job. That's all that matters.

Did you have to find a vocal teacher that empathized with what you're saying here? I'm thinking of a vocal teacher who might say, "You're going to have to choose between singing this or that simply because of your vocal apparatus and the technique we're going to have to focus on."
In my opinion, someone who would say that is not a good vocal teacher. A great teacher works with who you truly are and where your heart is coming from. Good vocal technique applies to every genre. That doesn't change.

There's a proper way to use your voice, and an improper way, and you can apply that proper way to just about any genre of music.

I had an amazing voice teacher, Peter Eldridge, who knows how to bring out the best in everyone. I chose the Manhattan School of Music because he was there. I didn't apply to any other schools. Studying with Peter and going to MSM probably led me down a clearer path towards a career more focused on jazz. Otherwise, I probably would have ended up auditioning for the musical theater program at New York University [NYU].

It's funny, because I read in the press all the time this misconception that supposedly I once said [in a mellow yet melodious voice], "I was a Broadway vocalist and my husband steered me towards jazz," and that's total bull.

Well, that's the story that is often told regarding women in the arts, that the husband comes in and sets everything straight.
It's so silly. [in a Southern belle voice] "Well, my man told me to be a jazz signer!" Forget about it! I'm a feminist. Even though he's my beloved husband who I've been with since I was 20 years old, whenever somebody says I did something because he told me to, my hackles rise! [laughs] My husband and I are equal partners. My career is a result of my own decisions.

Is jazz singing something you can define, even if it's a complicated definition? Is there something that separates a jazz singer from a different kind of singer?
The elements of jazz singing that remain constant include some sort of improvisation and some sort of alteration of the song's melody to further communicate a message. But the definition of "jazz" and "jazz singing" is changing. You just can't easily define jazz. It's almost more a feeling. There are people who don't even want to use the word "jazz" anymore.

For instance, we have jazz records that don't swing. People are doing all kinds of amazing things, exploring all kinds of instrumentation and repertoire. Which is wonderful and as it should be, as long we get to hold onto the traditions as well, because it would be an awful tragedy if they were gone. I will always swing some standards, because that is something that I believe in, something that I don't ever want to go away.

But I love hearing what other people who aren't necessarily swinging standards are doing too. My album *The Heart of the Matter* has all kinds of weird stuff on it and is the polar opposite to my last record, which was a traditional standards record. But that's what artists do! We do all kinds of different things.

Why jazz standards? Why should a singer who is just beginning to explore his or her voice sing a song written years ago by Cole Porter or Rodgers and Hammerstein?

Because jazz standards are building blocks of history; they're national treasures.

I have heard people say musicians shouldn't play standards anymore. My response to that is, "Should we also stop playing Mozart? Should we quit performing Shakespeare's plays? Should we stop staging great choreography?"

I think any singer who is trying to pursue a career in jazz needs to find his or her way around standards. The forms, melodies, and harmonies are all beautifully constructed. They're called "standards" for a reason. The Great American Songbook is an artistic national treasure.

You sing and have recorded songs by Ivan Lins, Buffy Sainte-Marie, and the Beatles, as well as your own compositions. I wonder if 50 years from now, jazz musicians will still be playing standards. Do you think we'll have a new set of standards?
We'll have both! I always think of the latter stuff as "volume two" of the Great American Songbook, but it's not exclusively American composers. You can't consider a "volume two" of great popular songs and not include Joni Mitchell, a Canadian, or John Lennon and Paul McCartney, who are British.

Gil Goldstein, who did the arrangements for *The Heart of the Matter*, creates such a distinctive sound with his arrangements. Did working with Goldstein provide a different kind of challenge for you as a singer?
In my teaching in the last year, I've been dealing mostly with lyrical interpretation, and I wanted to make an album to reflect my own progress in that area. I'm 35; I'm a mother, and as a result of these changes, I have become a better lyrical interpreter.

Gil was really the obvious choice for the arrangements, because he writes from the heart. I had worked with Gil before, so I already knew about the magic. His arrangements are challenging, and he doesn't baby-sit me, which I appreciate immensely.

When it comes to lyrics, is there something about Gil's arranging that you especially like, something that brings out the content of the lyrics?
Like I said, Gil really writes from the heart. He doesn't write things just because they're hip. He considers the lyrics and considers the performer. He knows me so well. We recorded "Until It's Time for You to Go," the Buffy Sainte-Marie song, and he played accordion on the track, and what he plays is so beautiful. Like me, he gets weepy over this stuff. It's so cute. We'll both be in the studio like all choked up. [laughs]

The music industry has changed dramatically in the past couple decades. From your perspective, what are some of the changes musicians are going to have to adapt to as we move further into 21st century?

We need our audiences to adapt. We need our older audiences to be okay with digital music. For the most part, they already are. My granddad is 91 and he's got an iPod. He's cool! He's totally hip. We need our older audiences, the people who are still buying the discs, to be okay with adapting.

We sell a lot of CDs at shows, I think because I'm there to sign them! Most musicians do that when on the road. You shake a hand, you sign an autograph, you say 'hi' for a minute, and you *thank* the person. That's a better experience than ordering something off of Amazon.

But CD sales are down, which means recording budgets are lower, and we can't always do everything we'd like to do in the studio. I mean, I made my new record in three days! When I did my album *Surrender* back in 2007, we just took forever and messed with every tiny detail. "Oh, we don't like this ... let's book more studio time!" These days it's like, "We're gonna do it tight, we're gonna do it old school. We're just gonna get in there and do our jobs." And that's what we did with *The Heart of the Matter*. We made a record that's just as beautiful as *Surrender*, but with a much lower budget. It can be done. You just have to work hard and be creative.

Are you seeing more women in the music industry now as opposed to when you started?

I do see more female instrumentalists, which is nice. There have always been a lot of singers. It's okay and acceptable to be a singer.

I was doing an interview the other day, and I actually said I chose the voice because it's the instrument I love, not because I'm a lady. Not because I'm a *pretty* lady. [laughs] Now, I have a glamorous persona, which is my own doing. I am that chick. I'm a glamorous broad. But, there's a lot of sexualizing of women in this industry, and there's just no place for that in our genre. If that's who you are as a person, if you want to put on the sexy dress and the high heels, then hell yeah! But if somebody is telling you to do that, and you don't want to, then absolutely not.

I come from a generation that's naturally fairly feminist. Our mothers were fighting for all kinds of women's rights in the 1960s and 70s, and we grew up with these iconic, feminist, musical heroes. We were raised a certain way. Women of my generation are strong and hopefully, the ones that are coming after us are as well.

There doesn't have to be "women in jazz." It can just be we're all musicians, and that's it. That would be nice! [laughs] We're all just people, and it should not matter what our gender is when it comes to what instrument we choose or how we are regarded in the music industry.

Jennifer Leitham

Near the end of my interview with bassist, singer, and composer Jennifer Leitham, Leitham offers some advice:

"I would tell anybody, no matter what profession they plan to enter, whether it's music or not, to just be great at what you do.... I may not have a college degree, but I've never stopped studying. I study every day. I'm always striving to better myself."

Leitham is not kidding when she says she never stopped studying. Growing up in the 1950s in a blue-collar community in Reading, Pennsylvania, and lacking parental support for her desire to pursue a career in music, she skipped school to work various low-paying jobs to earn money for an electric and then upright bass, and lessons studying improvisation and the Great American Songbook with her "musical father figure," Al Stauffer.

When Leitham began what she describes as her "voyage through jazz history," she was experiencing what the American Psychiatric Association would eventually classify as gender dysphoria,[84] a diagnosis for the sometimes overwhelming distress experienced by those whose gender identity does not match their birth anatomy. Before she transitioned to Jennifer, Jennifer was John Leitham. While John, Jennifer became one of the most respected and sought-after bassists in the country, joining the Woody Herman Thundering Herd in 1981, playing with [trumpeter and *Tonight Show* bandleader] Doc Severinsen, and playing and recording with [pianist] George Shearing and [vocalist] Mel Tormé. During all of this, Jennifer was leading a double life, one she would ultimately reconcile by undergoing sex reassignment surgery in 2002. Many supporters during her transition included several high-profile jazz musicians, including [drummer] Ed Shaughnessy, [bassist] Ray Brown, [multi-instrumentalist] Benny Carter, and the aforementioned Severinsen, who expresses nothing but praise for Leitham and her musical talent in the documentary about her career, *I Stand Corrected*.

The majority of my interview with Leitham deals with music and the level of commitment she has dedicated to her craft. As she recalls her first gig with Woody Herman, receiving the call for what would become a long gig with Tormé, and the inspirations behind several of her compositions and songs, her descriptions are candid and enlightening. She also offers some provocative insights regarding jazz education, and how independent labels and crowdfunding are benefiting the future of this music. Near the end of the interview, I ask her what advice she has for a young person (or any person) who is experiencing gender dysphoria, and her response is heartfelt and helpful.

Jennifer Leitham. Photo by Bob Barry.

Where were you born?

I was born in Illinois, but I didn't stay there very long. My family is from Reading, Pennsylvania, and that's where I was raised.

When did you first begin playing a musical instrument?

I was in a talent show in the fourth grade back when the Beatles were a big deal and appeared on *Ed Sullivan*. I guess that would have been 1964. I was supposed to be Paul McCartney in a group that would mimic the Beatles. I had a fake toy guitar, and I liked the way it felt holding it left-handed. That was my first instrument. All of the strings fell off except the bottom two, so all I could do was play melodies or bass lines. I had a knack for listening to a record and then playing what I heard before I knew a thing about music.

I didn't play an instrument formally until my senior year in high school. I played a little clarinet in the fourth grade. But the band director didn't want me in the band because I kept improvising! [laughs] That foreshadowed what was to come.

Your first musical adventures were in a rock band. Is that correct?
Yes. I also sang in the chorus. You could say my singing voice was really my first musical instrument. I was in my high school chorus and was chosen to do solos and sing in some smaller groups. This drew some attention to my voice, which made me popular among the rock-band set. Rock bands wanted me to sing lead vocals because I had an extremely high voice. I could sing really high without going into falsetto. But I never thought I was going to be a musician for life. It just sort of happened to me.

After a couple years of playing in bands, I realized that I was going to need to study music if I was going to play professionally. Music was the only thing that felt like a calling to me; it was the thing that gave me solace. Music was an activity I used to escape from all the other things going on inside my head. I could just sit in a room by myself and just concentrate on music. That heart, mind, body, soul connection was something I'd never experienced before.

I started taking electric bass lessons with a guy named Chuck Anderson. I was living in King of Prussia, Pennsylvania, at this time. One day, when I came in for my lesson with Chuck, there was a string-bass teacher named Al Stauffer teaching in the studio. The waiting room was just outside the studio so I could listen to Al teach. And I just loved how he demystified the process. He didn't come off like he had some "secret." He had really interesting ideas about means to an end, about learning a certain principle, and how that principle will lead to another. That appealed to me.

Al Stauffer became my main teacher. He helped me get a string bass. He helped get it changed to left-handed because in those early days, when I was mimicking Paul McCartney, I just thought that was how basses were played! I was so naïve about it. I thought guitars were played right-handed and basses were left-handed! But it felt comfortable to play left-handed, so I stuck with it.

When you began taking string-bass lessons, were your parents supportive of your musical goals?
I didn't really receive any support from my family. I mean, all of my instruments I bought with my own money.

I had sort of screwed up in my senior year of high school. I was dealing with gender dysphoria, and sort of lost heart for anything in the world except playing music. Thank goodness I had music! I would skip school and hitchhike across town to work in a car wash and then hitchhike back to work in a fast food joint at night just to earn the money I needed to buy an instrument. So, no, I did not have parental support.

Were you listening to jazz at this time?
Not until I began studying the string bass. Al was really like a musical father figure to me. He set up my whole career. He played with an incredible French pianist named Bernard Peiffer, and hearing the two of them was something I'll never forget. The way they played together was magical, the highest state of improvisation you can imagine, and they inspired me to learn more about jazz. Al put me through the process of studying improvisation as well as learning the Great American Songbook.

I began my own voyage through jazz history and found various periods that I stuck with. When I first got into jazz, I was playing in rock bands, but playing some of the more involved music of the day like Emerson, Lake & Palmer and Yes. I guess the first jazz music that interested me was [pianist] Chick Corea and Return to Forever's album *Hymn of the Seventh Galaxy*. I loved that record, and I started to research Chick Corea. I went back to his first Return to Forever record and then listened to earlier recordings like *Tones for Joan's Bones*. I discovered Corea played for Miles Davis, so I checked out Miles Davis and then John Coltrane.

At some point, I picked up the Oscar Peterson Trio's album *Affinity* for 99 cents at a Woolworth's. That album opens with the Bill Evans composition "Waltz for Debby," and Oscar's arrangement goes from 3/4 into 4/4 time. And then they go into a "two" feel, and at that point, they're flying. They've lifted off the ground. The groove sounded so good to me!

That record inspired me to research [bassist] Ray Brown's playing, which then led me to [bassist and cellist] Oscar Pettiford. I kept going back in my listening, further and further. If I had gone to a music school, my thesis would have been on Oscar Pettiford and Ray Brown!

You didn't go to a music conservatory?
No, I just took private lessons. Al Stauffer was my main teacher, but throughout my career I've been really fortunate to cross paths with several giants of the bass. Milt Hinton was a dear mentor as was Slam Stewart.

I thought about going to a music school, but my career kept taking me up and up and up. I was so busy playing that I didn't have time for school.

In hindsight, I kind of wish I had gone to a music school. It would have made getting a teaching gig much easier, especially these days. I probably missed some classical ensemble playing that might have helped me.

Some of the musicians I've interviewed for this book did not go to a music conservatory or college.

It's not like I didn't have teachers. Al Stauffer was a great teacher for me. After I stopped playing with Woody Herman's band I continued to take lessons from him. When I played with Woody Herman I met [bassist] Slam Stewart; when I played Colombo's nightclub I met [bassist] George Duvivier, and these guys were coaching me. They were coaching me in the business and how to handle my career. They were certainly talking me up to people.

Had you played in a big band before you got that call from Woody Herman?

Sure, lots of times. Before playing with Woody Herman's big band, I was doing show work. I played with a traveling act in the Catskills that was a little big band, just four horns and three rhythm players, and we played written arrangements. Then I was called to play in the Pocono Mountains in a resort house band. While I was there, I was recruited to play in [drummer] Buddy Rich's band, but I chickened out! [laughs] I was too afraid. Buddy would've looked at me and I looked like this frail thing, this girlish person. I thought he might fire me because of my looks. I had heard real horror stories about him, so I said no. I'm probably the only musician in the business who turned down both Buddy Rich and Frank Sinatra! [laughs] Yikes!

Before I played in Woody Herman's band, I had played with [guitarist] Larry Coryell at the Main Point. I played with [singer] Gloria Lynne at, I think it was Dino's Upper Lounge in West Philly. A really fun African-American hang. I really loved playing there. I played a couple of times with [saxophonist] Hank Mobley and [drummer] Philly Joe Jones in Germantown. At that time, they were just looking for a kid who would work cheap. [laughs] I probably played passably. I certainly wasn't a formed player when I played with those guys, but it was a great experience.

But by the time Woody Herman gave you a call, you were playing at a professional level.

Right! I was in the house band at Palumbo's in South Philadelphia, which would have been the equivalent of playing on a television show or in Vegas. We played acts! That's what I was doing in the Poconos as well.

It seems like with each playing experience, you had to learn to do something new with the bass. If you were playing with a singer, your role is going to be different than when you're playing with a big band. Were these things you just had to learn on the bandstand?

Yes! They say some musicians have a "knack" or whatever. I'm not sure if I'd call what I had a "knack"; I was just a very serious student of the genres of jazz. I did my homework. I researched and listened a *lot*. Listening is the most important thing. I emulated the masters. The goal of any musician is to have your own style, but at that time, I was in a research period, researching how it was done in the best possible way.

In a commercial sense, this research is what made my career possible, because in those days, it was very valuable to understand and have respect for the traditions.

Playing in Woody Herman's band was the best education I could have had in music. Woody was such a great teacher without trying that hard, you know? A great example of this would have to be the very first time I played the *real* Woody Herman jazz book. The first time I played with Woody we played a dance gig, and the music was really easy stuff, it was right up my alley. Woody told me after the gig, "Kid, you swing your ass off. You got the job!" and I just went crazy. I was whooping it up and jumping up and down on the bus.

So the next night we were booked at Blues Alley in Washington, D.C., a *real* jazz club, you know? And Woody calls all of the barnburners. We hadn't played any of the barnburners the night before. We played "Caldonia," and it was so *fast*. For fun, the trumpet section would time the choruses with stopwatches. A chorus of blues would go by in six and a half seconds!

Everyone had to take a solo on "Caldonia" and the last soloist was me! And I had never known you could play that fast. [laughs] So I'm trying to impress everybody with my harmonic knowledge and play these interesting bass lines and meanwhile, the music is going [sings an incredibly fast, swinging rhythm], the bass line quarter notes were really more like sixteenth notes.

At the end of the gig, as we're getting back on the bus, Woody came up to me and said, "Kid, it's not a crime to repeat notes." [laughs] With just that one sentence, I got it right away. The next night, I was playing [sings a steady, swinging, simpler bass line] and not trying so hard and it swung like crazy. He was a great teacher.

You also played with Doc Severinsen and Mel Tormé. How did they come into your musical orbit?

I was in Woody's band in 1981. After playing with Woody, I moved back to Philadelphia and stayed there for a couple of years. My ex and I got married during that time, and I played with some really great people in Philadelphia. But my ex had family in California, so we moved there in 1983.

Right away I met Ed Shaughnessy, the drummer in *The Tonight Show* band. I started playing in Ed's quintet and then his big band, which was called the Energy Force. I played with Ed's quintet on *The Tonight Show* in 1984, and Ed introduced me to Doc. Doc would call me to play in *The Tonight Show* band when [bassist] Joe DeBartolo was busy. I didn't really play on *The Tonight Show*, but I would play when the band did industrial shows and there were some recordings that I did with Doc as well.

I was playing with some really great people in Los Angeles, like [trumpeter and singer] Jack Sheldon, [saxophonist] Bob Cooper, [trombonist] Bill Watrous, [guitarist] Tommy Tedesco, and [trumpeter] Buddy Childers—I'm leaving many names out. My reputation was growing, and not just as a bass player for big bands.

One night in 1987, I came home from a gig and the phone was ringing. It was 3:30 a.m. I picked up the phone, and it's [pianist] George Shearing's manager asking me if I could be in San Jose at 10:00 a.m. He said, go ahead and book yourself a flight. I had to buy a seat for my bass. They reimbursed me for the tickets, of course. A limo picked me up at the airport and at 10:00 a.m. I'm rehearsing with George Shearing at the Paul Mason winery in Saratoga, California. Then later, this limo pulls up and out pops Mel Tormé. I didn't know I was going to be playing for Mel Tormé! [laughs] I thought it was just going to be me and George. A few minutes later, we're rehearsing with Mel Tormé and his drummer Donny Osborne. That weekend we played shows that were recorded for Concord Records for the album *A Vintage Year*. My whole career changed with that late-night phone call. I became Mel's regular bassist soon after.

Did you have a manager or an agent at this point in your career?
No. It's always been word of mouth. I would love to be able to find an agent or a manager, but so far, no luck.

These opportunities seem so serendipitous, but I think it's important to point out that you were playing all of these other gigs that weren't as high profile. All of that goes into being ready for these exciting opportunities to play with people like Mel Tormé and George Shearing.
The only thing you can control in the music business is the level of your playing. This philosophy certainly worked for me. At all times you have to try and keep your playing ability at the highest possible level, so when lightning strikes and that call comes out of nowhere, you're ready for it.

Listening to your trio on recordings like *The Real Me*, and the compositions you've written for that group, I hear how many musical roles the bass can play in jazz. Your bass is often in the foreground as the lead instrument.
My trio is my artistic outlet. If I'm putting my individual stamp on what I do it's with that trio. As a bass player, you are often in a supportive role, and I do play that role in my trio, but my bass gets to shine more. I enjoy being a side person and playing somebody else's music and making it sound as good as I possibly can. But my trio is me uncompromised.

When did you begin composing music?

I always wrote. My electric bass teacher Chuck Anderson would give me these very mechanical exercises to do, and I would come up with these little tunes from doing the exercises. And he encouraged that. I also wrote songs when I was playing with the rock and roll bands.

I think the writing has stretched me as much as anything. It's mysterious how it works. Each tune has its own little history. There's no one formula for composing for me.

How did you come to write the solo bass composition "Keni's Song"?

I wrote that song during the period I was transitioning. I was experiencing wild mood swings, and it came out of one of the happier mood swings. I have a friend in Milwaukee, Wisconsin, who sort of helped coach me through my trials during that time and showed me support and a real family kind of love. I wanted to pay tribute to her.

At that time, no one was paying attention to me in a musical sense. I was being ostracized and shunned consistently. I was also recuperating, recovering from some complications from my surgery and, just like in high school, playing the bass was the only joy I could find. I would put on little solo performances in my friend's living room.

Having all of that time to myself allowed me to retool my playing. I worked on a lot of new studies, new scales, harmonic studies, interval exercises, cello sonatas, things I hadn't touched on before with that degree of repetition. As a result of all of that retooling, and new life adjustments, these solo bass pieces came out, and "Keni's Song" is one of those pieces. I almost wrote that tune in one long improvisation. It just flowed.

The lyrics to your song "Stick It in Your Ear" are pretty self-explanatory. Is this a mission statement?

[laughs] That's a tune I wrote a long time ago. I wrote it for my record *The Southpaw* [1992]. Bob Cooper and Buddy Childers played on the original recording, but we did it as an instrumental. Actually, when I wrote that melody, I was thinking of Mel Tormé. I thought it would be fun to have Mel sing this. I wrote a set of lyrics for that melody back then, but I don't remember what I wrote. But Mel did tell me, "If you ever record this, I'll do it for free!" I should have taken him up on that!

There's a lot of music on *The Real Me* that I had already recorded. I rerecorded it because I was worried nobody was going to play my music on the radio anymore because they wouldn't know what to say about my name change, from John to Jennifer. So, I rerecorded "Turkish Bizarre," I put lyrics to "Split Brain" and recorded that again. This music has been played a lot on the radio, especially in California and on a few stations around the world. I have little knots of followers all around the U.S. and Canada, as well as Europe and Japan.

For "Stick It in Your Ear," I tried to harken back to the lyric I wrote with Mel in mind. The title was already in place before the lyrics. The lyrics are a double entendre. They could also mean, "Hey, *listen* man. You gotta listen to this music!"

I read that you will be using the crowdsourcing platform Indiegogo to fund your next recording project.
I've been an independent artist since I recorded *Two for the Road* in 1999, a duo record I did with Jimmy Bruno. Since then, I haven't even tried to get a record company interested.

I don't see a lot of encouragement of older musicians in the mass-marketed jazz world. I just don't see it. The bigger labels seem to want young, fast, pretty pussycats, you know? [laughs] I'm as vain as the next person, but I know I'm not a young, fast pretty pussycat anymore! I'm under no illusion that I'm going to be some big star. I make music because I love to make music. So for me, I don't think it makes sense to go after a deal with a large record label. For the record, I wound up having a successful Indiegogo campaign.

The industry itself is nothing like it was back in the 90s.
I'm not complaining. I love making records and I love having my own voice. Compliments like yours regarding *The Real Me* and how it is such an individual statement pleases me to no end. I can't tell you how flattered I am by that. And that's my goal, to make records that have my personality all over them. I'm a pretty competent producer, and I know about recording techniques and how to get the best sound for my bass. From the writing to the final mix I have the means to create an album that speaks from the heart. Maybe it would be interesting to work with a producer one day, someone who would take the reins in the recording process, and see how I would function in that situation. But I'm not looking for that right now.

I have had jazz educators at the university level tell me, "We are training kids for jobs that don't exist."
That's a really good point. I was involved in jazz education for a long time. I still teach privately, but I'm not affiliated with a school right now.

But artists such as yourself show that you can carve a niche market for your music, that you can fund your projects using platforms like Kickstarter and Indiegogo. Many of the musicians I've interviewed for this book are doing this.
Real, artistic music, music that pushes the envelope, has been pushed aside by

forces in marketing and education as well. We've institutionalized jazz. Earlier in this interview, I was talking about how I researched the traditions and became very good at playing those traditions. But for me, being able to play those traditions informed the originality of my playing. Jazz should be about creativity.

Institutionalizing jazz to a point where you are expected to have a college degree before you can be taken seriously as a player is turning a lot of younger musicians off from those traditions. Basically, what you're hearing from a lot of younger players right now is just odd meter modal playing. Jazz as it is marketed in the commercial world is mostly stagnant. And all of the outlets you're talking about, including crowdfunding, that's where the creative artists are going.

I don't feel that education is a bad thing. But, I do think that in addition to the traditions of learning the Great American Songbook, and learning what people have done before, there should be a little more room for creativity in jazz education. It should not only be about emulating the Count Basie Orchestra or making Duke Ellington into a master's thesis or a doctoral study. Duke Ellington was about blood and guts and heart and soul. His music was of its time and it was brilliant, but it's treated today like classical music. When it's regurgitated with transcriptions of exactly how it was played back then, to me that's crazy. The individual players in those bands and Duke's brilliance in orchestrating for their unique abilities were a big part of his genius, and it was one of a kind. The groove of the Basie band should be studied, and imitated, but it needs to be a deep immersion, not a test at the end of the week.

Given the way jazz is set up in the institutional sense, and in the way people are choosing to book shows and market the music, I don't think we'll ever see another Charlie Parker. Only people who come from wealth or patronage will have a chance in the future. There's never going to be this lightning bolt of a musician who changes the art form and takes it to a whole new place based purely on the merits of the music. It has to be bankrolled these days. I just don't see another Bird coming along. The only hope for jazz in my humble opinion is in independent artistry.

What I think is going to happen in the future is a grassroots type of music that embraces elements of jazz as well as elements of different kinds of ethnic music, music from around the world, that will catch people's ears, and people will grab a hold of that. The commercial part of jazz may reluctantly embrace some of this, but the next wave of creative jazz will come from the grassroots.

Many of the younger musicians I've interviewed for this book are incorporating musical styles from around the world into jazz.
You're seeing this in a lot of music. I love this new wave of bluegrass they're

calling "newgrass" that incorporates elements of classical and jazz in it, like what Béla Fleck and Chris Thile are playing. These are two musicians who are steeped in tradition who are pushing the boundaries of their genre.

Have you checked out [clarinetist] Anat Cohen?
Oh, I know her. She's magnificent, a very authentic player in a lot of genres. I think she's a great lady.

What advice would you give to a young person or any person reading this interview who is experiencing gender dysphoria?
Don't be afraid. The fear is the biggest enemy. The hardest trial for me, in going through what I dealt with, was being afraid.

I came up in a different time. Today, there are more resources now for transgender people. Attitudes and prejudice about transgender people in the jazz world are still pretty much the same; sometimes it's very blatant, sometimes it's not, but it's just as insidious. You can't always be sure if these attitudes are the reason why you are being rejected or shunned, but it's always in the back of your head. But you can't let fear rule your life.

If you're feeling like I felt, find somebody to talk to. Find a really good counselor. Most major colleges offer LGBT support for students. Seek out counseling. I didn't overcome my fear until I found counseling, and when I did, it was a process. It didn't happen overnight, but when I stopped being afraid of what people would think about me, I began to flourish both as a person and as a musician.

Being transgender is just a part of the human experience. We're all in this together. We're all normal. There's nothing negative about it. Once we can break down all of the ridiculous stereotypical thinking and ignorance surrounding the subject of transgender people, we will all be a lot safer and more productive.

I can understand someone being afraid, because there is, literally, terrible violence that is done to people who are gender variant. Discrimination is rampant. But it's going to get better if people are honest about who they are. Hopefully, I've had a hand in making things a little better for people by just being open and honest about myself. Overall, things are a lot better now than when I transitioned. I transitioned in 2001 and it was a completely different age.

In my case, I was almost fortunate to have had the issues that I had, because it made me really happy to be alone in a room and practice. It informed my craft. To this day, I like being alone playing my bass. I would tell anybody, no matter what profession they plan to enter, whether it's music or not, to just be great at what you do. Be really conscientious about educating yourself about what you do. I may not have a college degree, but I've never stopped studying. I study every day. I'm always striving to better myself.

Just keep bettering yourself. Don't let your gender identity issues become your focus. I mean, for people who are cisgender, how many hours a day do they spend fixated on what gender they are? If you're trans, you're trans! That's okay! Don't get sidelined by trying to prove something, just be who you are, be a good person, be great at what you do, and someday it will all take care of itself.

Ellen Seeling

While a small number of musicians demurred after being contacted with a request for an interview for this book (some expressed being "burnt out" on "women" projects), several did welcome the opportunity to be a part of a project solely focused on the contributions of women to jazz. That said, the majority of these interviews are about music, not gender. However, the following interview with trumpeter, bandleader, educator, and activist Ellen Seeling is an example of an in-depth conversation that unapologetically embraces both subjects.

In 1969, Seeling was accepted into Indiana University, one of the top five music schools in the U.S., and is the first woman to graduate from IU with a jazz degree. ("Bachelor's of Music in Jazz Studies is the official name on my diploma," says Seeling.) While still in school, she recorded and toured with the legendary all-female progressive rock band Isis (named after the Egyptian goddess), one of two all-female rock bands based in New York City at the time with a record deal (the other being Fanny, led by guitarist June Millington). The experience was life-changing, and led to her being asked to tour with singer songwriter Laura Nyro in a band that included jazz musicians Mike Maneri on vibraphone and Richard Davis on bass. Both opportunities coincided with the women's rights movement, and were empowering for Seeling both as a musician and a woman.

Ellen Seeling. Photo by Jane Higgins.

"Growing up, it was very daunting to not see many other women like me playing the trumpet," says Seeling, "but I just kept going.... I loved music, and after playing with Isis and Laura Nyro, I had a support system of other women musicians.... And it kept me going."

Seeling relocated to New York City in 1975, and since then, has enjoyed a successful and wide-ranging career performing and recording with musicians across the musical spectrum of jazz, rock, and funk, all while remaining a vocal advocate for women's rights, especially when it comes to the bandstand and academia. After relocating to the West Coast, Seeling and her partner Jean Fineberg founded both the Jazzschool for Women and the Girls' Jazz and Blues Camp to provide music education opportunities for women in a supportive environment. In 1997, Seeling and Fineberg founded the Montclair Women's Big Band, which features some of the most talented women jazz players in the Bay Area. Seeling is also the chairperson for Jazz Women and Girls Advocates, a relatively new organization dedicated to promoting "the visibility of women and girl instrumentalists of all ethnicities in jazz and to advocate for their inclusion in all aspects of the art form."

Seeling's activism and formidable musicianship continues to inspire both women and men who believe jazz is a progressive, not regressive, form for artistic expression. But I can't help but wonder what opportunities for women in jazz would be like without Seeling and others like her who are speaking out against gender discrimination in jazz. I also wonder what, if any, changes we will see in this field a decade or two into the future.

....

When did you first begin playing an instrument?
I started playing the trumpet at the age of 12 while attending a small rural Catholic school in southern Wisconsin. I grew up in Waukesha County, which is near Milwaukee. Back then, in the 1950s, the area was fairly rural. We lived in what we used to call a subdivision, sort of out in the middle of miles and miles of farmland, small forests, and open fields. It was great place to grow up.

My school didn't have much of a band program. I was sort of interested in playing music, but more involved in sports.

When they started a band program at my school, I initially wanted to play drums, but my dad said no. He didn't want to hear all of that banging going on in the basement. Then I wanted to play violin, but there was no string program at my school. I liked the trumpet too, so that's what I chose to play in the school band.

Did your mom or any other family members play music?
My dad played the trumpet, although I never heard him play because he quit

when he got married. [laughs] My dad always had good records around the house, a lot of classic big bands, both white and black bands. He had records by Les Brown and Glenn Miller, but he also loved Louis Armstrong and Dizzy Gillespie. He did try playing professionally for a year or so when he got out of the navy after World War II, but he couldn't make any money. He was doing one-nighters with what they used to call "tenor bands," in the Midwest. That's a really tough way to make a living and not much fun, and when he got married and settled down, he just didn't play anymore.

My mother played piano when she was younger and also sang. I have four sisters, and I remember all of us would sing around the house with my mother. We were all members of our church choir. So there was a lot of music in the house, but my parents weren't really musicians.

What kind of music did you play in the school band?
I don't really remember, probably elementary-school band music. It certainly wasn't jazz. I didn't get any of that until I got to high school, although I was listening to it at the time, and really loved it.

I think it's really important for kids to listen to music when they're young, especially jazz players, because so much of jazz isn't notated. You just sort of have to know it, and the only way to know it is to listen to the people who play it. Listening enables you to develop some sort of conception of the sound, even before you actually begin playing an instrument.

And your listening library was your dad's record collection.
Yes. I still have some of the old 78s of Charlie Parker, Dizzy Gillespie, Woody Herman, Benny Goodman—I must have thirty or forty 78s out in my garage somewhere.

When you listened to these records, would you pick up your trumpet and try to replicate what you were hearing?
No, I was pretty busy just learning the instrument. The trumpet is . . . daunting. It really is. It's very physical. It's not an instrument you can play a couple of times a week and really learn to play well.

My parents couldn't afford private lessons for me, but my band director at school would give me lessons every once in a while. I had books I would work out of on my own and learn songs, but not necessarily jazz.

After eighth grade, my family moved from sort of a rural setting into Milwaukee County, which was more urban. So, taking my dog and disappearing into the woods for an afternoon was no longer something I could do, and my interests shifted.

When I got to high school, there was a stage band that played big band repertoire. I worked really hard to get into that band. I was playing catch up, and making it into the stage band was a big deal. Once I got in to the stage band, I really got into music.

While in high school, did you decide that you wanted to play music for a living?
Yes. Once I got into the stage band, pretty much all of my extracurricular activities were music. I loved music. It takes a couple years before you're able to play anything on the trumpet. It's really slow going. But once I got a handle on the instrument, I got more and more enthusiastic about playing music for a living.

When I was a junior in high school, I started to get gigs with really good local professional big bands. I don't even really remember how that happened. I guess somebody heard me play at one of the high school jazz-band contests and got my contact information from my band director and just called me up for a gig.

There were no other kids in those bands; it was all adult men, grown-up guys. Some were professional musicians, others were really good amateurs with "real" jobs. Once I started working and making some money, I was totally hooked. I didn't have money for lessons or even a really good instrument until I started working. My family didn't have money. My dad was a tool and die maker, which was a good job, but he was supporting all of us. My mother didn't work.

After high school, you attended Indiana University. Did IU have a jazz program in place at that time?
They did not have a jazz degree program the year I started, but the school was in the process of convincing the school of music's administration that they should offer one. There was a jazz department run by David Baker, who is a very famous jazz educator and one of the first to be associated with a major university. The school of music at Indiana is one of the top five music schools in the country. You might not think of a Midwestern state as having such a music program, but the music programs at the land-grant colleges in the Midwest are quite good.

After high school, I initially went to the University of Wisconsin extension in Milwaukee. They had a music department but no jazz program to speak of, not even a jazz ensemble. I was so discouraged with the music program and with what I *wasn't* learning, that I dropped out after the first semester. I got a full-time job running a punch press in a factory in Milwaukee and decided to work and save up enough money to go to a real school. After UWM, I wanted to make a fresh start, so I applied to other schools as an incoming freshman instead of a transfer.

In 1969, I got accepted to IU, but when I got there, I was informed the school had raised the tuition by $300 a semester. I thought I had enough money saved for a year, but it turned out I only had enough for a semester. So, after the first semester, I was back working 24 to 28 hours a week and going to school at the same time.

These were the early days of jazz education in the colleges . . .
Right.

. . . and you were a part of the first wave of students.
I remember that first year sitting with a number of my student friends who were also interested in jazz and trying to get people to sign a petition to convince the university administration to offer a jazz degree, which they finally did.[85]

You were the first woman to graduate from IU with a degree in jazz studies.
Bachelor's of Music in Jazz Studies is the official name on my diploma.

Did you go to New York City right after graduating?
I was sort of back and forth for a while. I dropped out for a year because they kept raising the tuition and I couldn't afford it, even though I was working. At one point, I was working something like 32 hours a week, taking out loans and getting grants but still barely making tuition and paying my living expenses. And the program there was very rigorous. I couldn't slack off on the practicing and all the other stuff. So, I dropped out for a year so I could get my residency status and come back to school and pay tuition as a resident. During that time, David Baker was nice enough to let me continue to play in the ensembles and audit some classes.

In December of my senior year, I got a call from Carol MacDonald, who was the lead singer of Isis, one of the first all-woman rock bands in New York City with a record deal. There were just two all-female rock bands in New York at that time. One was Fanny, led by June Millington, who is still around, and the other was Isis. Both bands were what they called back then progressive rock bands. Isis had a horn section, kind of like Chicago or Blood, Sweat & Tears.

Carol had gotten my name from [tuba and baritone saxophone player] Howard Johnson, who had come to IU to do a clinic with the big band. I believe I was the only woman in any of the big bands, and possibly the only woman in the jazz department at that time. I was getting to play and do some soloing, and he heard me. Isis was going to record an album in New Orleans with Allen Toussaint producing in Toussaint's new studio, but their regular trumpet player couldn't do it, and she was looking for a replacement. On Howard's recommendation, Carol called me up and asked me to go to New Orleans with Isis, sight unseen, because there just wasn't anybody else in New York who could do the gig. I mean, this is how scarce women jazz and commercial trumpet players were back then.

Isis flew me down to New Orleans over Christmas vacation. I met and hung out with the band and spent all day and all night in the studio for about two weeks and did my first record. I think that was also my first time on an airplane! It was very heady! [laughs] A total rush, you know? Talk about getting hooked on something!

That's an amazing story. Did recording with Isis lead you to decide to move to New York City and dive into the world of playing commercial music?
Well, sort of. After I finished the album, I went back to Indiana to finish my degree. A month or two later, Carol called me again and said, "The band is going on the road this summer and we need a trumpet player. Are you interested?" I said, "Sure!" I managed to work it out with David to finish up all of my course work ahead of schedule so that I had time to complete my degree and make it to New York in time to head out on the road with this crazy women's rock and roll band.

Isis toured for the summer. I had applied to go to graduate school at IU as a trumpet performance major. (The school didn't offer a graduate jazz degree at that time.) When school started in August, I left the band and went back to IU, but you know, it was never the same after that. [laughs] I was just never the same. I started working on my grad degree in trumpet, but I was stuck studying all this stuff I didn't want to study, learning all this repertoire I didn't want to learn, and that's when this crazy series of events happened to me, and I don't know why.

I was at IU, feeling pretty miserable, when I got a phone call. I picked up the phone and it was Laura Nyro. I don't know if you know her music....

Oh, yes. I do!
At first, I thought it was a hoax. I picked up the phone and a voice said, [gently] "Hello, this is Laura Nyro." I waited a second and said, "Yeah, right! And I'm Miles Davis and I have to go now. Good-bye." And I hung up on her! A few minutes later, the phone rang, and it was her, again, and I thought, "Maybe I should talk to this person?"

The conga player in Isis was a very good friend of Laura's, and Laura was getting ready to do a big comeback. She decided she was going to go on the road and do a series of live recordings, and that her band was going to be a jazz band. Alex Foster was her horn player, and the rhythm section included Mike Maneri on vibes, John Tropea on guitar, Richard Davis on bass, and Nydia Mata from Isis on congas. Laura told me Alex was leaving, and asked if I would be interested in auditioning for her horn section. Although I had no idea what she had in mind, I said, "Hell, yes!"

She also called Jean Fineberg, whom I had met in Isis, who played tenor saxophone and flute. Laura's plan was to replace Alex with two or three horn players.

To get ready for the audition, I went out and bought her latest album, *Smile*. There were several tunes on there she wanted me to learn by ear. She didn't send me any music. Michael and Randy Brecker played the horns on that album. She flew me to her band's first gig at Symphony Hall in Philadelphia, and my audition was to do the sound check with the band, which consisted of all of these guys, these big name musicians I had been listening to since high school. If I sounded good at the sound check, I had the gig.

It was very scary but I was not one to back down. I just sort of did it, and Laura seemed to think I was okay. I played the show that night, and then she offered me the gig, which ended up being a year's worth of recording and live performances around the country, including Carnegie Hall.

I went back to school and checked in with David Baker about this gig, this gig that was like a gig from heaven. It paid decently, I was going to be playing with a dream band and travel all over the country, and it was my entrée to New York City. After the tour, I would have enough money to move to New York.

But David Baker told me, "Don't take the gig. Stay in school."

Wow! That surprises me!
I thought about what he said and realized that this gig was the reason *why* I went to school, to be ready for an opportunity like this. So I left school, went to New York, and I never went back.

Do you think David Baker wanted you to finish the graduate degree in order to become an educator like him?
Well, I don't know what he was thinking. I had a very different perspective on what he said then than I do now. Back then, I was in my early 20s, and I thought maybe he was looking out for me. But I remember, as a grad assistant, he gave the jobs of running the other bands and teaching classes to the guys. My job as a grad assistant was basically to be his secretary in his jazz history class, even though I was just as good a player, had been around longer, and had a better professional track record than the guys. So, I didn't really think about it then. But as I got older, I got more and more angry about the whole thing. I'm so glad I didn't take his advice.

Even today, this is something musicians run into, where they begin playing professionally while they are in school and ask themselves if they should finish their degree or drop out. But it's important to put your story and this decision you made into a historical context, with the women's rights movement developing as you were evolving as a musician.
I never saw another female play the trumpet until I went to IU where there

were two other women in the music program: Sandy Steinberg, who's in L.A. now and is still playing, and Michelle Kaufman, who was a classical player. She was a monster player, the best classical player at IU while I was there.

By the time I got to New York, there were two other commercial female trumpet players that I knew about, one being Laurie Frink, who was a really well-known, well-respected trumpet player. She and I knew each other and played together.

Growing up, it was very daunting to not see many other women like me playing the trumpet, but I just kept going. I figured I could do it. I loved music, and after playing with Isis and Laura Nyro, I had a support system of other women musicians. I had a support system, and it kept me going.

At IU, did you have a similar kind of support system? Did you hang out and jam with other jazz musicians?

I'm sure the program at IU has since evolved but back then, there were some glaring omissions in the jazz degree programs. We did not get any combo instruction. The combo thing went on in the practice rooms with the guys, after hours, and I was not invited to those things. But between going to school and working different jobs, I didn't have time to stop to think about the things that were going on around me, like, not getting invited to jam sessions. I just worked as hard as I could to get what I wanted.

When I got out of college, I became more aware of our situation as women performers in music, particularly in commercial music and jazz. Hanging out with the older women in Isis was a really good education for me. The original core group of Isis had played together previously as Goldie and the Gingerbreads.

I've heard of them. Sort of inspired by the British beat music, right?

Yes. They opened for and toured with the Rolling Stones in Britain and had some radio hits. Three of the women in that band became the core of Isis. Goldie was Goldie Zelkowitz, now Genya Ravan, who is a pretty well-known singer and record producer. The keyboard player was Margo Lewis. She went on to run her own talent agency, Talent Consultants International, and managed Bo Diddley for 25 years or something—she still manages his estate. Ginger Bianco was the drummer. Carol MacDonald was the guitar player and became lead singer of Isis.

These women were powerful. They knew who they were. They knew that the business was messed up, and they just hung together. That was a powerful bunch of women to be around in the 70s. I was really lucky to get in with that group. It was a wonderful support system and gave me a lot of opportunities to play in front of large audiences.

I don't know if anyone else has opened up this topic for you, but I think an unspoken but very important aspect, or characteristic, or quality of a lot of women musicians who are well known, or somewhat well known, or able to make a living playing jazz is that they are lesbians. I think part of what kept them going was their connection with other women and not caring that much about what the guys thought.

It's sort of unspoken in women's sports and in women's music that a large percentage of the women are not straight. I think that tends to help them bond with each other in a way that may be different than straight women. Not that I don't have a lot of straight women friends and colleagues whom I love. Most of the women in my band are straight. But there's a connection and level of support that goes really, really deep among women who do not rely on men.

The culture around jazz can be very homophobic ...
Ya think?

... but there are plenty of gay jazz musicians throughout history.
Oh, absolutely.

It's amazing to me that among the practitioners of such a progressive art form, that there is such a degree of homophobia and sexism.
I want to speak a little bit to how virulently "male" this art form is. There are men that will exclude women from the history of jazz at all costs, and will denigrate their contributions and their very existence.

Wynton Marsalis is so obsessed with the history of the music, but when it comes to jazz, its plasticity, the ability for the music to change and grow, he's totally arrested. He's a one-man moldy fig conspiracy. I can't even watch Ken Burns' jazz documentary because it had Marsalis and Crouch as its consultants. I'm so disappointed in Ken Burns for the way in which he presented the music and completely cutting women out of their rightful history in jazz.

There *is* a history of women in jazz, all anyone has to do is watch Judy Chaikin's film *The Girls in the Band* to understand that.

It may be hard for women musicians born in 1970 and afterward to imagine and understand what life was like in the U.S. in the 1950s before the women's movement. The younger musicians I've interviewed for this book share a laudable, positive attitude and have told me, "Of course I can play as well as men. It's a non-issue." But while there has been some significant progress, women are still underrepresented when it comes to how the history of jazz is told, the programming of jazz festivals, and in academia. To not acknowledge that this underrepresentation exists strikes me as being a bit naïve.
It's extremely naïve. I encounter this with the younger players in my band who are embarrassed by my activism and not on board with it.

You're encountering what I'm describing?

Yes, and it's very annoying. [laughs]

Let me just say that these musicians are young, and they don't have perspective with this issue. I also think that with women it's a little bit of a survival thing. If women really stop and look, clear-eyed, at what is going on around them, and copped to it, it is so discouraging. Some women might just shut down and stop what they're doing.

I can't tell you how many of my friends, all really good players, who, when they got to their 30s and 40s and found they couldn't make a living because of discrimination against women in this music, just quit. And they're doing something else now, you know? They're doing something besides playing music.

The discrimination in jazz ruins women's lives. I'm not saying it's easy for guys. It's not easy for *anybody* in jazz. But it's a whole lot easier for men than it is for women, and the younger players don't see that. They do see a lot more women around them than I did, but what they don't see are women with sustainable careers in music, and that's because of the gender discrimination.

Younger players have had the benefit of role models as teachers, because a lot of women who could not make a full-time living as performers have taken to teaching. There are a lot of women teachers, although not in the high-powered universities, that's for sure. You can take a look at any high-powered university's jazz department, and you may see a pianist or a singer, but you're not going to see any women on the faculty. I've been looking at the faculty of jazz department's for years and it's disgusting. I see no women in the jazz department at Indiana University or at Northridge, or UCLA, or USC. I don't know how the universities get away with it. Until somebody starts grousing about it and threatening universities with lawsuits, the institutions will not change.

I see more women students and more women playing, but I don't see any women in the Jazz at Lincoln Center orchestra. I see only one woman out of 45 acts on the Detroit Jazz Festival. I see just one woman on the summer session of the San Francisco Jazz Festival. I see no women headliners at this year's [2014] Newport Jazz Festival. [sarcastically] Thank you, George Wein.

The Mary Lou Williams Jazz Festival has ceased programming exclusively women. But why do they have guys running that festival? At least Billy Taylor had a sensibility about it. I know the reason why my band got to play that festival is because [pianist] Marian McPartland called Billy Taylor up and told him to hire us. I had been trying to get my band on that festival years before that. But this is how the guys' networks operate. Women don't get those kinds of powerful endorsements from other women, because first of all, there are hardly any powerful women.

I get so tired of women being afraid to stick up for themselves. Many women think they have to keep everything cool, that everybody has to like them,

The Montclair Women's Big Band. Photo by Jane Higgins.

and they shouldn't rock the boat. I don't want to discourage the young women who are playing jazz, but I think they need to wake up and get on the bandwagon.

In 2009, you founded the Girls' Jazz and Blues Camp at the Jazzschool. What do the girls who come to these camps come away with as a result of being a part of and participating in these camps?
It's life changing for these girls. Absolutely. And they will tell you that. I have pages of quotes not only from students in the girls' camp but from participants in the women's camp, the Jazzschool for Women, as well, which we started three years ago.

The camps are a life changing and unique experience for both girls and women. It reminds me of when I left college and joined Isis. That's what it's like for them. They have access to excellent faculty at these camps, faculty who are some of the best female jazz and commercial music players from the Bay Area. Yes, they get excellent music instruction, but they get it in an environment where they don't have to be afraid that they are going to be blindsided, that they're going to get hit upside the head if they're not constantly vigilant. It's an environment where the musicians feel comfortable enough to try and improvise and aren't worried about somebody making fun of them. We had 56 girls in the camp last summer. It is, as far as I know, the only camp of its kind anywhere.

I don't believe music has to be competitive in order for a musician to become a great player. I think competition keeps people down. In my big band, the Montclair Women's Big Band, we're supportive of each other. Maybe men play better when they're threatened or scared? Personally, I don't think so, although competition can foster other qualities. Competition can make a musician work harder and more aggressive, I suppose, and that's part of jazz, and I like that part. But to constantly be in fear of being put down or of losing your gig or being embarrassed in front of your bandmates is not a good atmosphere in which to develop musically.

Mindi Abair

PART TWO

I read a review of one of your performances where the reviewer describes you as "a kinetic force" onstage.
I never heard that! I love that.

Can you pinpoint a time in your career where you feel like you made that transition to having that kind of stage presence? Where it was clear to everyone in the audience that you are the bandleader?
I don't think there's any one point that I became a bandleader, or that I found who I am onstage. All of those guys that tell you on the way up, "You know, you gotta pay your dues...." I think they're right.

For me, I always wanted to be a bandleader. In college, I started my own band. I was always working towards that, voraciously. But what I was also doing that I think is priceless, is playing every night. At school, I went to classes, and practiced in the practice rooms. But at night, I'd go out and play, six or seven nights a week, four or five sets a night. Doing that, you create who you are. You become comfortable with your instrument. You become comfortable being on stage with your instrument. You become comfortable with your surroundings and the people around you. Malcolm Gladwell wrote a great book called *The Outliers*, where he chronicles what he thinks it takes to succeed. One of the things in the book is he believes it takes 10,000 hours of practice or doing anything, be it playing a musical instrument or becoming a great writer or whatever it is. And I've got to say, looking back, I've done my 10,000 hours to become who I am. I played every night for years and years and that allowed me to become really comfortable with who I am as a player, saxophonist, and singer.

The reason I wrote *How to Play Madison Square Garden* is I think it's helpful to understand not only how your instrument works and what it takes to be a better player, but also what it takes to be onstage. Do you want people to buy a ticket to your next concert? Well, there's a few things you can do to hopefully draw them in and create fans, instead of just playing a club every night but not connecting with people.

But I think every artist is different. Every musical situation is different. At the very beginning of the book, I discuss how important it is to figure out who you are as a performer. Are you a Jackson Browne-type who's going to go out there with a guitar and sing and get political? Then you don't need to come up with flash pots onstage or have raining fire during your set. Or, do you want to be like [the rock band] Kiss and make it a huge production and have things blowing up onstage while wearing huge heels and makeup? Are you heavy metal or are you a balladeer?

Knowing who you are as a performer and as a musician is everything you need to build a show based on who you are and what your strengths are. I toured with the Backstreet Boys on their millennial tour, and that was quite a show. Very choreographed, from the lighting to the stage moving with us, to people flying around and everything. We definitely did the same stuff every night. You couldn't change it. But then I'd go out on the road with my band, and it would be a different show every night. Each night, I would do a different set list, maybe changing it up in the middle, depending on how I feel and what I'm feeling from the audience.

So when it comes to building a live performance, I don't think there's a right or wrong way to do it.

What is it like playing on a television show as huge as *American Idol*? Is the sound onstage weird? Are you nervous with all of the cameras pointing at you? Can you describe what that experience is like for a musician?
Well, with the *Late Show with David Letterman*, I couldn't even see all of the band members. The way I'm positioned onstage, I can see the audience, but only some of the band members, and Dave is positioned way to my left. It's a whole different reaction time. It's a whole different way of playing music. Unlike when I play with my band, where I'm able to see everyone and run around with everyone, on *Letterman*, I have this place where I have to stand. What's interesting is that I'm a very prepared bandleader. I write up a set list in advance and pass it out to the guys before we go onstage. Whereas with the *David Letterman Show*, Paul Schaffer and those guys have been doing this for 30 years, and they fly by the seat of their pants. They're machines! So 15 seconds before a guest comes on, Paul's like, "Ooo! I got an idea! Let's do *this* song!" Key of . . . something? Go! And that's a whole different way of approaching music and a band. It's like a ride! I told him at the end of my first day, "This is absolutely a drug," because not many people work that way, that quick and making that much music on the fly. It's amazing, and it's fun.

There is extreme pressure when you're talking about TV when you know how many people are watching. I remember the first time I was on *American Idol*. I was walking onstage and just thinking, "Whoa. 26 million people. Wow. I've played for a lot of people live. Upwards of 80 to 100 thousand people. But we've got eyeballs on a TV screen. So don't screw up!" [laughs] I'm not usually a nervous person when I'm playing music, but that experience definitely put an edge on me.

Do you do anything to remedy that? Like deep breathing or drinking some water before you go out there?

I don't. I usually talk myself out of getting nervous. I tell myself, "You know what? You've done this a million times before. Go out and have fun and don't let the fact that millions of people are watching get to you. This is what you do. Just go out and rise above." Some people do have secrets for dealing with nervousness, and I wrote about some of that in my book, how to deal with stress and stage fright.

From your perspective, are you seeing more women in the music industry now? Maybe not just as artists, but in management, in the recording studios, or in publicity?

I think in many ways the glass ceiling has broken. It hasn't completely broken in all genres and places in music. There are definitely many more male executives in the business than there are female. But, I think more and more, it's just who is right for the job. And I love that. I always went into musical situations with no chip on my shoulder thinking, "All right. I'm going to go in and play, and if I'm right for the job, I'm going to get it. If I'm not, I'm not." You hope that the color of your skin doesn't prevent you from getting a job or that being a man or a woman doesn't. It does sometimes. But hopefully, it's the exception rather than the rule. I can name some gigs I got because I am a woman, and some gigs I did not get because I am a woman.

I do find that there are more women out there doing their thing because it's less odd now, you know? It's just more acceptable, which is beautiful. One day nobody's even going to think about it.

People have asked me, why does your book need in its title "Women in Jazz"? Why can't it just be "Musicians"?

One day it will be. But we're not done with it. It's not like no one thinks about it anymore. I think it's important to have this conversation, to talk to people about their experiences.

I love the way Diana Krall sings. I love the way Al Green sings. But I'm not going to hire Al Green for the same thing I'd hire Diana Krall for. They are very different. I love the way Ella Fitzgerald sings. I love the way Charlie Parker plays the saxophone. Everyone's different and I tend to look at things that way. When a person has a talent, it doesn't matter if they're a woman or a man or what their sexual orientation is or what the color of their skin is. It's about talent. I think I'm not alone in believing that.

Notes

Introduction

1 "You Don't Know Jazz" by Dr. Lewis Porter, wbgo.org, June 9, 2011. http://www
   .wbgo.org/blog/you-dont-know-jazz-with-dr-lewis-porter.
2 Liner notes to the album *Orchestrion* by Pat Metheny, November 2009.
3 "Rocking the Cradle of Jazz," by Sherrie Tucker, *Ms. Magazine*, 2004.
4 Ibid.
5 Ibid.
6 Frank Sinatra, "The Way I Look at Race," *Ebony*, July 1958.
7 "Lady sings the blues: Dee Dee Bridgewater brings it on for Billie Holiday at
   Wortham Center," by Chris Becker, *Culturemap Houston*, March 15, 2012.
8 *Q: The Autobiography of Quincy Jones*, by Quincy Jones, Doubleday, 2001.
9 "Mary Lou Williams" from *Reading Jazz: A Gathering of Autobiography, Reportage,
   and Criticism from 1919 to Now*, edited by Robert Gottlieb, Vintage Books, 1996.
10 Ibid.
11 *Harlem Nocturne*, by Farah Jasmine Griffin, Basic *Civitas* Books, 2013.
12 Ibid.
13 *Peggy Gilbert and Her All-Girl Band*, Jeannie Gayle Pool, Scarecrow Press, 2008.
14 "Oral History with Carol Kaye," Rock and Roll Hall of Fame Museum, 2005.
   YouTube video. http://youtu.be/F9WQTrr3GZ4.
15 *Swing Shift: "All-Girl" Bands of the 1940s*, by Sherrie Tucker, Duke University Press,
   2000.
16 "Zildjian Wishes Artist Viola Smith a Very Special Happy Birthday and asks, Can
   playing drums help you live to 100?" November 29, 2012. http://zildjian.com
   /News-Events/2012/11/Happy-Birthday-Viola.
17 *Harlem Nocturne*, by Farah Jasmine Griffin, Basic Civitas Books, 2013.
18 Ibid.
19 "Rock n Roll Suicide: Beverly Kenney (1932-1960)," The Lonesome Beehive, May
   4, 2011. http://lonesomebeehive.wordpress.com/2011/05/04/rock-n-roll-suicide
   -beverly-kenney-1932-1960.
20 "From Beatles Fans to Beat Groups: A Historiography of the 1960s All-Girl
   Rock Band," by Christine Feldman-Barrett, Feminist Media Studies, DOI:
   10.1080/14680777.2013.866972, 2013.

21 *When Everything Changed: The Amazing Journey of American Women From 1960 to the Present*, by Gail Collins, Little, Brown and Company, 2009.

22 Ibid.

23 Ibid.

24 "First Vanity, Now Insurrection: Jane Eyre, That Girl, and Miley Cyrus," by Chris Becker, March 2011, Houston Press Blogs, Art Attack http://blogs .houstonpress.com/artattack/2011/03/jane_eyre_that_girl_and_miley.php.

25 *Miles: The Autobiography*, by Miles Davis with Quincy Troupe, Touchstone, Simon & Schuster, 1989.

26 "Soul Couture," by Dean Van Nguyen, *Wax Poetics*, Winter 2013.

27 "The History of Jazz Education: A Critical Reassessment," by Kenneth E. Prouty, from the Journal for Historical Research in Music Education, Indiana State University, April 2005.

28 Ibid.

29 "The Case for Girls," by Anya Kamenetz, *Fast Company*, December/January 2011.

30 "John Zorn: One Future, Two Views," John Zorn interviewed by Bill Milkowski for *JazzTimes*, March 2000.

31 *Mister Jelly Roll: The Fortunes of Jelly Roll Morton, New Orleans Creole and Inventor of Jazz*, by Alan Lomax, Duell, Sloan and Pearce, New York, 1950.

32 Liner notes to the album *Orchestrion* by Pat Metheny, November 2009.

33 "John Zorn: One Future, Two Views," John Zorn interviewed by Bill Milkowski for *JazzTimes*, March 2000.

34 "With *Another Country*, Cassandra Wilson continues to expand the boundaries of jazz," by Chris Becker, Culturemap Houston, October 18, 2012.

35 Marian McPartland also started her label Halcyon Records that same year.

36 "Jazz in the New Depression," Connie Crothers interviewed by Against the Current for Solidarity, September/October 2009. http://www.solidarity-us.org/site /node/2369.

37 *How Music Works*, David Byrne, McSweeney's, 2012.

38 Ibid.

39 However, there are a small number of similarly themed documentaries that are in progress at the time of this writing.

Dee Dee Bridgewater

40 *Digging: The Afro-American Soul of American Classical Music*, "Billie Holiday," by Amiri Baraka, University of California Press, 2009.

41 Ibid. p. 220. Baraka writes, "Our history, our lives, our struggle, our ecstasy are all inside our arts, and our artists are still griots, historians, and poets, carrying word from bird, from the oldest ancestry, to prepare us for the future."

42 In 1969, long before the advent of the Internet and mp3s, jazz vocalist Betty Carter took control of her music by creating a label she named Bet Car Records.

Terri Lyne Carrington

43 The "one" refers to the first beat of a measure of music. Carrington is saying for
    television, the energy of a musical performance must be at its peak right from
    the very beginning of a musical cue.

44 The full quote is, "If 'jazz' means anything at all, which is questionable, it means
    the same thing it meant to musicians 50 years ago—freedom of expression. I
    used to have a definition, but I don't think I have one anymore, unless it is that
    it is music with an African foundation which came out of an American environ-
    ment." *The World of Duke Ellington*, by Stanley Dance, Da Capo Press, 2000.

Brandee Younger

45 Jazzmobile, Inc. is a non-profit, educational outreach organization founded in
    New York in 1964 by Dr. William "Billy" Taylor, who also created the Mary Lou
    Williams Women in Jazz Festival, and Daphne Arnstein.

46 On February 26, 2012, 17-year-old Trayvon Benjamin Martin was shot and killed
    by George Zimmerman for the crime of being black and walking and eating
    candy in a white neighborhood in Sanford, Florida. Martin was unarmed. Zim-
    merman, who went on to have several violent encounters with the police, was
    charged and acquitted of second-degree murder and manslaughter.

Eliane Elias

47 The term "standards," known alternately as "the Great American Songbook,"
    refers to a repertoire of songs, composed from the 1920s to the 1960s, for Broad-
    way and movie musicals or as popular songs of their time.

Val Jeanty

48 *Shadow Dancing in the USA*, by Michael Ventura, Tarcher, 1986

49 Jean-Claude succeeded his father, Francois ("Papa Doc") Duvalier, as president
    "for life" of Haiti in 1971. He fled Haiti in 1986 in the wake of increasing social
    unrest, and a military council ruled the country for the next several years.
    Duvalier returned to Haiti in January 2011, and eventually was ordered to appear
    in court to face charges of corruption and human rights abuses committed while
    he was President. He died of a heart attack on October 4, 2014.

50 "Comp" is short for "accompany." When a musician in an ensemble is soloing,
    the rhythm section provides improvised rhythmic and harmonic accompani-
    ment (or "comping") that supports and interacts with the solo.

Lenaé Harris

51 "No Bop Roots In Jazz: Parker" by Michael Levin and John S. Wilson, *DownBeat
    Magazine*, 1949.

52 *The Real Book*, published by Hal Leonard Corporation, is a compilation of lead
    sheets for several standard and contemporary jazz compositions. There are actu-
    ally several editions of *The Real Book* available, each transcribed for a different
    clef (treble or bass) or transposing instrument.

Sofia Rei

53 Solfège exercises are vocal exercises where the singer sings vowels (a, o, u, etc.) or a different syllable for each note of the Western scale (do, re, mi, fa, sol, la, ti, do).

54 The original members of Mycale included Ayelet Rose Gottlieb, Basya Schechter, Sofia Rei, and Malika Zarra. Schechter was replaced by Tammy Scheffer, who was later replaced by Sara Serpa.

Mazz Swift

55 In classical music performance, a conductor uses a baton, hands, and facial expressions to guide the musicians through the score and control the tempo and dynamics of the music. Conduction®, developed by composer Lawrence D. "Butch" Morris (b. 1947, d. 2013), is a similar series of conducting gestures used to direct musicians in the spontaneous creation of music. Conduction can also be used to improvise with the musical elements of a notated composition. For more information, visit www.conduction.us.

56 After the Côte d'Ivoire election of 2010, the first election in the country since a 1999 coup that deposed then President Henri Kona Bedie, civil war broke out, pitting forces loyal to Laurent Gbagbo, President of the Ivory Coast since 2000, against those supporting opposition candidate Alassane Ouattara. Over 3,000 people died during the conflict. On April 11, 2011, Gbagbo was taken into custody by pro-Ouattra forces backed by French forces. At the time of this writing, President Ouattara is seeking re-election for a second term.

Aurora Nealand

57 *The Year Before the Flood: A Story of New Orleans*, by Ned Sublette, Lawrence Hill Books, 2009.

58 *New Orleans: A Cultural History (Cityscapes)*, by Louise McKinney, Oxford University Press, 2006.

59 Founded in 1963, the Preservation Hall Jazz Band is named after New Orleans' Preservation Hall in the French Quarter. They play traditional New Orleans-style jazz.

60 Hurricane Katrina of August 2005 was one of the five deadliest hurricanes in U.S. history.

Nicole Rampersaud

61 Rampersaud is referring to two different method books, each a collection of transcribed solos (by saxophonist Charlie Parker and trumpeter Clifford Brown, respectively) for musicians to study and practice.

62 The *Harvard Concise Dictionary of Music* defines a hocket as: "The rapid alteration of two or more voices with single notes or short groups of notes, one part sounding while the others rest."

Sharel Cassity

63 Sharel is talking about her ability to play a variety of different reed and wood-wind instruments.

Jacqui Sutton

64 http://jacquisutton.com/biography
65 *The Warmth of Other Suns*, by Isabel Wilkerson, Random House, 2010
66 http://caselaw.lp.findlaw.com/scripts/getcase.pl?court=US&vol=396&invol=19
67 http://jacquisutton.com/biography
68 Ibid.
69 *Alan Lomax: The Man Who Recorded the World*, John Szwed, Penguin Group, 2010, p. 128.

Cheryl Bentyne

70 *Blissongs* is a meditative and sonically healing CD by Bentyne singing chakra tones and their accompanying syllables.

Diane Schuur

71 Tony Bennett's 1994 appearance on MTV *Unplugged* and its accompanying platinum-selling album *MTV Unplugged: Tony Bennett* revived his career. More recently, Bennett has enjoyed success performing with pop singer Lady Gaga.
72 The complete quote from Duke Ellington is: "I am an optimist. From where I sit, music is mostly all right, or at least in a healthy state for the future, in spite of the fact that it may sound as though it is being held hostage." *Music Is My Mistress*, by Duke Ellington, University of Michigan Press, 1973.

Jacqui Naylor

73 First launched in 1991, ProTools is a widely used computer software program that allows musicians to digitally compose, record, edit, and mix music. The fact that the software allows musicians to easily cut and correct mistakes made by a performer during the recording process is what Naylor is referring to.

Roberta Piket

74 Marian McPartland passed away on August 20, 2013.
75 "Roberta Piket's Suggested Listening: a Jazz Piano Discography," http://robertajazz.com/suggested-listening-jazz-piano-discography.

Jean Cook

76 "being matter ignited ... an interview with Cecil Taylor," by Chris Funkhouser, *Hambone*, 1994.
77 Musicians use the word "changes" to refer to the chords (or harmonies) of a song. A chord is created when two or more notes are played at the same time, and provides the musician soloing over the chord with a point of reference for the notes she or he chooses to play.

Samantha Boshnack

78 Carla Bley's *Escalator Over the Hill*, a conceptual masterpiece originally released as a 3-LP album, is perhaps the most obvious point of reference here. Bley's composition draws upon a huge range of musical genres, including rock, free jazz, Indian raga, and is infused with both a reverent and irreverent spirit I hear in Boshnack's compositions. I flag both Duke Ellington and Sun Ra as well, since both men were creating "world music" before that term became a genre, and to once again point out that jazz has always been a "globally inspired" music.

Connie Crothers

79 In jazz, the "head" is the first and last chorus of a tune in which the melody is stated without improvisation.

Malika Zarra

80 On July 17, 1996, shortly after takeoff, TWA flight 800 exploded off of Long Island and crashed into the Atlantic Ocean. Initially, there was much speculation that a surface-to-air missile launched by a terrorist group was the cause of the crash.

Nioka Workman

81 "A Fireside Chat With Reggie Workman," All About Jazz, April 16, 2003, www .allaboutjazz.com/a-fireside-chat-with-reggie-workman-reggie-workman-by -aaj-staff.php.

82 Extended techniques refer to non-traditional methods instrumentalists and singers use to produce unusual sounds. Some common extended techniques on the cello include playing the strings between the bridge and the tailpiece (sub-ponticello) or pressing down while bowing to produce a scratchy, distorted tone.

83 The Suzuki Method is a music-teaching method for children, created by Japanese violinist Shin'ichi Suzuki. With the Suzuki Method, children are taught to play their instrument before learning to read music, and parents collaborate with the teacher to play an integral role in the training process.

Jennifer Leitham

84 In the fifth edition of the American Psychiatric Association's *Diagnostic and Statistical Manual of Mental Disorders* (2013), people whose gender at birth is contrary to the one they identify with are diagnosed with gender dysphoria. This diagnosis is a revision of DSM-IV's classification "gender identity disorder," and is intended to better characterize the experiences of affected children, adolescents, and adults.

Ellen Seeling

85 In 1968, the baccalaureate in Jazz Studies was approved and jazz band became a major ensemble. http://www.music.indiana.edu/departments/academic/jazz /history.shtml